Subseries of Lecture Notes in Computer Science

T0230135

485

K. Furukawa    H. Tanaka
T. Fujisaki  (Eds.)

# Logic Programming '89

Proceedings of the 8th Conference
Tokyo, Japan, July 1989

Springer-Verlag

# Lecture Notes in Artificial Intelligence (LNAI)

# Lecture Notes in Artificial Intelligence

Subseries of Lecture Notes in Computer Science
Edited by J. Siekmann

# Lecture Notes in Computer Science

Edited by G. Goos and J. Hartmanis

**Editorial**

Artificial Intelligence has become a major discipline under the roof of Computer Science. This is also reflected by a growing number of titles devoted to this fast developing field to be published in our Lecture Notes in Computer Science. To make these volumes immediately visible we have decided to distinguish them by a special cover as Lecture Notes in Artificial Intelligence, constituting a subseries of the Lecture Notes in Computer Science. This subseries is edited by an Editorial Board of experts from all areas of AI, chaired by Jörg Siekmann, who are looking forward to consider further AI monographs and proceedings of high scientific quality for publication.

We hope that the constitution of this subseries will be well accepted by the audience of the Lecture Notes in Computer Science, and we feel confident that the subseries will be recognized as an outstanding opportunity for publication by authors and editors of the AI community.

Editors and publisher

# Lecture Notes in
# Artificial Intelligence

Edited by J. Siekmann

Subseries of Lecture Notes in Computer Science

# 485

K. Furukawa   H. Tanaka
T. Fujisaki  (Eds.)

# Logic Programming '89

Proceedings of the 8th Conference
Tokyo, Japan, July 12–14, 1989

Springer-Verlag
Berlin Heidelberg New York London Paris
Tokyo Hong Kong Barcelona Budapest

**Volume Editors**

Koichi Furukawa
ICOT Research Center
Mita Kokusai Building 21F, 4-28 Mita 1-chome
Minato-ku, Tokyo 108, Japan

Hozumi Tanaka
Department of Computer Science
Tokyo Institute of Technology, 12-1 Oh-okayama 2-chome
Meguro-ku, Tokyo 152, Japan

Tetsunosuke Fujisaki
IBM, Thomas J. Watson Research Center
P.O. Box 704, Yorktown Heights, New York 10598, USA

CR Subject Classification (1987): D.1.1, D.1.3, D.3.1–3, F.4.1–2, I.2.1, I.2.3–5,
I.2.7

ISBN 3-540-53919-0 Springer-Verlag Berlin Heidelberg New York
ISBN 0-387-53919-0 Springer-Verlag New York Berlin Heidelberg

Printing and binding: Druckhaus Beltz, Hemsbach/Bergstr.
2145/3140-543210 – Printed on acid-free paper

# Foreword

This volume of the Springer Lecture Notes in Artificial Intelligence contains selected papers presented at the Eighth Logic Programming Conference (July 12-14, 1989, Tokyo). It is the successor to Volumes 221, 264, 315 and 383.

The contents cover various topics of logic programming: reasoning, programming language, concurrent programming, knowledge programming, natural language processing and other applications.

The first section contains one invited talk by Prof. Donald Michie, the chief scientist of the Turing Institute. The title of his presentation is "Human and Machine Learning of Descriptive Concepts". The paper is based on the oral presentation of his talk and is transcribed from ICOT Journal, No. 27, 1990. It introduces various research results on learning conducted by Prof. Michie's group at the Turing Institute including data classification, extraction of classification rules of propositional level and inductive inference of predicate logic formulas.

The second section , "Reasoning" contains three papers. The first paper, by J.Yamaguchi, discusses the issue of concept classification, particularly exceptional cases, and relates the problems to non-monotonic reasoning. The second paper, by F. Dong and H. Nakagawa, introduces a new class of program called conditional programs and discusses their declarative semantics using the perfect model semantics proposed by Przymsinski. The third paper, by Y. Shi and S. Arikawa, tries to formulate time-bounded reasoning and discusses such issues as the soundness, completeness, truth maintenance and reliablility of the inference procedure.

The third section, "Logic Programming Language", contains one paper by A. Yamamoto, which gives a theoretical foundation of EFS (Elementary Formal System) as a logic programming language. It can be regarded as a constraint logic programming language on strings, and therefore could be useful in natural language processing.

The fourth section is on "Concurrent Programming", and contains two papers. One is by J. Tatemura and H. Tanaka, presenting a debugger for a parallel logic programming language, Fleng, introduced by M. Nilsson. The second paper, by H. Numazaki et al., proposes a parallel generalized LR parser, an extension of Tomita's algorithm, written in a concurrent logic language, GHC.

The fifth section is on "Knowledge Programming", and contains one paper by Y. Hosono et al. The paper describes a system called "Knowledge Media Station" which provides users with a flexible and powerful tool for incorporating and organizing knowledge represented by a well-formed language with various types of knowledge using a hypermedia framework. Hosono also tries to show that logic programming and hypermedia meet in several respects.

The sixth section is about "Natural Language Processing" and contains two papers. The first paper, by H. Tsuda et al., presents a kind of constraint logic programming language, called cu-Prolog, for combinatorial problems. The paper also describes cu-Prolog's application to JPSG (Japanese Phrase Structure Grammar) parser. The way cu-Prolog solves the constraints is based on program transformation, which is unique and very powerful. The second paper of this section , by T. Tamura et al., proposes an efficient table-driven bottom-up parser written in Prolog.

The last section is about "Applications". Two papers are presented. The first one is by T. Shintani and proposes a consistency maintenence mechanism in subjective judgements based on an AHP (Analytic Hierarchy Process) pairwise comparison method. The consistency maintenence is done by the TMS (Truth Maintenance System) embedded in a Prolog-based production system. The second paper, by H. Nakamura et al., describes a logic design assistance system built on top of a temporal logic based language called Tokio.

We hope that reader will find useful information in these proceedings. Finally we thank program committee members, reviewers and authors for their cooperation and patience. We especially would like to thank the reviewers from the IBM Watson Research Center for their thorough efforts to improve the quality of the English as well as the contents of all submitted papers.

Tokyo, Winter 1990

Koichi Furukawa
Hozumi Tanaka
Tetsunosuke Fujisaki

# Table of Contents

## Knowledge Programming

## Natural Language Processing

## Application

# HUMAN AND MACHINE LEARNING OF DESCRIPTIVE CONCEPTS

Donald Michie

The Turing Institute

George House, 36 North Hanover Street, Glasgow G1 2AD, U.K.

I am speaking today of machine learning, because I believe that its study is the logical and necessary next step for the ten years which lie ahead of us. My reason is that we have a common goal inspired by the idea of the automatic creation and management of large bodies of knowledge; — not mere data or mere information, but organized, structured knowledge of human type. The current status of machine learning is illustrated in Fig. 1A.

The knowledge enterprise requires not only powerful methods of automatic deduction, which are capable of deriving facts from theories, but also the history of human knowledge accumulation, which we call "science", proves to us that it is also necessary to have powerful mechanisms for constructing theories from facts. The second of these processes is known as "inductive inference", the logic oriented branch of machine learning.

The first process of deductive reasoning by machine and incorporation into programming language has seen much progress, particularly in the last ten years. But when we move to learning, to inductive inference, we find the situation rather undeveloped.

In the area of commercial application, rather simple methods of rule induction at the propositional level of Boolean formulas and decision trees, machine learning has been very successful, and continues to generate substantial financial payback for those companies in various parts of the world for whom specialist induction engineering companies develop applications.

For routine commercial requirements, GOOD (and highly lucrative); needs expert structuring.

For high-level scientific and educational requirements, PROMISING BEGINNINGS: non-monotonic adaptation of predicate-logic algorithms required.

**Fig.1A  Status of Machine Learning**

However, the methods and algorithms of learning are very restricted and incomplete, and in particular, the methodology requires the use of a human expert, who understands the domain in detail to structure the problem into sub-problems, sub-sub-problems, and so forth, in the style of structured analysis or structured programming.

In the context of logic programming, we have to say that it is necessary for a human to construct the new sub-predicates or intermediate predicates that are required in order to complete each machine-generated theory.

At the end of my talk today, I will speak about new work at the Turing Instutute by Stephen Muggleton. Using the more powerful target language of predicate calculus, the automatic construction of new predicates required for descriptive concepts has actually been achieved.

In general, when we speak of the requirement of higher level learning, the fully-automated construction of complex descriptions and theories, we have to say that we have promising beginnings, and have met with many difficulties. The most important is that there is a requirement in higher level learning for non-monotonic adaptation of predicate-logic algorithms. So that we have to see machine learning in the logic context as inherently non-monotonic. This is the most active current theme in logic learning at the Turing Institute. I am interested to see from the table of contents or programme for this Conference that similar problems are under active study here.

A straightforward definition of what is meant by machine learning is given in Fig. 1B.

Machine learning of AI-type, as I define it, uses sample data, or training data — we call this the "training set" — to generate an updated basis, a modified or augmented representation, for improved performance in classifying subsequent sampled data from the same source, and also —

DEFINITION: a machine learning system (AI-type) uses sample data (training set) to generate an updated basis for improved performance on subsequent data and also communicates its internal updates in explicit and operationally effective form.

**Fig.1B**

this is the characteristic AI feature — the system must be able to communicate its augmented basis or augmented representation to the user in terms which the user can understand and mentally check. Otherwise, the machine has simply generated a description, and not a concept. In Artificial Intelligence we are interested in the development of information structures which can be interpreted by the human brain.

This requirement that the newly generated theories and descriptions should be understandable to the human is not simply an academic requirement. In our contract work for commercial, for industrial and other institutional sponsors, we find that the customer normally requires that the rule base which we develop using indictive tools must be intelligible to his own specialists in house. And in some cases, this requirement that the machine generated rules should be understood is a necessity.

In recent work for an Industrial Space Agency in America, called "Wespace", we were involved in their requirement to launch a fully operational commercial space station in 1992. This is not the same as the NASA Space Station. This is an industrial space station that aims to be a self-financing business from renting space and facilities on board the space station to companies who require to manufacture pharmaceuticals or other products under conditions of zero gravity and a hard vacuum.

Now, that station will orbit the earth every hour and a half to two hours, but they only plan a single ground control station, with the result that only for 18 minutes during the orbit is there communication with the human experts on the ground (See Fig. 2).

If, meanwhile, the system has encountered problems, and has utilized machine learning routines in order to fix or adapt to these problems, then it is necessary that the report which it gives during that 18 minutes window of opportunity should be short and easy to understand

WESPACE'S INDUSTRIAL SPACE FACILITY

PLANNED LAUNCH: 1992.

ONLY ONE GROUND STATION.

→18-MINUTE WINDOW IN EACH 90-MINUTE ORBIT

Hence interest in having as fall-back an adaptive altitude controller, required to be
•simple
•robust
•conceptually transparent

**Fig.2**

for the human engineers. So, there is a natural requirement that the learning system should produce augmentations of the rule base which are simple, which are robust, and which are conceptually transparent.

In the case of the space station application, what is required is a controller which can adapt its behaviour and generate new strategies when unexpected and novel situations occur. Such an adaptive controller acts as a fall-back or insurance mechanism to support a conventional controller developed according to classical numerical methods of control theory. But when the unexpected happens in the orbiting satellite, the clients require a learning mechanism that can innovate with the construction of new strategies.

This is similar to what might happen when a human riding a bicycle discovers that the handle bars have come off in his hand. He now has a new situation. The existing control strategies are no longer precisely applicable. And if he is intelligent and resourceful, he may be able, by a trial and error learning process, to master the riding of the bicycle in its new form, without even falling off once.

In such a situation, and in almost all the commercial applications of machine learning, what is required is to develop from data a logical simulation of a function. But the function is of a restricted and simple kind, usually called a "heuristic model". That is to say, the function maps from a space of situations to a space of actions, a direct mapping. Such functions correspond to what we call "skills", including mental skills, in humans. I distinguish the word "skill" from the word "understanding".

---

• Heuristic-model: situations → actions (compiled knowledge; "skill")

• Causal-model: situations × actions → situations (interpreted knowledge; "understanding")

---

**Fig.3**

The type of model is different (See Fig. 3).

One can think of a heuristic model as having arisen by a process similar to compilation, either by generalization and inductive learning over the facts of experience, which is how most human skills are acquired, or alternatively, as has now been demonstrated by Ivan Bratko and his colleagues, and confirmed in our Institute, by generating efficient compiled skills from the use of a more complex logical model which is demonstrated in the lower half of the diagram. We call these more complex models "causal models". Instead of mapping directly from situations to actions, they map from situation-action pairs to situations. In other words, a causal model is used to predict — to predict the next state.

One method which has been successful is to use a causal model to generate a complete set of low level strategy rules, a complete exhaustive set of situations paired with actions, and then, to use inductive inference to compress these gigantic dictionaries down into small, elegant, understandable human-type, heuristic rules.

In this case, one arrives at a set of heuristic rules which can be certificated as correct with respect to the initial logical model of the causality of the situation. There is an account of this methodology as applied to the diagnosis of cardiological disorders, published by Bratko and others in "Machinbe Intelligence 11". A more extensive account is now available from MIT Press.

Machine learning, as has been said, is in that early stage when the problem is challenging and difficult. Our research policy is always to try to do what can be done today, rather than to move to more difficult stages in advance of having solved the easier stages. So we concentrate at present on the development of logical models of heuristic skills.

But we must remember that in this category also belongs much of the activity of the trained intellectual, when performing fairly routine

```
┌─────────────────────────────────────────────────────────────────────┐
│                    ┌─────────────────────────┐                        │
│                    │    MACHINE LEARNING     │                        │
│                    └─────────────────────────┘                        │
│                                                                       │
│                    AT PROPOSITIONAL-LOGIC LEVEL                        │
│                    ───────────────────────────                        │
│                      (e.g. decision-tree induction)                   │
│                                                                       │
│    Some problems and solutions:                                       │
│    •Validation of induced rules (interactive highlighting)            │
│    •Numerical attributes (entropy-based splitting)                    │
│    •Default assumptions ("exception programming")                     │
│    •Structuring (expert partitioning into goal hierarchies)           │
│    •Noisy data and uncertain inference (the CART and C4 algorithms;   │
│      Bayesian semi-decision trees)                                    │
│                                                                       │
│    Missing capabilities:                                              │
│    •Variablisation                                                    │
│    •Discovery of new intermediate attributes and general             │
│      predicate-construction                                           │
│                                                                       │
│    Hence the need for PREDICATE-LOGIC LEVEL                            │
└─────────────────────────────────────────────────────────────────────┘
```

**Fig.4**

mental tasks, for example, algebraic simplification, logical manipulations, all the lower level processes of the human mathematician.

I am first going to survey the progress and difficulties at the propositional level of machine learning, where nearly all the successful applications and the present-day action is concentrated. Then I shall show why, for really complex problems, the limitations of the language for expressing theories are too great, and it becomes necessary to move to the level of predicate logic (See Fig. 4).

A mong the problems that I will discuss is the validation of induced rules. This is overwhelmingly important, because there is a widespread conception among less technical people that somehow expert programs generated automatically by inductive inference are less reliable than handcrafted programs, and less open to methods of validation. This fear is groundless, as I will show. I will illustrate one particular technique, which I call "interactive highlighting" of the parts of the induced theory which correspond to generalization steps, automatically highlighting these for subsequent validation.

Secondly, there is the problem of numerical attributes. Machine learning originally developed in a logical framework. How do we incorporate attributes, variables with numerical values? There is a method developed by Quinlan, and also by an American group, called "entropy-based splitting" of a numerical range into discrete intervals, which can then be handled as logical variables.

The use of default assumptions and the non-monotonic extension of a description at the propositional level is now routinely performed in commercial work and is incorporated as a feature in a number of commercially available rule induction packages, under the name "exception programming". I will give an example.

Then there is the question of structuring. As I mentioned, at present the only dependable agent we can employ to partition a domain into a goal hierarchy is the domain specialist himself.

There is also the problem of noisy data, data which is incomplete, or has been corrupted by some random interference, and the need to have confidence factors, and to perform reasoning in a probablistic style. There are practical solutions to that problem that come academically from the group of Breiman, Friedman, Olshen and Stone, and also from Quinlan, which is the basis of most commercial rule induction.

There is another approach, on which I am personally engaged, of redeveloping, re-deriving the whole of propositional-level rule induction from the axioms of Bayesian probability, and combining this with principles developed in the 1940's by Abraham Wald under the tile "Sequential Analysis". This seems to give promise of similar results, but is less ad hoc, and with a broader and clearer interpretation.

The two capacities that we severely miss in all machine learning at the propositional level are not sufficient to disable machine learning for the great majority of practical applications. But it is the minority of applications, where the theory which has to be built by machine is really complex, that we enter the interesting territory. That territory is bared to us unless we move to a more powerful language. Essentially there are two reasons. One is that structures — explicit structures such as decision-trees, or other structures equivalent to Boolean expressions-lack variables, so that generalization by substituting variables for constants is denied to us.

Even more important, we are dependent on human knowledge for discovering essential intermediate attributes or predicates. In general, the construction of new predicates has to be done by the human. We would like to remove that limitation and automate it. This requires moving to the predicate logic level, with which I will conclude my talk.

---

ID3

Given: a collection of positive and negative instances, where each instance is the description of an object in terms of a fixed set of attributes or properties.

Produces: a decision tree for differentiating positive and negative instances

---

**Fig.5**

Let us start at the simplest level of constructing a simple Boolean expression, possibly in the form of a decision-tree, from ground level example cases.

Fig. 5 gives a statement of the task which algorithms such as Quinlan's ID3, or Michalski's AQ algorithms, or Bratko's Assistant, all address in common.

Given a collection of positive and negative instances of some concept, where each instance is a description — a low level description of an object simply in the form of a list of attribute values or properties, the algorithm produces a decision tree, or similar machine executable and human understandable expression. This can be used on new cases sampled from the same source, to classify them either as positive or negative cases — to classify the new material usually called the "test set", according to whether each case is an example of the concept or a counter-example.

I am going to assume that everyone here is familiar with the basic nature of ID3, which is the most commonly used algorithm for performing this type of propositional level induction. If not, I will be happy to go through the details in discussion time or afterwards.

I now want to consider the various problems that I listed earlier, each with its solution.

The question of validation was most important in an application in which we were involved some years ago, that arises from the last stage of descent of the Space Shuttle. NASA was concerned about the pilot's decision whether to use the autolander or whether to control the spacecraft manually. The decision is taken on the basis of information about a number of attributes such as visibility, errors of measurement, the aerodynamic stability of the craft, the attitude, whether there was head wind or tail wind, atmospheric turbulence.

| | stab | errors | sign | wind | mag | vis | Class |
|---|---|---|---|---|---|---|---|
| 1] | — | — | — | — | — | no | useauto |
| 2] | no | — | — | — | — | yes | notauto |
| 3] | yes | lx | — | — | — | yes | notauto |
| 4] | yes | xl | — | — | — | yes | notauto |
| 5] | yes | mm | negative | tail | — | yes | notauto |
| 6] | — | — | — | — | out | yes | notauto |
| 7] | yes | ss | — | — | light | yes | useatuo |
| 8] | yes | ss | — | — | med | yes | useauto |
| 9] | yes | ss | — | — | strong | yes | useauto |
| 10] | yes | mm | positive | head | light | yes | useauto |
| 11] | yes | mm | positive | head | med | yes | useauto |
| 12] | yes | mm | positive | tail | light | yes | useauto |
| 13] | yes | mm | positive | tail | med | yes | useauto |
| 14] | yes | mm | positive | head | strong | yes | notauto |
| 15] | yes | mm | positive | tail | strong | yes | useauto |
| 16] | yes | mm | negative | head | — | yes | notauto |

**Fig.6**

```
[vis      ] :

    yes : [errors   ] :

        ss : [stab   ] :
                yes : [mag    ] :
                        light : useauto
                        med : useauto
                        strong : useauto
                        out : notauto
                no : notauto

        mm : [stab      ] :

            yes : [sign      ] :

                negative : notauto

                positive : [mag        ] :
                        light : useauto
                        med : useauto
                        strong : [wind       ] :
                                        head : notauto
                                        tail : useauto
                        out : notauto
                no : notauto
        lx : notauto
        xl : notauto
    no : useauto
```

Decision tree with the cases decided by generalization highlighted.

**Fig.7**

After an unsuccessful attempt by the NASA engineers, headed by Roger Burke, the designer of the autolander, using dialogue acquisition to develop a rule base for giving the pilot advice in real time, they temporarily abandoned the project as being too difficult. Then, they were fortunate enough to be included in a course on inductive programming delivered in Austin, Texas, by Radian Corporation. The instructor, Dick Shockett, encouraged them during the course to tackle this problem by induction from examples — in this case, the examples being interactively generated by the human expeeeerts. The first fifteen lines of Fig. 6 give the set of examples with which they terminated a successful day spent in developing a decision tree rule.

Those fifteen examples generated the decision tree shown in Fig. 7.

The important point is the question of validation. This rule, having been constructed in one day in Austin, Texas, was then sent to Houston, and subjected to exhaustive validation trials on the Shuttle simulator at Houston at very great expense. That expense could have been greatly reduced if this exception programming, or validation-directed induction feature had already been available. Re-running the program now, the system automatically highlights, as you see in Fig. 8, those parts of the rule which are not direct logical deductions from the initial set of examples, but which represent the use of a generalization step; and hence, are probably true, but not guaranteed correct.

Those that are highlighted can then be expanded automatically to generate additional examples corresponding to cases which did not appear in the initial examples set.

If you allow for the expansion of the "don't care" symbol, and also allow for a redundant overlap, there are, in fact, three additional cases that are covered by the additional line, sixteen, and by concentrating simply on those cases which have been automatically highlighted, the validation process can be greatly accelerated.

The next problem I want to consider is the treatment of numerical values. I shall illustrate with a real case which was studied by Barry Shephard during his thesis work as a graduate student before he joined the Turing Institute. It came from a branch of the food industry, concerned with chocolates, a company called "Rowntree" of York, who sell a brand of chocolates called "Black Magic".

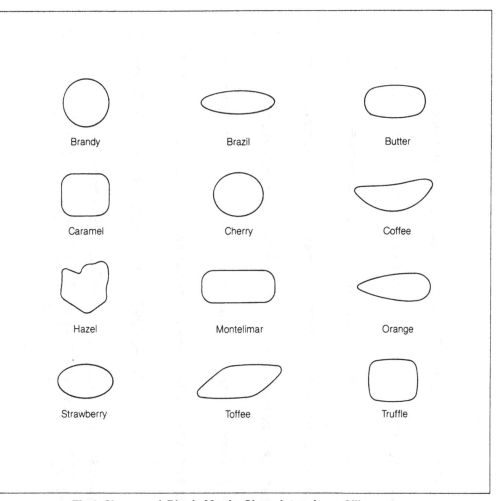

**Fig.8 Shapes of Black Magic Chocolates from Silhouettes**

The different chocolates have different shapes. Rowntree's problem was that they want to have the right-shaped, the correct chocolates packed into the correct place in the box by a robot that can recognize these shapes by television camera, by visual recognition.

The normal approach at the low level in vision is to generate many numerical attributes measuring such quantities as the aspect ratio or the total area, or the irregularity of the perimeter, etc., and from that, to develop a classification rule.

Typical sample data are shown in Fig. 9, exactly as would appear to a statistical data analyst, who might tackle it with one of the statistical

| Area | Prornd | Circity | Boxness | Bx2ness | Asprat | AS2rat | Elong | Perim | CLASS |
|------|--------|---------|---------|---------|--------|--------|-------|-------|-------|
| 143 | 58 | 83 | 71 | 79 | 88 | 91 | 119 | 122 | brandy |
| 139 | 61 | 79 | 72 | 78 | 84 | 85 | 113 | 118 | brandy |
| 127 | 59 | 88 | 73 | 77 | 91 | 94 | 124 | 114 | brandy |
| 117 | 61 | 81 | 74 | 78 | 85 | 85 | 106 | 108 | brandy |
| 127 | 59 | 85 | 73 | 77 | 91 | 91 | 115 | 114 | brandy |
| 136 | 58 | 80 | 70 | 77 | 85 | 88 | 116 | 120 | brandy |
| 131 | 61 | 79 | 71 | 79 | 81 | 86 | 112 | 114 | brandy |
| 125 | 58 | 86 | 74 | 77 | 91 | 91 | 127 | 114 | brandy |
| 135 | 60 | 79 | 70 | 79 | 83 | 88 | 117 | 117 | brandy |
| 87 | 58 | 62 | 76 | 80 | 62 | 64 | 79 | 95 | brazil |
| 87 | 54 | 58 | 73 | 79 | 58 | 62 | 98 | 98 | brazil |
| 94 | 54 | 57 | 76 | 76 | 59 | 59 | 100 | 103 | brazil |
| 82 | 54 | 53 | 74 | 76 | 55 | 55 | 74 | 96 | brazil |
| 79 | 54 | 55 | 72 | 77 | 57 | 59 | 108 | 94 | brazil |
| 84 | 56 | 58 | 73 | 75 | 61 | 63 | 81 | 95 | brazil |
| 95 | 55 | 55 | 73 | 76 | 58 | 59 | 81 | 103 | brazil |
| 88 | 51 | 55 | 70 | 81 | 55 | 61 | 107 | 102 | brazil |
| 91 | 57 | 53 | 72 | 78 | 54 | 58 | 75 | 98 | brazil |
| 91 | 44 | 53 | 68 | 93 | 48 | 61 | 93 | 113 | butter |
| 92 | 44 | 55 | 60 | 85 | 54 | 72 | 103 | 112 | butter |
| 88 | 50 | 59 | 61 | 88 | 53 | 75 | 69 | 103 | butter |
| 95 | 50 | 57 | 58 | 86 | 54 | 77 | 72 | 107 | butter |
| 101 | 44 | 55 | 65 | 88 | 50 | 67 | 93 | 118 | butter |
| 98 | 48 | 52 | 62 | 86 | 49 | 66 | 62 | 111 | butter |
| 103 | 51 | 55 | 68 | 91 | 49 | 63 | 59 | 111 | butter |
| 99 | 59 | 54 | 76 | 90 | 48 | 56 | 54 | 101 | butter |
| 106 | 52 | 55 | 59 | 89 | 50 | 72 | 57 | 111 | butter |
| 107 | 53 | 72 | 60 | 90 | 75 | 93 | 115 | 111 | caramel |
| 119 | 64 | 74 | 62 | 87 | 78 | 93 | 104 | 106 | caramel |
| 117 | 64 | 73 | 61 | 86 | 80 | 93 | 106 | 105 | caramel |
| 109 | 63 | 75 | 62 | 87 | 78 | 94 | 105 | 102 | caramel |
| 114 | 58 | 74 | 62 | 91 | 77 | 93 | 108 | 110 | caramel |
| 119 | 50 | 69 | 60 | 84 | 75 | 90 | 133 | 121 | caramel |
| 109 | 67 | 76 | 63 | 87 | 82 | 94 | 104 | 100 | caramel |
| 121 | 56 | 76 | 62 | 86 | 81 | 95 | 102 | 114 | caramel |
| 126 | 55 | 74 | 61 | 86 | 80 | 95 | 115 | 118 | caramel |
| 97 | 59 | 80 | 71 | 77 | 86 | 88 | 118 | 100 | cherry |
| 87 | 60 | 85 | 73 | 82 | 87 | 91 | 119 | 94 | cherry |
| 94 | 58 | 88 | 75 | 78 | 91 | 91 | 121 | 99 | cherry |
| 92 | 61 | 76 | 71 | 80 | 84 | 84 | 113 | 96 | cherry |
| 93 | 59 | 83 | 74 | 79 | 88 | 88 | 122 | 98 | cherry |
| 97 | 59 | 87 | 71 | 79 | 90 | 96 | 128 | 100 | cherry |
| 103 | 60 | 83 | 69 | 79 | 88 | 94 | 120 | 103 | cherry |
| 94 | 58 | 81 | 71 | 80 | 86 | 90 | 121 | 100 | cherry |
| 91 | 60 | 82 | 73 | 78 | 88 | 88 | 114 | 96 | cherry |
| 113 | 47 | 53 | 70 | 70 | 59 | 59 | 84 | 121 | coffee |
| 110 | 45 | 56 | 65 | 68 | 66 | 68 | 78 | 122 | coffee |
| 114 | 45 | 52 | 70 | 70 | 58 | 58 | 82 | 124 | coffee |
| 110 | 46 | 57 | 67 | 69 | 65 | 66 | 55 | 120 | coffee |
| 117 | 47 | 53 | 64 | 69 | 61 | 65 | 73 | 123 | coffee |
| 108 | 48 | 55 | 64 | 68 | 65 | 68 | 71 | 116 | coffee |
| 105 | 49 | 58 | 66 | 72 | 64 | 68 | 73 | 114 | coffee |
| 97 | 43 | 53 | 70 | 70 | 59 | 59 | 88 | 116 | coffee |
| 102 | 44 | 52 | 63 | 69 | 62 | 65 | 83 | 118 | coffee |
| 114 | 54 | 79 | 69 | 79 | 84 | 89 | 128 | 113 | hazel |
| 128 | 53 | 75 | 68 | 74 | 85 | 85 | 114 | 121 | hazel |
| 123 | 58 | 82 | 71 | 75 | 89 | 91 | 128 | 114 | hazel |
| 135 | 55 | 84 | 70 | 76 | 91 | 95 | 108 | 122 | hazel |
| 122 | 53 | 71 | 68 | 76 | 82 | 82 | 120 | 118 | hazel |
| 118 | 57 | 76 | 69 | 81 | 79 | 86 | 96 | 112 | hazel |
| 128 | 56 | 75 | 69 | 78 | 82 | 85 | 97 | 118 | hazel |
| 120 | 52 | 77 | 66 | 78 | 84 | 91 | 122 | 118 | hazel |
| 130 | 55 | 81 | 67 | 79 | 88 | 95 | 112 | 120 | hazel |
| 159 | 61 | 69 | 59 | 86 | 66 | 91 | 71 | 126 | montel |
| 150 | 51 | 71 | 62 | 87 | 69 | 89 | 105 | 133 | montel |
| 144 | 59 | 70 | 64 | 86 | 67 | 85 | 79 | 122 | montel |
| 147 | 52 | 67 | 71 | 89 | 62 | 74 | 84 | 131 | montel |
| 162 | 51 | 68 | 62 | 86 | 65 | 86 | 90 | 139 | montel |
| 141 | 55 | 67 | 58 | 87 | 66 | 89 | 88 | 125 | montel |
| 137 | 62 | 71 | 60 | 88 | 68 | 92 | 83 | 116 | montel |
| 144 | 47 | 62 | 62 | 88 | 62 | 79 | 101 | 136 | montel |

**Fig.9**

multivariate methods, such as multiple regression. These are consistently found in our work to be less accurate than decision-rule induction methods.

In the right-hand column is entered the decision class, namely, which of the eight kinds of chocolate.

The basic ID3 algorithm and similar algorithms applies a top-down divide-and-conquer partitioning of the problem, using as its choice function the principle of minimizing entropy. some years ago, Andrew Blake, working with us in Edinburgh, proposed that the problem of partitioning the range of a numerical variable into a small number of logical intervals could be tackled by using identically the same entropy minimizing method.

This method has proved extremely successful, and is routinely used everywhere in the world in which rule induction is in industrial application. It corresponds quite well with experience of the behaviour of human experts who do not, in fact, process numerical data in the way that a multivariate statistics model does.

On the contrary, your doctor is not interested in the precise value of your temperature. All that he records in his mind, and all that he remembers, is whether your temperature is normal, or sub-normal, or whether it is a mild fever, or whether it is a high fever. Four or five logical categories are the maximum in which human experts divide experience of numerical quantities. This behaviour is closely simulated by rule induction methods.

Fig. 10 shows the decision tree is generated from those particular data by a commercial rule induction package called "Extran", which generates its rule in the format you have already seen. This particular package also has facilities for automatic conversion of the rule into FORTRAN.

In comparative trials with statistical multivariate methods, this method of logical rule induction showed up very favorably. It has two further advantages against statistical methods, including the fashionable approach known as "neural networks" or "neural computing". The latter belongs to a specialized subset of the category of multivariate statistical analysis.

First, rule induction detects which attributes are relevant, and which are not. This rule only incorporates five out of the initial set of nine attributes.

```
[asprat] :
            < 72 : [bx2ness] :
                        < 83 : [area] :
                                    <96 : brazil
                                    > =96 : coffee
                        > =83 : [area] :
                                    < 122 : butter
                                    > =122 : montel
            > =72 : [area] :
                        > 105 : cherry
                        > =105 : [boxness] :
                                    < 65 : caramel
                                    > =65 : [prornd] :
                                                < 58 : hazel
                                                > =58 : [bx2ness] :
                                                            < 76 : hazel
                                                            > =72 : brandy
```

The rule as finally extracted. Note the use of only five of the original nine attributes.

**Fig.10**

Secondly, it is presented in a form which the human user finds easy to follow and mentally check for himself.

The next example concerns default assumptions, related to the problem which at predicate calculus level is known as "non-monotonic inference". But even in propositional level rule induction, it is observed that human induction of a concept typically proceeds by an initial overgeneralization, followed by successive refinement. And yet, the examples that I have shown so far do not have this feature.

Let me take a very simple and trivial example of developing a rule to help a robot decide whether to take its umbrella when going on a journey.

The problem definition provides four attributes, namely, whether the weather is sunny, rainly, or blustery; — that is, windly; whether the robot is inside or not; whether it's in the car; and finally, whether it is already soaked — already wet.

As shown in Fig. 11, there are two decision classes: Use and don't use. In the middle of the diagram is a sufficient set of examples to define a complete strategy. Please note that the hyphen symbol is a "don't care" symbol, and consequently, this Table, when fully expanded, consists of 24 fully instantiated example cases (3 x 2 x 2 x 2). The rule induced by the

| Problem definition: | rain | | | | |
|---|---|---|---|---|---|
| | 4 | | | | |
| | weather | logical | wet | dry | blustery |
| | inside | logical | yes | no | |
| | incar | logical | yes | no | |
| | soaked | logical | yes | no | |
| | 2 | | | | |
| | use | use an umbrella | | | |
| | dontuse | don't use an umbrella | | | |

| Cases: | | weather | inside | incar | soaked | decision |
|---|---|---|---|---|---|---|
| | 1 | dry | — | — | — | dontuse |
| | 2 | blustery | — | — | — | dontuse |
| | 3 | — | yes | — | — | dontuse |
| | 4 | — | — | yes | — | dontuse |
| | 5 | — | — | — | yes | dontuse |
| | 6 | wet | no | no | no | use |

Rule:
```
weather
    wet : inside
            yes : dontuse
            no  : incar
                    yes : dontuse :
                    no : soaked
                            yes : dontuse
                            no : use
    dry : dontuse
    blustery : dontuse
```

**Fig.11 The Example Set and Induced Rule of the Umbrella Problem**

system is shown at the bottom of the figure.

The point I want to establish is that the human style of constructing a theory is to start from an assumption which may be an optimistic assumption, as in this case, or may be pessimistic. If it's to do with the use of umbrellas, and the agent originates in Scotland, then he will take the pessimistic assumption. The initial rule will be "always take your umbrella". Then successive refinement reconstructs a theory every time it encounters a refutation.

But first, Fig. 12 (a) illustrates the philosophy of the optimist.

The optimist has a very simple world. He starts with the assumption that you do not use an umbrella, which serves him well until he meets the case that the weather is wet; he is not inside; he is not in the car; and he is not soaked already. And that single conjunctive case is picked up by the system. Notice the syntax that is used in Extran. When you see those brackets, it means that all the cases that are enclosed within the brackets are given priority; — given precedence, when they clash with any individual members of the expansion of the original "no" case.

So, that is the optimist's representation of the problem. It is very compact.

| weather | inside | incar | soaked | Class |
|---------|--------|-------|--------|-------|
| — | — | — | — | dontuse |
| > | | | | |
| wet | no | no | no | use |
| < | | | | |

**Fig.12 (a) The Umbrella Example Set using Exception Programming**

| weather | inside | incar | soaked | Class |
|---------|--------|-------|--------|-------|
| — | — | — | — | use |
| > | | | | |
| dry | — | — | — | dontuse |
| biustery | — | — | — | dontuse |
| — | yes | — | — | dontuse |
| — | — | yes | — | dontuse |
| — | — | — | yes | dontuse |
| < | | | | |

**Fig.12 (b) The Umbrella Example Set from a Different Viewpoint**

The pessimist case is interesting, because it gives a better feel for the successive steps of non-monotonic refinement. As shown in Fig. 12 (b) the initial assumption, because you come from Scotland, is that you always use your umbrella. Now, you must imagine these exception examples coming sequentially in time. So that successive alteration of the theory is possible, according to how many of these refutations have been encountered.

In the limit, the two processes of refinement converge on identically the same decision tree, namely, the decision tree that we saw earlier induced from the more conventional kind of example set.

You might say that in the limit, the denotation in the form of the final executable theory is the same, but the connotation, as illustrated by the very different appearance of the declarative representation in terms of examples, is different. But they map in the limit to the same denotation.

This method is rapid. On large industrial problems, rates of construction of expert system rule bases typically proceed at more than a hundred lines of FORTRAN or a hundred lines of PASCAL, a hundred lines of C, per programmer day. So, we see a gain of more than ten-fold in the rate of construction of reliable code. Further, in the case of applications where the dialogue method is not applicable, because the human expert is unable fully and completely and accurately to articulate the rules, then rule induction is the only feasible method.

I spoke next about structuring, and the limitation that decision tree induction suffers from, namely, requiring an expert to partition the original large, messy, multi-attribute problem into a hierarchical system of procedures.

If this is not done, the system may well deliver a complete and correct decision tree, but one which fails the criterion of being AI type; in other words, fails to be intelligible to the user.

In Alen Shapiro's thesis work in Edinburgh, and subsequently in Glasgow, be took as his target, a descriptive concept in a chess end game, which is beyond the power of chess experts and masters to articulate. There are no accounts of the theory of how you adjudicate an adjourned game in this particular end-game in any of the chess literature.

So, the enterprise was: The knowledge does not exist. Can we automatically manufacture it by machine? Fig. 13 shows the product's initial form. The result is, as you see, unsatisfactory.

In the final form shown in Fig. 14 the domain is broken down into a hierarchy of predicates and sub-predicates, which is comprehensible to the human master. Yet it depended on the insight of the specialist to form the higher-level predicates.

For the question of automatic generation of structures which involve the invention by machine of new predicates, we require to pass on to the predicate calculus level. I will talk about a system developed by Steven Muggleton, called "CIGOL".

As illustrated in Fig. 15, the name "CIGOL" simply comes from the word "LOGIC", spelled backwards. Its fundamental set of operations is based on the inversion of Robinson's resolutionalgorithm. It accepts unit-clause examples as the training set. It inverts resolution. It performs the search in the inverse direction to resolution, using a set of three operators; — truncation, absorption, and intraconstruction. Of those three, it is the third operator, intraconstruction, which is concerned with the development of new predicates. The other two perform generalizations of other kinds.

The task of the search is to modify incomplete theories, including the augmentation of such theories, so as to increase their coverage. It uses compactness, that is, the compactness of the total non-redundant representation, including whatever example cases still have to be retained, together with whatever theory has so far been incrementally constructed.

```
No. of examples in final working-set = 175.                    f: spcop
No of nodes in final tree = 82.                                  f: rxmsq
Time taken to generate rule = 963 CPU second.                    f: WON
                                                              t: qxmsq
rimmx                                                             t: NOT
    f: bxqsq                                                      t: WON
        f: wknck                                                t: NOT
            f: bkxbq                                             t: NOT
                f: wkna8                                    t: bknwy
                    f: bkblk                                    f: NOT
                        f: katri                                t: simpl
                            B: NOT                                f: r2ar8
                            W: WON                                    f: WON
                            N: wkpos                                  t: NOT
                                f: reskr                            t: NOT
                                    f: wkcti                    t: WON
                                        f: NOT             t: blxwp
                                        t: r2ar8               f: mulch
                                            f: dsopp               f: bkona
                                                f: thrsk               f: bkxcr
                                                    f: bkspr               f: wkov1
                                                        f: skach               f: bkon8
                                                            f: WON                 f: bkxbq
                                                            t: NOT                     f: thrsk
                                                        t: NOT                             f: skach
                                                    t: NOT                                     f: skrxp
                                                    t: WON                                         f: reskr
                                                t: NOT                                                 f: WON
                                            t: NOT                                                     t: NOT
                                    t: rxmsq                                                         t: NOT
                                        f: wtoeg                                                 t: NOT
                                            1: dsopp                                             t: WON
                                                f: WON                                         t: NOT
                                                t: dwipd                                   t: bknwy
                                                    L: WON                                     f: NOT
                                                    G: skewr                                   t: WON
                                                        f: WON                             t: NOT
                                                        t: NOT                             t: NOT
                                            N: WON                                     t: NOT
                                            t: qxmsq                               t: NOT
                                                f: NOT                         t: NOT
                                                t: WON                     t: WON
                                        t: hdchk
```

**Fig.13 An Unstructured KPa7KR WTM WFW/not WFW Decision Tree**

CIGOL generalizes incrementally from positive examples. Its weakness in its old form, until very recently, was that the original CIGOL does not generalize over counter-examples. It is capable of a limited form of learning from counter-examples simply by retaining in memory individual refutation instances. But it does not generalize over the refutation instances. So, until recently, the non-monotonic property of alternately generalizing and specializing was not provided.

However, in the last two months or so, Muggleton and Bain have successfully introduced a new version of CIGOL, NM-CIGOL, which stands for "non-monotonic CIGOL". Its general approach is to use the negation by

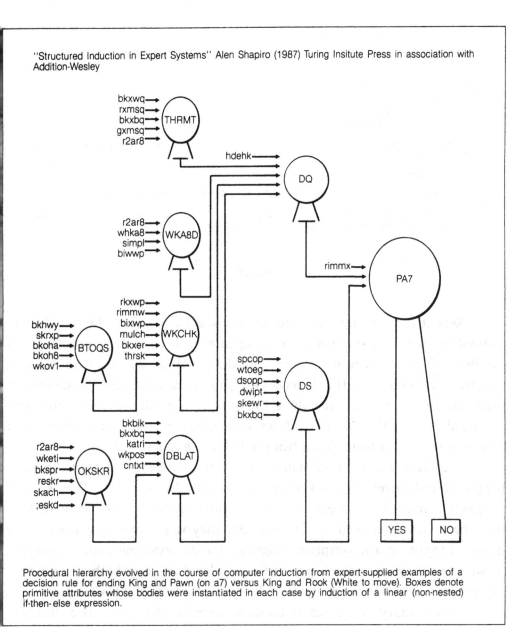

"Structured Induction in Expert Systems" Alen Shapiro (1987) Turing Insitute Press in association with Addition-Wesley

Procedural hierarchy evolved in the course of computer induction from expert-supplied examples of a decision rule for ending King and Pawn (on a7) versus King and Rook (White to move). Boxes denote primitive attributes whose bodies were instantiated in each case by induction of a linear (non-nested) if-then-else expression.

**Fig.14 Expert-derived Structure for a Complex Problem**

failure variant of the closed world assumption, which is implemented, of course, in the PROLOG language. They have a working "closed world specialization algorithm", which on trivial test examples does the right things, and it does generate a most general correct specialization. In other words, the generalization over the set of counter-examples is as conservative as it can be.

---

CIGOL ("LOGIC" spelled backwards)

accepts unit-clause example
inverts resolution
uses operators: truncation
         absorption
         intraconstruction

to modify incomplete clausal theories so as to augment their coverage, using compactness criterion to constrain search.

CIGOL generalises incrementally from positive examples.

CIGOL does not generalise over negative examples which contradict its current theory.

NM-CIGOL ("non-monotonic CIGOL") uses Negation by Failure to implement in Prolog a Closed World Specialisation Algorithm, which generates a most-general-correct-specialisation.

---

**Fig.15**

Recently, we made tests, not of the new CIGOL, but the old CIGOL, against the power of various learning agents, to learn a hard problem — a problem of considerably greater complexity than the Shuttle landing problem. It belongs to the general category of data integrity predicates, a predicate to say whether positions taken from a particular space in chess are legal or illegal positions. After a hundred training examples, each learning agent was tested on a hundred test examples.

The first category of learning agents consisted of four leading propositional level dicision tree induction algorithms. The second category consisted of fifteen teen-age school children, who were divided into three sub-sets, according to whether they were given a symbolic or a pictorial input as a description language for the examples, and according to whether they were given positive examples only, or whether a mixture of positive and negative examples. The final category was CIGOL.

In summary, with small training sets of that size, the children tested with about 80 percent accuracy on the test material, and CIGOL achieved a similar score. The state of the art decision tree induction algorithms did somewhat poorly, and were only able to produce performance at the level of 80 percent, if provided with a very large example set — a training set of a thousand cases.

I also gave the same material to fourth-year mathematics students in the University of Strathclide, where I was engaged in teaching a course on data analysis. They not only had more than an hour, which is all that the children had: they had as long as they liked. They also had a range of data analytical tools including statistical and rule induction tools. I am sorry to tell you that their performance was not as impressive as that of the teenage school children. Possibly that's the price paid for being distracted by too many software tools, rather than being allowed peace and quiet in which to think.

In conclusion, the next step is to test NM-CIGOL, the non-monotonic version, on this hard test problem. The theoretical prediction is that it should be fully efficient. But in our environment, over the years, we have acquired a fairly experimental bias. Consequently we never believe our theoretical extrapolations until the matter has been proved by systematic comparative trials.

**CHAIRMAN**: Thank you very much.

There is very little time, so, I would like to accept only a few questions. Any questions? Comment?

**(Q.)**: I have been interested in CIGOL, and I have been at the last Machine Learning — International Machine Learning Conference. And many of the excitements generated at that Conference about CIGOL were that that was presented as having the ability to invent predicates; — a W operator for invention of predicates.

How do you evaluate that CIGOL correctly learns invention?

**D. Michie**: Predicate invention is a fact. It is efficient. The unknown question is just how valuable that predicate invention capability really is.

**(Q.)**: Okay. Is that tested against the examples? Or against any formal understanding of what invention is?

**D. Michie**: The formal understanding is embedded in the theoretical derivation of the algorithm.

I do not understand the distinction between the theoretical derivation of predicate invention and your form of words, which says, we want to find out what it really is.

**(Q.):** Well, in my learning programs, I say: "Well, I want to learn this." CIGOL says: "I want to invent predicates."

**D. Michie:** No, CIGOL also says: "I want to learn this." And in the course of its attempts to learn that concept, it generates intermediate predicates as being possibly helpful.

Now, as you will be familiar, it presents interactively on the screen the new predicate. For example, if it is trying to larn how to sort, from examples of sorted and unsorted lists, it may invent an intermediate predicate, which you or I would call "partition", shall we say. It presents a PROLOG program on the screen with an ID number, and asks the user: "Is this a useful sub-predicate?" "Is it a useful concept?" And if the oracle says "yes", then it asks the user "please name it." So, then, the user types in "partition". And then, it continues with its goal.

**(Q):** So, that was my question. In fact, the user is providing the validation of the invented predicates?

**D. Michie:** The evaluation. Yes.

**(Q):** That's it. Thank you.

**CHAIRMAN:** Other questions?

**(Q):** Can I ask one question? Also in CIGOL, the system invents intermediate predicates. And as far as I know that it invents if the intermediate predicate you need is one — one predicate. If you need maybe more than one, what is the situation?

**D. Michie:** CIGOL is an incremental learning system. If a satisfactory solution to the problem requires the invention of two or three subpredicates, then, the discovery proceeds incrementally.

**CHAIRMAN:** Incrementally. Thank you. Any other questions? Okay.
I would like to finish this session. Thank you very much.

# The Classification and Boundary Problem

Jinsei Yamaguchi

*Dept. of Information Sciences, KANAGAWA UNIVERSITY*

*2946 Tsuchiya, Hiratsuka, Kanagawa 259-12, JAPAN*

**Summary:** We propose the concept of "the classification and boundary problem" and review a few types of reasonings in our daily life from the angle of this problem. As a typical example, we treat the topic of a realization of non-monotonic reasoning based on a logic programming.

**Key Words:** AI, non-monotonic reasoning, logic programming

## §0. Introduction

It is important that we recognize various intrinsic difficulties which occur when AI is realized by computers. As one methodology to this inclusive recognition, a nice(and/or simple)naming of the target hardship is rather useful. The most famous among many such namings might be, so to speak, "the frame problem ". Here, we would like to propose a concept named "the classification and boundary problem ", which can also be viewed as an abstract issue in AI. Since both spring up from the same field, i.e., AI, they intervene in each other. As a typical example which is located at the conjunction, there is the topic of non-monotonic reasoning. Similar to the case of the frame problem, the classification and boundary problem would be unsolvable in its ultimate meaning (in the same sense that it is impossible to discover the eternal scientific truth ). However, it seems that humankind can easily resolve classification and boundary problems in its daily life. From this fact, we had better face the difficulty in an active manner (by which we are trying to explore a secret of man's way of thinking),rather than with a negative pessimism. As one possible technique to overcome the problem, we try to formalize the concept. By doing so, we can abstract a pattern from various kinds of classification and boundary problems. Then, by applying the pattern to a particular case, we can comprehend the proper character of it. Paying attention to this character, we might be able to obtain some strategy (at an abstract level) which would be available. If this is realized, then there occurs a possibility that we can feedback the strategy to the case as heuristics. The main theme of this paper is to propose the concept of the classification and boundary problem and to apply the concept to non-monotonic reasoning as a particular case.

In § 1, we propose the concept of the classification and boundary problem and confirm that this concept appears almost everywhere in our way of thinking. In § 2, we reinterpret non-monotonic reasoning from the angle of this problem and, at the same time, abstract the reinterpretation. By so doing, we notice that there is a phase where this resoning technique works effectively. § 3 is devoted to treating the topic of realization of non-monotonic reasoning based on logic programming, in order to suggest that the idea can be useful in a practical aspect. As the theoretical backbone of this realization, we present a Boolean-valued interpretation of non-monotonic reasoning in § 4. Through this Boolean-valued technique, the conventional notion of non-monotonicity can be generalized. Finally in § 5, we list our original claims stated in this paper as a conclusion.

## § 1 . The Classification and Boundary Problem

The catchphrase "AI is a field of study which puts weight on a technique of the treatment of vague information in our daily life" is true in a sense. Just take the notion of "beauty" for instance. Let's try to divide the set of all women in the world into two categories of "beautiful"and "ugly". Then, we at once recognize a naive problem of whether an average woman belongs to the former category or the latter. This is an essential question, considering the fact that a similar question can still survive even if we introduce an ad hoc criterion "average" in order to refine the division. Restating this question in one word, we can say that this is "the problem concerning the boundary when the intended domain(whether it is continuous or discrete) is divided somehow or other." As one way to escape the difficulty, the technique of introducing the notion of the fuzzy set has been proposed for many years. In a fuzzy fashion, it is announced that the straight division into two (or three) classes is the inelegant point, and that representing "beauty" by using a membership function line is the graceful cutting to avoid such senselessness. However, matters under the heavens are not at all improved by employing this strategy. Using a word of fuzzy logic, the above is only r-educed to the problem of how to determine the membership function. Given the set of all women, the decision of the membership function corresponding to "beauty" is influenced by a person's subjective intention in one way or other. Though we don't further continue the argument in this direction, we can recognize that the classification and boundary problem is still important even in the field of fuzzy inference.

With the observations stated above in mind, we give the name "the classification and boundary problem" to "our deliberate concern as to the boundary generated by classifications of the intended domain (the set of objects of the target knowledge) using certain kinds of criteria." Watching a variety of topics in AI with this mental process of recognition, we can obtain a systematic and synthetic viewpoint at an abstract level. One aspect of our Boolean-valued methodology is the strategy with which we grasp this viewpoint formally and describe the content at the level of knowledge representation and inference. Our aim in this paper is to analyze the notion of non-monotonic reasoning from the angle of the classification and boundary problem with the help of Boolean-valued interpretation.

## § 2. Non-monotonic Reasoning

In the previous section, we offer a unified viewpoint in the field of AI, that is, the importance of the classification (of the intended domain of knowledge) and the boundary (attached to each class by certain kinds of criteria). In this section, we show that this viewpoint can be applied to non-monotonic reasoning. As an instance, let's consider the case of the domain $D = \{x \mid x \text{ is an animal}\}$. As one classification of $D$, there is an equivalence relation $\approx$ according to a taxonomy which defines equivalence classes like "animal", "bird",…,etc. On the other hand, we can divide $D$ by the attribute-of-action relation $\approx'$ which animals properly have, to produce equivalence classes like "walk", "fly", "swim",…, etc. (It is not an essential matter at all whether we consider a class like "walk and fly".) Here,in general,it is interesting that there often happens to be a case that an equivalence class $[\ ]_{\approx}$ defined by $\approx$ and an equivalence class $[\ ]_{\approx'}$ defined by $\approx'$ have common elements which form a major subset $[\ ]_{\approx} \cap [\ ]_{\approx'}$ of both $[\ ]_{\approx}$ and $[\ ]_{\approx'}$. In the following, as usual, select the case of $[bird]_{\approx}$ and $[fly]_{\approx'}$. Then, the conjunction $[\text{bird}]_{\approx} \cap [\text{fly}]_{\approx'}$ occupies the majority in both $[\text{bird}]_{\approx}$ and $[\text{fly}]_{\approx'}$ . In other words, $[\text{bird}]_{\approx} - [\text{fly}]_{\approx'}$ becomes a set of exceptional(abnormal) elements in $[\text{bird}]_{\approx}$ in the sense of the attribute and $[\text{fly}]_{\approx'} - [\text{bird}]_{\approx}$ becomes a set of exceptional elements in $[\text{fly}]_{\approx'}$ in the sense of the taxonomy. This fact becomes the basis of non-monotonic reasoning. In this sense, we should not miss the point that the concept of the classification and boundary (the symmetric difference of two equivalence classes) also intervenes in the notion of non-monotonic reasoning.

Now, observing non-monotonic reasoning from this angle, we obtain the next inference scheme which is just the same as the fuzzy inference scheme.

$$\frac{A'(x), \quad A(x) \rightarrow B(y)}{B'(y)} \qquad \cdots (1)$$

Applying this scheme to the above instance, we obtain

$$\frac{(\text{Tweety is a bird}), (x \text{ is a normal bird}) \rightarrow (x \text{ can fly})}{(\text{Tweety perhaps flies})}$$

In the case of fuzzy inference, the reasoning ends in this form of conclusion with a certainty factor. However, in the case of non-monotonic reasoning, we further try to judge the conclusion by means of data *at hand*. That is, looking at the list of exceptional elements(the exception of "bird" w.r.t. "fly" ), we get the result:

$$\begin{cases} \text{Tweety can fly (certainty factor 1), if Tweety does not appear as an} \\ \qquad\qquad\qquad\qquad\qquad\qquad \text{exception (default reasoning)} \\ \text{Tweety can't fly (certainty factor 0), otherwise.} \end{cases}$$

Note that in the case of the former,there still remains the possibility that, though Tweety does not appear in the data *at hand* ( because of the lack of complete information ), he will appear as an exceptional element in the future.(increment of information or "the effect of time") Then,of course, the status of Tweety changes to the latter at that point in time In any case, both fuzzy and non-monotonic inferences put weight on the reasoning type (1). The main difference is whether a minor revision (based on 2-valued philosophy) is undertaken or not.

As stated above, some kinds of non-monotonic reasoning can be abstracted to the problem of "dividing a domain D by two equivalence relations and comparing the resulting two equivalence classes which overlap each other in major part." This viewpoint is the aspect that we can employ as a heuristic of AI. For example, we often experience in our daily life that our original aim is to divide D by $\approx$ but an algorithm to determine $\approx$ precisely becomes rather complex (or, sometimes, it is even impossible to determine precisely because of the lack of complete information ). In such a case, we usually try to temporarily divide D by $\approx'$ which is almost equal to $\approx$ except for minor changes (in case of incomplete information, "minor" means unknown parts) and is simpler than $\approx$ in the sense of algorithm. ( In the case of incomplete information, nothing is more complex than the unknown.) Then we adjust the difference between $\approx$ and $\approx'$ (shortly) afterwards. It is obvious that this becomes a non-monotonic reasoning owing to the existence of adjustment. In the following, we are going to apply this idea (comprehension of non-monotonic reasoning by means of the adjustment of two equivalence relations) to an inference based on logic programming.

**Remark:** Since the arguments go parallel, we focus our attention only on the idea with no time lag,i.e.,the case that our knowledge concerning D does not increase as time goes by. ┤

As a preparation,let's mathematically formalize the notions of "exception" and "boundary" which are naively (or rather vaguely) used above. As the preliminary notions :

**Definition 2-1** Let X,Y be arbitrary sets. Then,
(1) $|X|$ is the cardinal number of X.
(2)
$$order(X) = \begin{cases} n+1 & \text{,if } 10^n \leqq |X| < 10^{n+1} \\ |X| & \text{,otherwise.} \end{cases}$$
(3) $X \ll Y$ iff $order(X) < order(Y)$.
(4) $X \ll_n Y$ iff $X \ll Y$ and $|X| < 10^n$ . ┤

Using these notations,we define :

**Definition 2-2** Let X be an arbitrary set and $\approx$ , $\approx'$ be two different equivalence relations over X. ( Then, $\approx \cap \approx'$ is also an equivalence relation.)
(1) "The exceptional set $Q_n(\approx - \approx')$ of order n for $\approx$ w.r.t.$\approx'$ " is defined as
$$Q_n(\approx - \approx') = \{a \in X \mid [a]_{\approx \cap \approx'} \ll_n [a]_{\approx} \}.$$

Similarly,we can define

$Q n(\approx' - \approx) = \{a \in X \mid [a]_{\approx \cap \approx}, \quad \leqq_n [a]_{\approx'} \quad \}.$

(2) "The boundary $K n(\approx, \approx')$ of order $n$ w.r.t. $\approx$ and $\approx'$ " is defined as

$K n(\approx, \approx') = Q n(\approx - \approx') \cup Q n(\approx' - \approx).$

The following images might illustrate the above concepts intuitively.

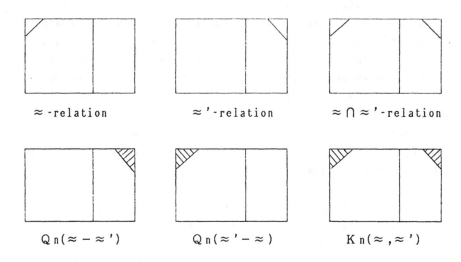

≈-relation          ≈'-relation          ≈ ∩ ≈'-relation

$Q n(\approx - \approx')$          $Q n(\approx' - \approx)$          $K n(\approx, \approx')$

*Figure 1*

From the definition, we at once notice that

**Proposition 2-3**  In case of $\approx \subset \approx'$, $Q n(\approx - \approx') = \emptyset$, and so $K n(\approx, \approx') = Q n(\approx' - \approx)$. Similarly, $K n(\approx, \approx') = Q n(\approx - \approx')$ if $\approx' \subset \approx$.  □

In the following, as a typical candidate of the domain to which the notions of exceptional set and boundary are applied, we take an Herbrand base ( or an Herbrand universe ) from a viewpoint of logic programming.

## § 3.  ≡.B.F.E.-unification

Let P be a Horn clause program, $B p(U p)$ be the Herbrand base (universc) of $P$ and $A(\Pi p,V)(\ T(\Sigma p,V)\ )$ be the set of all atoms( terms ) used in $P$ (whose variables are supposed to be picked from $V$). Convent-ional realizations of non-monotonic reasoning based on logic programming have been putting their weight mainly on the deriving of negative infor-mation through CWA or negation as failure. Contrastingly, the aim of th-is section is to show that the idea of the previous section can be util-ized to derive positive information on the basis of logic programming. For this purpose, let's extend the notion of syntactical unification to the following more general form.

**Definition 3-1**  Let $\equiv$ be an equivalence relation over $A(\Pi p,V)$.
(1) $\equiv$ is "substitution-transitive" iff
$\quad(\forall A,B \in A(\Pi p,V))(\forall\theta:$ substitution$)(\ A \equiv B \rightarrow A\theta \equiv B\theta\ )$.
(2) Let $\equiv$ be a substitution-transitive equivalence relation over $A(\Pi p,$
$\quad V)$. Then, $\theta$ is a $\equiv$-unifier for $A,B \in A(\Pi p,V)$  iff $A\theta \equiv B\theta$. $\dashv$

**Example 3-2**  Let $E$ be an equational theory over $T(\Sigma p,V)$. Using $E$, we can define an equivalence relation $\equiv_E$ over $A(\Pi p,V)$. Then, the well-known $E$-unification becomes $\equiv_E$-unification in the above sense. ( From the nature of $E$, it is obvious that $\equiv_E$ becomes substitution-transitive.)
$\dashv$

   Here, we can extend the notion of SLD-resolution to SLD($\equiv$)-resolution by using $\equiv$-unification ( based on the $\equiv$-unifier) instead of syntactic-al unification. Let's denote thus obtained logic programming paradigm as $(P,\equiv)($, more accurately, $(P_-,\equiv)\ )$. The key point in this paradigm is the algorithm to determine whether $\theta$ is a $\equiv$-unifier for $A,B \in A(\Pi p,V)$ ( $\equiv$-mgu, if possible) or not. This is the place where the above idea is available. To be more precise, suppose there is another (substitution-transitive) equivalence relation $\equiv'$ (over $A(\Pi p,V)$ ) such that:

1. $\equiv'$ is equal to $\equiv$ except on the boundary in the above sense, i.e.,
    for any $\sigma,\tau \in B p - Kn(\equiv,\equiv')$, $\sigma \equiv \tau$ iff $\sigma \equiv' \tau$,
    where $Kn(\equiv,\equiv')$ is defined as above from $\equiv \upharpoonright B p \times B p$ and $\equiv' \upharpoonright$
    $B p \times B p$.
2. Compared with $B p$, the number of exceptions $|Kn(\equiv,\equiv')|$ becomes
    relatively small.
3. $\equiv'$ becomes substantially simpler (compared with the original $\equiv$ as a
    whole) from a viewpoint of algorithmic realization. In other words,
    we suppose the existence of $\equiv'$ such that checking whether $\theta$ is a $\equiv$
    -unifier for $A,B$ becomes more complicated than checking whether $\theta$ is
    a $\equiv'$-unifier for $A,B$.

In this situation:

Definition 3-3    Suppose the enumeration of $Kn(\equiv,\equiv')$ is easy. Then, $\equiv'$ is called

⎧ an extended good-approximation of $\equiv$ ,    if $\equiv \subset \equiv'$

⎨ a reduced good-approximation of $\equiv$ ,    if $\equiv' \subset \equiv$

⎩ a good-approximation of $\equiv$ ,    otherwise.    ┤

The following images might illustrate the above concepts intuitively.

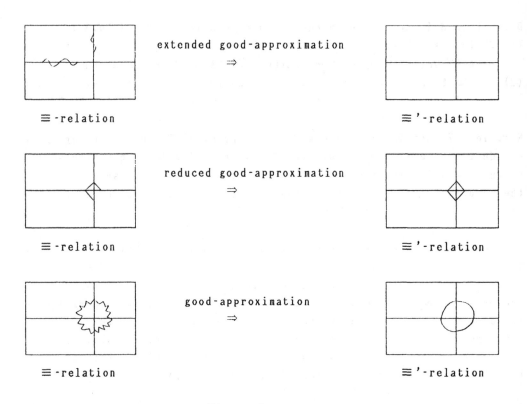

extended good-approximation
$\Rightarrow$

$\equiv$-relation    $\equiv'$-relation

reduced good-approximation
$\Rightarrow$

$\equiv$-relation    $\equiv'$-relation

good-approximation
$\Rightarrow$

$\equiv$-relation    $\equiv'$-relation

*Figure 2*

Now, just consider the case where we realize $\equiv$-unification by using an extended good-approximation $\equiv'$ of $\equiv$. In this case, when we want to obtain the answer for the query, say, $\leftarrow q$ w.r.t. $(P_\equiv , \equiv)$, we employ the following technique:

1. use the $\equiv'$-unifier instead of the $\equiv$-unifier.
2. On the $\equiv'$-derivation tree, if a branch b is a $\equiv'$-success branch(in

the usual sense that the leaf node is empty) with the set of substit-
utions $\theta_1, \cdots, \theta_n$ and the set of input clauses $C_1, \cdots C_n$, then check
whether "a wrong ground substitution" $\rho$ w.r.t. $\theta_1, \cdots, \theta_n$ may exist
or not. Else, do nothing.

Here, a wrong ground substitution $\rho$ is a substitution which corresponds to the difference between $\equiv$ and $\equiv'$. That is, since $\equiv \subset \equiv'$,
we might find a substitution $\rho$ such that
$$C_i{}^+\theta_i \cdots \theta_n \rho \equiv' B\theta_i \cdots \theta_n \rho \quad \text{but} \quad C_i{}^+\theta_i \cdots \theta_n \rho \not\equiv B\theta_i \cdots \theta_n \rho$$
where B is the i-th selected goal corresponding to $C_i$ for some $1 \leqq i \leqq$
n.

Here, note the fact that, since $Kn(\equiv, \equiv')$ is finite, the set of all
wrong ground substitutions are at most finite.

3. If the set of wrong ground substitutions is not empty, say, $\{\rho_1, \cdots,$
   $\rho_k\}$, then "modify" the answer substitution $\theta (= \theta_1 \cdots \theta_n)$. Else, do
   nothing.

   Here, the modification means that
   if $\theta$ is not fully grounded, then list the set of exceptions
   $$[q\theta\rho_1, \cdots, q\theta\rho_k]$$
   and add it as new information of counter examples for $q\theta$ w.r.t. the
   branch b. Else, abandon $\theta$. (If $\theta$ itself is already grounded, then
   $\rho$ is the empty substitution and so $q\theta - q\theta = \varnothing$ .)

4. Repeat the above process 2~3 until no more success branches remain,
   in case we need all possible answers for q (under the condition that
   the tree is ideal).

Since $Kn(\equiv, \equiv')$ is finite, the algorithm 2~3 is terminated for each
particular $\theta$, if there is any. In the above algorithm, the modification
is nothing but non-monotonic reasoning stated in the previous section.

Remark: A word of caution. When a program $(P_{\equiv'}, \equiv')$ is written, we should not use exceptional atoms in $P_{\equiv'}$ . In other words, a representative
of each equivalence class ( mod. $\equiv'$ ) which does not belong to $Kn(\equiv, \equiv')$
or a predicative name attached to each equivalence class must be employ-
ed in order to describe the $P_{\equiv'}$ part of the program. In this case, there
may *sometimes* happen that the $P_{\equiv'}$ becomes different from the $P_\equiv$ part of
the ( supposed to be original and/or imaginary ) program $(P_\equiv, \equiv)$. Even
if it happens, however, $P_{\equiv'}$ always becomes simpler than $P_\equiv$ as a whole
( because $Kn(\equiv, \equiv')$-part does not influence $P_{\equiv'}$ part ). So, we need
not worry about the merit of our performing the above technique. A more
precise argument concerning this aspect will be discussed in the other
paper.

The legitimacy of the above reasoning is assured when we grasp the $\equiv$-unification as a kind of constraint-solving. The difference between the conventional $\equiv$-unification and ours is the difference in realizations of the same equivalence relation. One is naively and directly done by $\equiv$ and another is tactically and indirectly done by $\equiv'$ and $Kn(\equiv,\equiv')$. That is, the former is to try to apply a solver w.r.t. $\equiv$ to each newly generated constraint.( For example,from the goal $\leftarrow q$ and an input clause $C$ , a constraint $(\exists \xi)(q\xi \equiv C^+\xi)$ is generated to obtain an answer $\eta$ and to deduce a new goal $\leftarrow C^-\eta$ .) On the other hand, the latter is to firstly try to find a default answer to the query by using a simpler solver w.r.t. $\equiv'$ and then modify each answer by $Kn(\equiv,\equiv')$ at the final stage. In this latter tactic, as can be seen in the above, not only an answer substitution $\theta$ is obtained, but the "history" $q\theta_1 \equiv' C_1^+\theta_1$, $\cdots$ of each answer $\theta (= \theta_1 \cdots \theta_n)$ should be recorded in order to pass the final judgement by $Kn(\equiv,\equiv')$. At a first glance, it apparently seems that redundant elaborations have been done. This, however, is not so at all. The former is substantially equivalent to the technique of carrying out a $Kn(\equiv,\equiv')$-check at each $\equiv'$-derivation step. At the same time, since histories select only succeeding branches, they can serve a variety of tasks like the verification of the correctness of answers (concerning substitutions), the investigation of inference process (concerning clauses), program debugging etc, all of which are important from the viewpoint of programming environment (especially when the time lag of the non-monotonicity exists ). Moreover, the form of the answer we admit (a general answer with exceptions) is important. By permitting this form of answers, we can widen the range of knowlede representation based on the logic programming paradigm.

In general, there ought to be a form of constraint-solving which uses a $\equiv'$-unification at first where $\equiv'$ is a good-approximation of $\equiv$ and modifies both the $\equiv'$-success set and the $\equiv'$-finitely failed set at the final stage by using the boundary $Kn(\equiv,\equiv')$. We call this kind of constraint- solving " the $\equiv.B.F.E.$-unification ($\equiv$-but-finite-exception unification)". The precise definition of this general notion and concrete examples of its applicational form will be treated in the other paper.


## §4. $\mathbb{B}$-valued Interpretation


As the theoretical foundation of the realization of non-monotonic reasoning based on a logic program ($P_{\equiv},\equiv$) discussed in the previous section, we $\mathbb{B}$-valued interpret the realization. At the end of this section, you will notice that the $\mathbb{B}$-valued interpretation is really needed to verify the non-monotonicity of the $\equiv$.B.F.E.-unification. Let's begin our argument with the definition of the $\mathbb{B}$-valued unification.

Definition 4-1 Let $\sim$ be a substitution-transitive relation over $A(\Pi p, V)$ and $\mathbb{B}$ be a complete Boolean algebra. Suppose a map $[\![\ ]\!]: Bp \to \mathbb{B}$ is given. Then,
(1) a substitution $\theta$ is a $\mathbb{B}$-valued unifier for $A, B \in A(\Pi p, V)$ w.r.t. $\sim$ and $[\![\ ]\!]$ iff
　　$A\theta \sim B\theta$
　　and
　　$[\![A\theta\rho]\!]=[\![B\theta\rho]\!]$ for any ground substitution $\rho$ for $A\theta$ and $B\theta$.
(2) The $\mathbb{B}$-valued unification of $A, B \in A(\Pi p, V)$ w.r.t. $\sim$ and $[\![\ ]\!]$ means the process of:
　　(i) finding a $\mathbb{B}$-valued unifier $\theta$ for $A, B$ w.r.t. $\sim$ and $[\![\ ]\!]$
　　and
　　(ii) calculating the $\mathbb{B}$-value $\bigwedge_{\rho:\,ground} [\![A\theta\rho]\!]$.　　　　　　　┤

　　Now, suppose two equivalence relations $\equiv, \equiv'$ s.t. $\equiv'$ is an extended good-approximation of $\equiv$, are given. Then, we can define a boundary $Kn$ $(\equiv, \equiv')(= Qn(\equiv' - \equiv))$ on $Bp$ from the two equivalence relations $\equiv \restriction Bp \times Bp$ and $\equiv' \restriction Bp \times Bp$ as in §3. Our purpose is to recover the original $\equiv \restriction Bp \times Bp$ and $\equiv' \restriction Bp \times Bp$ by using $\sim$ and $[\![\ ]\!]$.

Remark: The equivalence relation defined by $\sim$ and $[\![\ ]\!]$ need not be exactly equal to the original $\equiv, \equiv'$ over $A(\Pi p, V)$. All we need is the coincidence over $Bp$. (For arguments concerning this aspect, see [8].) ┤

For this purpose, let's take $\sim$ to be the transitive closure of $\equiv \cup \equiv'$. Next, define $[\![\ ]\!]_\equiv$ and $[\![\ ]\!]_{\equiv'}$ so that, for any $\sigma, \tau \in Bp$,

　　$[\![\sigma]\!]_\equiv = [\![\tau]\!]_\equiv$　iff　$\sigma \equiv \tau$
and
　　$[\![\sigma]\!]_{\equiv'} = [\![\tau]\!]_{\equiv'}$　iff　$\sigma \equiv' \tau$　　　　　　　…(2)
and
　　$[\![\sigma]\!]_\equiv = [\![\sigma]\!]_{\equiv'}$　if　$\sigma \in Bp - Kn(\equiv, \equiv')$.

Though there are many possible candidates for $[\![\ ]\!]_\equiv$ and $[\![\ ]\!]_{\equiv'}$ which satisfy above conditions, we can always choose two of them *under the condition that $\mathbb{B}$ is large enough* so that, for any $\sigma \in Bp$,

$$[\![\sigma]\!]_{\equiv} \in F \cup I \quad \text{and} \quad [\![\sigma]\!]_{\equiv'} \in F \cup I$$

and

$$[\![\sigma]\!]_{\equiv} \in F \quad \text{iff} \quad (P,\equiv) \vdash \sigma \qquad\qquad \cdots(3$$

and

$$[\![\sigma]\!]_{\equiv'} \in F \quad \text{iff} \quad (P,\equiv') \vdash \sigma$$

where $F$ is a complete filter over $\mathbb{B}$ and $I$ is the dual ideal of $F$. ( $F$ is supposed to represent a *relatively true* region in $\mathbb{B}$. For the precise argument, see [7],[12].)

By definition, it is easy to see that, for any $A,B \in A(\Pi p,V)$,

$\theta$ is a $\equiv$-unifier for $A,B$ iff $\theta$ is a $\mathbb{B}$-valued unifier for $A,B$ w.r.t. $\sim$ and $[\![ \ ]\!]_{\equiv}$

and

$\theta'$ is a $\equiv'$-unifier for $A,B$ iff $\theta'$ is a $\mathbb{B}$-valued unifier for $A,B$ w.r.t. $\sim$ and $[\![ \ ]\!]_{\equiv'}$ .

In this setting,

**Definition 4-2** A non-monotonic reasoning w.r.t. $Kn(\equiv,\equiv')$ over $(P_{\equiv}, \equiv)$ is performed based on $\mathbb{B}$-valued interpretation
iff
$(\exists \sigma \in Kn(\equiv,\equiv'))([\![\sigma]\!]_{\equiv'} \in F$ and $[\![\sigma]\!]_{\equiv} \in I)$.
In this case, the set $Nm =\{\sigma \in Kn(\equiv,\equiv') \mid [\![\sigma]\!]_{\equiv'} \in F$ and $[\![\sigma]\!]_{\equiv} \in I\}$
is called "the non-monotonic set" w.r.t. $Kn(\equiv,\equiv')$.

This means that, for any $\sigma \in Nm$, the status of a sentence $\sigma$ which was supposed to be "right" (or "positive") ($[\![\sigma]\!]_{\equiv'} \in F$) has turned out to be "wrong" (or "negative") by the interpretation $\equiv$ ($[\![\sigma]\!]_{\equiv} \in I$) through the oracle of the boundary $Kn(\equiv,\equiv')$. Then, we notice that an inference based on the $\mathbb{B}$-valued unification w.r.t. $\sim$ and $[\![ \ ]\!]_{\equiv'}$ becomes a default reasoning. Note that the above notion of ($\mathbf{2}$-valued philosophical) non-monotonicity is defined by means of a model theoretic concept rather than a proof theoretic concept. However, since the $\mathbb{B}$-valued unification is directly related to $[\![ \ ]\!]$, we can surely apply the above notion of non-monotonicity to the $\equiv$-refutation procedure described in the previous section. ( For any $\sigma \in Nm$, $(P_{\equiv'},\equiv') \cup \{\leftarrow \sigma\}$ has a refutation, but $\sigma$ is removed by $Kn(\equiv,\equiv')$.)

Here, we can't reject the possibility that there might be $\sigma \in Kn(\equiv, \equiv')$ such that

$[\![\sigma]\!]_{='} \in F$ and $[\![\sigma]\!]_{=} \in F$

In general, there often exist two elements $\sigma, \tau \in Bp$ such that:

1. both $\sigma$ and $\tau$ belong to the success set $Sp(\equiv)$ $(=\{\sigma \in Bp \mid (P,\equiv)$ $\vdash \sigma\})$ of $(P,\equiv)$, and so $[\![\sigma]\!]_{=} \in F$ and $[\![\tau]\!]_{=} \in F$.
2. $[\![\sigma]\!]_{=} \neq [\![\tau]\!]_{=}$ .
   ( success set $Sp(\equiv)$ is $\mathbb{B}$-valued ordered.)
3. $[\![\sigma]\!]_{='} = [\![\tau]\!]_{='} \in F$
   ( the distinction by $\equiv$ ceases to exist in $\equiv'$).

In this case, there may be answer substitutions $\theta, \theta'$ for $(P_{='},\equiv')\cup$ $(\leftarrow q)$ such that

a) $(\exists\rho,\rho')(q\theta\rho = \sigma$ and $q\theta\rho' = \tau)$ but $\sigma$ is removed by the $Kn(\equiv,$ $\equiv')$- check in this path
b) $(\exists\xi)(q\theta'\xi = \sigma)$ but $\sigma$ is not removed by the $Kn(\equiv,\equiv')$-check in this path.

This (, in addition to (2) and (3),) is the reason why the $\mathbb{B}$-valued interpretation of the $\equiv$.B.F.E.-unification is needed to explain its non-monotonic property. On the grounds of the above observation, we are interested in the following wider notion of non-monotonicity.

**Definition 4-3** A non-monotonic reasoning in a wider sense w.r.t. $Kn(\equiv,$ $\equiv')$ over $(P_{=},\equiv)$ is performed iff there exists $\sigma \in Kn(\equiv,\equiv')$ s.t.
1). $(P_{='},\equiv')\cup(\leftarrow q)$ has a refutation with the answer substitution $\theta$ such that $(\exists\rho)(q\theta\rho = \sigma)$
2). $\sigma$ is removed by the $Kn(\equiv,\equiv')$-check. ┤

Note that this definition is a proof theoretic one and this is just what we have done in the previous section. In the above, we don't mention whether the $\mathbb{B}$-value $[\![\sigma]\!]_{=}$ belongs to $I$ or not. This suggests to us a more abstract and wider framework of the notion of a non-monotonicity through a $\mathbb{B}$-valued interpretation. For example, under the general $\equiv$.B.F. E.-unification, a change of maps something like

$$(\forall\sigma \in Bp - Kn(\equiv,\equiv'))([\![\sigma]\!]_{='} = [\![\sigma]\!]_{=})$$
and
$$(\exists\sigma \in Kn(\equiv,\equiv'))([\![\sigma]\!]_{='} \neq [\![\sigma]\!]_{=})$$

should be permitted for further AI theoretic notions.

Before closing the section, let's point out the following important aspect. So far, we have presented that we can grasp the concept of non-monotonic reasoning within the framework of classical logic via the $\mathbb{B}$-valued philosophy. This fact is based on the property that we reduce the (originally model theoretic) notion of maps to a (object level) program $(P,\sim,[\![\ ]\!])$ and, by so doing, can change maps one after another. Here, if we are allowed to use an analogy, the change of maps corresponds to "routine revision" in the sense of McDermott & Doyle [3].

§ 5 . Conclusion

In the following, we list our original claims stated in this paper.
1. We suggest that the notions of fuzzy inference and non-monotonic reasoning, etc, which are used in our daily life, can be captured by a simple uniform framework which is characterized by the naming of " the classification and boundary problem ".
2. As an application of non-monotonic reasoning to the paradigm of logic programming, we use a default reasoning based on a universal unification. As the result, each answer in this system has, in general, the form of (the set of) "general answer + finite exceptional counter examples for it".
3. A new " $\mathbb{B}$ -valued interpretation" of non-monotonic reasoning is proposed. Using this, we can precisely comprehend how a person's blief changes.

Notice: Any person or group who want to borrow any part of the idea stated in this paper should get in touch with the author.

References

[1] Hanks,S. and McDermott,D., "Default Reasoning, Nonmonotonic Logic, and the Frame Problem", Proc. of AAAI-86, 328-333, 1986.
[2] McCarthy,J., "Circumscription: A Form of Non-monotonic Reasoning", Artif.Intell., Vol.13, 27-39, 1980.
[3] McDermott,D. and Doyle,J., "Non-monotonic Logic I", Artif.Intell., Vol.13, 41-72, 1980.

[4] Reiter,R., "A Logic for Default Reasoning", Artif.Intell., Vol.13, 81-132, 1980.

[5] Yamaguchi,J., "Boolean-valued Logic Programming Language Paradigm: LIFE-$\Omega$ —Philosophical Background—", NEC LR-5196,1987.

[6] Yamaguchi,J., "Boolean-valued Logic Programming Language Paradigm: LIFE-$\Omega$ —Theoretical Background of LIFE-Ⅰ,Ⅱ,Ⅲ—",NEC LR-5197,1987.

[7] Yamaguchi,J., "Logical Completeness of LIFE-Ⅱ and LIFE-Ⅲ and Its Applications to the Foundation of Logic Programming",NEC LR-5346,1987.

[8] Yamaguchi,J., "Universal Unification from a Viewpoint of LIFE-Ⅱ",NEC LR-5347,1987.

[9] Yamaguchi,J., "Boolean-valued Logic Programming Language Scheme:LIFE-Ⅲ—A Summary—",NEC LR-5357,1988.

[10] Yamaguchi,J., "Two-lane Unification and A.B.F.E. -unification —One Step Toward an Application of LIFE-Ⅱ—",NEC LR-5426,1988.

[11] Yamaguchi,J., "F-LIFE: a L-fuzzy Inferential System", NEC LR-5544, 1988.

[12] Yamaguchi,J., "Boolean-valued Logic Programming Language Scheme:LIFE-Ⅲ [1]Inferentially Transforming Logic Programs",(in Japanese)5th Conference Proceedings Japan Soc.Software Sci.&Tech.,1988,237-240.

[13] Yamaguchi,J., "Boolean-valued Logic Programming Language Scheme:LIFE-Ⅲ [2]A Technique to Execute a Logic Program Efficiently",(in Japanese)5th Conference Proceedings Japan Soc.Software Sci.&Tech.,1988, 241-244.

[14] Yamaguchi,J., "LIFE-Ⅲ [3]Relativized Completeness", Proc. of the 3rd Annual Conference of JSAI,1989,33-36.

[15] Yamaguchi,J., "LIFE-Ⅲ [4]A Fuzzy Inferential System",(in Japanese) 6th Conference Proceedings Japan Soc.Software Sci.&Tech.,1989,121-124.

# Semantics of Non-monotonic Reasoning based on Perfect Model

fangqing DONG        hirosi NAKAGAWA

Dept. of Electrical and Computer Eng.
Yokohama National Univ.

### Abstract

Because of the lack of general semantics for non-monotonic formalisms, the relationship between the major forms of non-monotonic formalisms has not been understood very well. Recently, it has been proposed by C.Przymusinski that perfect model semantics for logic programming is also suitable for some special cases of non-monotonic formalisms. The importance of this result is not only for shedding new light on these two fields, but also for establishing a close relationship between main forms of non-monotonic formalisms. However,these understandings are achieved only in stratified programs. In this paper, we introduce a new class of programs called conditional programs, define its declarative semantics by least exceptional models, show its relation with perfect model semantics and non-monotonic logics, and give a procedure about how to transform a conditional program into a general program. This new semantics of conditional programs shares a lot of common characteristics with logic programming and non-monotonic reasoning, such as priorities between predicates, minimizing extensions of predicates, and minimizing abnormality. A better understanding about the relationship between forms of non-monotonic formalisms can be achieved by least exceptional model semantics of conditonal programs.

## 1   Introduction

The declarative semantics for logic programming has been represented by the minimal model. However, it has been pointed out that this semantics is not suitable for general programs. Recently, perfect model semantics, a new approach to the declarative semantics of logic programming, has been proposed. In this semantics, priorities are given to all predicates occurring in a general program. The perfect model for a general program are defined by minimizing the extensions of predicates according to their priorities. The lower its priority is, the smaller its extension should be. Moreover, it has been shown that the perfect model semantics is equivalent to suitable main non-monotonic formalisms.

However, this new semantics is only adequate for the model-based semantics of some special cases of non-monotonic formalisms. Furthermore, we argue that the epistemological difficulty of how to reason about the defaults of real world should be considered.

In view of these problems, we introduce a new class of programs, called conditional programs, with negative predicate in head and define its declarative semantics which shares some common characteristics with perfect model semantics and non-monotonic reasoning, such as showing priorities between predicates, minimizing extensions of predicates according to their priorities, and minimizing abnormality etc. In section 2, we illustrate the perfect model for a general program and its relation with non-monotonic logics. In section 3, we define conditional programs and its declarative semantics by least exceptional models. In section 4, we show how to transform a conditional program into a general program on the equality of the least exceptional model of a conditional program with the perfect model of the corresponding general program. At last, we discuss the relationship between least exceptional model semantics and non-monotonic logics.

## 2 Perfect Model

Perfect model semantics[Przy88a] [Przy88b] is a new declarative semantics for logic programming and adequate for the model-based semantics of non-monotonic formalisms. In this section, we only consider general programs without functions and introduce their perfect models. Firstly, we give several concepts here.

The following clause is called general program clause, where $A$'s, $B$'s and $C$ are atoms.

$$A_1 \wedge \ldots \wedge A_n \wedge \neg B_1 \wedge \ldots \wedge \neg B_m \supset C$$

A set of finite general program clauses $P$ is called general program.

A general program $P$ can be represented by a dependency graph $G$ [Przy88b] [Geff88], whose vertices are predicate symbols occurring in $P$, and there is a directed edge from $A$ to $B$ iff there is a clause in $P$ such that $A$ occurs in its head and $B$ in its body. If $B$ is a negative premise of $A$, then the edge is called negative. If there is a directed edge from $A$ to $B$, and the edge is negative, then it is said that $B$ has lower priority than $A$. More generally, for any ground general program clause of $P$

$$A_1 \wedge \ldots \wedge A_n \wedge \neg B_1 \wedge \ldots \wedge \neg B_m \supset C,$$

we have the following priority relations.

$$A_i \leq C \quad 1 \leq i \leq n$$
$$B_j < C \quad 1 \leq j \leq m$$

By priority relation $<$ between ground atoms, Herbrand base $B_L$ could be decomposed into several strata according to the priorities of ground atoms. $\neg A$ should be true if $A$ could not be derived from low stratum to its stratum. More precisely, a model $M$ should be preferable to another $N$, if there is a predicate $A$ whose extension in $M$ is larger than the one in $N$, then there must exist a predicate $B$ whose priority is lower than $A$ and extension in $M$ is smaller than the one in $N$. These observations are formalized by the notation of a perfect model.

**Definition 2.1** $M \prec N$ and perfect model

*Let $M$ and $N$ be two distinct Herbrand models of general program $P$. Then it is said that $M$ is preferable to $N$, if for every ground atom $A$ in $M - N$ there is a ground atom $B$ in $N - M$, such that $B < A$. A model $M$ of $P$ is called perfect if there are no models preferable to $M$.* ∎

A general program $P$ is called stratified if it is possible to decompose the set $S$ of all predicate symbols occurring in $P$ into disjoint sets $S_1, \ldots, S_r$, called strata, so that for any ground atoms $A$ and $B$, we have:

$$if\, A \leq B \; then \; stratum(A) \leq stratum(B)$$
$$if\, A < B \; then \; stratum(A) < stratum(B)$$

where $stratum(A)$ is the number of stratum to which the predicate of $A$ belong.

For any stratified program $P$, we know that $P$ has an unique perfect Herbrand model.

It has been proposed that perfect model semantics for logic programs is equivalent to suitable main non-monotonic formalisms. So perfect model semantics can also be viewed as the common semantics for non-monotonic formalisms in some special cases.

The equivalence between perfect model semantics for stratified programs and the semantics of prioritized circumscription was shown in [Przy88b] as follows: suppose $P$ is a stratified program and $S_1, \ldots, S_r$ are strata of all predicate symbols occurring in $P$, then the perfect model of $P$ coincides with the model of prioritized circumscription $CIRCUM.(P; S_1 > \ldots > S_r)$.

For any stratified program $P$, let $W$ be the set of all positive clauses in $P$, $D$ be the set of defaults:

$$\frac{A_1 \wedge \ldots \wedge A_n : \neg B_1, \ldots, \neg B_m}{C}$$

generated from the clauses of $P$ which have at least one negative premise

$$A_1 \wedge \ldots \wedge A_n \wedge \neg B_1 \wedge \ldots \wedge \neg B_m \supset C \, ,$$

then the default theory $(D, W)$ has exactly one extension whose unique minimal model is the perfect model of $P$.

# 3 Least Exceptional Model

Perfect model semantics for general programs and its relation with main non-monotonic formalisms have been presented in section 2. Perfect model semantics could be viewed as the semantics for non-monotonic formalisms. This semantics, however, is only suitable for the problems in which negative knowledge is implemented by NAF. Moreover, according to [Delg88] [Delg87], there are two general limitations with non-monotonic logic. First, one cannot generally reason about defaults. Second, epistemological difficulty with those approaches is that their semantics rests on the notion of consistence. If commonsense assertions about real world were represented by default logic, tacit abnormal knowledge should be clarified firstly, but it is not so easy to reason about it. On these reasons, we try to represent commonsense assertions by conditional programs and discuss the declarative semantics of these programs.

The following clause is called conditional program clause, where $L$ is a literal, $A$'s and $B$'s are atoms.

$$A_1 \wedge \ldots \wedge A_n \wedge \neg B_1 \wedge \ldots \wedge \neg B_m \supset L$$

A set of finite conditional program clauses $D$ is called conditional program. $P\theta$ is said to be a ground conditional program clause of $D$, if $P\theta$ is a ground instance of $P$, where $P$ is a clause of conditional program $D$ and $\theta$ is a ground substitution whose ground terms belong to Herbrand universe of $D$ [Lloy84].

In this paper, any conditional program clause

$$A_1 \wedge \ldots \wedge A_n \wedge \neg B_1 \wedge \ldots \wedge \neg B_m \supset L$$

is used to represent knowledge normally true but with exception. For example, "all birds normally fly, but penguin is a bird that does not fly." can be represented by conditional program as follows:

$$bird(X) \supset flies(X),$$
$$penguin(X) \supset bird(X),$$
$$penguin(X) \supset \neg flies(X).$$

However, we should pay attention that some conditional programs are reasonable in commonsense, but may not have any Herbrand models. In this paper, we use interpretations, instead of models, to show the declarative semantics for conditional programs. The preferences for interpretations of a conditional program are determined by priorities between literals and priorities between contradictory clauses.

For any ground conditional program clause of conditional program $D$,

$$A_1 \wedge \ldots \wedge A_n \wedge \neg B_1 \wedge \ldots \wedge \neg B_m \supset L$$

1. The priority relations $\leq$ between literals are defined as follows:

$$A_i \leq L \quad 1 \leq i \leq n$$
$$\neg B_j \leq L \quad 1 \leq j \leq m$$

with transitivity rule:

$$if \ A \leq B \ and \ B \leq C, then \ A \leq C \ .$$

2. If $L$ is an atom, then priority relations $<$ are defined as follows:

$$B_j < L, \ 1 \leq j \leq m \ .$$

For Herbrand ground atoms, the priority relations $\leq$ and $<$ introduced in this section are also met the transitivity rules introduced in last section.

Our object is to make the models or interpretations which are minimized as much as possible, while clauses remain true as much as possible. If there are models for a conditional program, we would like to define intended models by minimizing extensions of predicates according to their priorities as much as possible. If there are no any models for a conditional program, we consider that there must exist some exceptional clauses which should be false and intended models could be determined if those clauses are removed from the conditional program. We would like to select intended interpretations of a conditional program by minimizing exceptional clauses as much as possible. The intended interpretations are called least exceptional models, because some clauses of the conditional program are ignored. Before giving the definition of a least exceptional model, we discuss how to show priorities between clauses and preferences for interpretations firstly.

**Example 3.1** For the following conditional program $D$,

$$D = \{A(a), A(b), B(b), A(X) \supset P(X), A(X) \wedge B(X) \supset \neg P(X)\}$$
$$p_1 = A(a) \supset P(a)$$
$$p_2 = A(b) \supset P(b)$$
$$p_3 = A(a) \wedge B(a) \supset \neg P(a)$$
$$p_4 = A(b) \wedge B(b) \supset \neg P(b)$$

There are 64 interpretations, but no models. Only eight of them are listed as following, where $A(a), A(b), B(b)$ are true and $B(a), P(a), P(b)$ remain to change. Denote by $P_{M_i}$ the set of all ground conditional program clauses which hold in $M_i$.

|       | $A_a$ | $A_b$ | $B_a$ | $B_b$ | $P_a$ | $P_b$ | $P_{M_i}$ |
|-------|-------|-------|-------|-------|-------|-------|-----------|
| $M_1$ | 1 | 1 | 0 | 1 | 0 | 0 | $\{ \qquad\qquad p_3, \quad p_4 \}$ |
| $M_2$ | 1 | 1 | 0 | 1 | 0 | 1 | $\{ \quad\quad p_2, \quad p_3 \qquad \}$ |
| $M_3$ | 1 | 1 | 0 | 1 | 1 | 0 | $\{ p_1, \qquad\quad p_3, \quad p_4 \}$ |
| $M_4$ | 1 | 1 | 0 | 1 | 1 | 1 | $\{ p_1, \quad p_2, \quad p_3 \qquad \}$ |
| $M_5$ | 1 | 1 | 1 | 1 | 0 | 0 | $\{ \qquad\qquad p_3, \quad p_4 \}$ |
| $M_6$ | 1 | 1 | 1 | 1 | 0 | 1 | $\{ \quad\quad p_2, \quad p_3 \qquad \}$ |
| $M_7$ | 1 | 1 | 1 | 1 | 1 | 0 | $\{ p_1, \qquad\qquad\quad p_4 \}$ |
| $M_8$ | 1 | 1 | 1 | 1 | 1 | 1 | $\{ p_1, \quad p_2 \qquad\qquad \}$ |

Firstly, we would like to select the interpretations which is minimized as much as possible, while clauses remain true as much as possible. $M_3$ and $M_4$ meet these conditions. $p_2$ and $p_4$ are contradictory to each other, $p_2$ fails in $M_3$ and $p_4$ fails in $M_4$.

The meaning expressed by $p_2$ is that if only $A(b)$ is known to be true, then $P(b)$ is also true. The meaning expressed by $p_4$ is that if only $A(b)$ and $B(b)$ are known to be true, then $\neg P(b)$ is also true. Because the premises of $\neg P(b)$ are more special than $P(b)$'s, the priority of $p_4$ should be higher than $p_2$, written $p_2 < p_4$. From the fact that $A(b)$ and $B(b)$ are known to be true, it is reasonable to regard that $\neg P(b)$ should hold and $P(b)$ should fail in commonsense. So $M_4$ is preferable to $M_3$. Generally, one interpretation $M$ is preferable to another $N$, if for every pair of contradictory clauses $P$ and $P'$ $P$ holds only in $M$ and $P'$ only in $N$, such that the priority of $P'$ is higher than $P$'s, as well as $M$ itself is minimized as much as possible. ■

We give some more examples to show how to decide priorities between clauses.

**Example 3.2**

$$D = \{A(X) \supset P(X),$$
$$A(X) \wedge B(X) \supset \neg P(X),$$
$$A(X) \wedge B(X) \wedge C(X) \supset P(X)\}$$

By the fact that the premises of $A(X) \wedge B(X) \supset P(X)$ imply the premises of $A(X) \supset P(X)$, we say that the premises of $A(X) \wedge B(X) \supset P(X)$ are more special than the premises of $A(X) \supset P(X)$, and the priority of $A(X) \wedge B(X) \supset P(X)$ is higher than $A(X) \supset P(X)$. On the same reason, the priority of $A(X) \wedge B(X) \wedge C(X) \supset P(X)$ should be higher than $A(X) \wedge B(X) \supset P(X)$. ∎

**Example 3.3**

$$D = \{ \ adult(X) \supset employed(X),$$
$$univ\_st(X) \supset adult(X),$$
$$univ\_st(X) \supset \neg employed(X) \ \}$$

$\neg employed$ could be derived from premise $univ\_st$ at one step. However, $employed$ is implied by the same premise $univ\_st$ at two steps. The reasoning path of $\neg employed$ is said to be shorter than $employed$'s with respect to the same set of premises $\{univ\_st\}$. So $univ\_st(X) \supset \neg employed(X)$ should have higher priority than $adult(X) \supset employed(X)$. ∎

For representing the priority relations between clauses abstractly, a new notation $R(L|P_1, ..., P_n)$ is introduced, which is a set of priorities between literals represented by ground conditional program clauses $P_1, ..., P_n$. For example, Suppose that

$$p_1 = A(a) \wedge B(a) \wedge C(a) \supset P(a),$$

then

$$R(P(a) \mid p_1) = \{A(a) \le P(a), B(a) \le P(a), C(a) \le P(a)\} \ .$$

Suppose that

$$p_2 = adult(john) \supset employed(john)$$
$$p_3 = univ\_st(john) \supset adult(john)$$

then

$$R(employed(john) \mid p_2, p_3)$$
$$= \{ \ univ\_st(john) \le adult(john),$$
$$adult(john) \le employed(john),$$
$$univ\_st(john) \le employed(john)\} \ .$$

The priority relation between groud clauses $P^+$ and $P^-$ is decided by the sets of priority relations between literals. The priority of $P^+$ is said to be higher than $P^-$'s , written $P^- < P^+$, if for any ground literal $B$

$$(B \le \neg L) \in R(\neg L|P^-, P_{11}, \ldots, P_{1n})$$

and

$$(B \le L) \notin R(L|P^+, P_{21}, \ldots, P_{2m})$$

then

1. $P^+$ is an ground atom, but $P^-$ not.

2. or,there is another literal $C$,

$$(C \leq B) \in R(\neg L | P^-, P_{11}, \ldots, P_{1n})$$

and

$$(C \leq L) \in R(L | P^+, P_{21}, \ldots, P_{2m}),$$

where $P^-, P_{11}, \ldots, P_{1n}, P^+, P_{21}, \ldots, P_{2m}$ are ground clauses of conditional program $D$, $P^+$ 's head is literal $L$,and $P^-$ 's the negation $\neg L$.

**Definition 3.1** $M \prec N$ *and least exceptional model*

Let $M$ and $N$ be the interpretations of conditional program $D$, $P_M(P_N)$ be the set of all ground conditional program clauses which hold in the interpretation $M(N)$, $P$ be the intersection of $P_M$ and $P_N$, $M_P(N_P)$ be the extension of $P$ in interpretation $M(N)$. If one of the following conditions is met, then we say that $M$ is preferable to $N$, written $M \prec N$.

(a) if for every ground atom $A$ in $M_P - N_P$, then there is a ground atom $B$ in $N_P - M_P$ such that $B < A$.

(b) if for every ground conditional program clause $P'$ in $P_N - P_M$, then there is a $P''$ in $P_M - P_N$ such that $P' < P''$.

If there are no interpretations preferable to $M$, then $M$ is called least exceptional.  ■

**Example 3.4** Let's consider how to decide the least exceptional models for the conditional program shown in example 3.1.

The interpretation $M_3(M_4)$ and the set of clauses $P_3(P_4)$ which hold in $M_3(M_4)$ are as follows:

$$M_3 = \{A(a), A(b), B(b), P(a)\}, \qquad P_3 = \{A(a), A(b), B(b), p_1, p_3, p_4\},$$
$$M_4 = \{A(a), A(b), B(b), P(a), P(b)\}, \quad P_4 = \{A(a), A(b), B(b), p_1, p_2, p_3\}.$$

By the following facts:

$$p_2 \in P_3 - P_4, \quad p_4 \in P_4 - P_3, \quad p_2 < p_4,$$

we know $M_4 \prec M_3$ according to definition 3.1. For any another interpretation $M_i$, we can also prove that $M_4$ is preferable to $M_i$. Then it is known that $M_4$ is a least exceptional model of this conditional program.  ■

**Example 3.5** For the conditional program shown in example 3.2, $M$ and $N$ are two of its interpretations.

$$M = \{A(a), B(a), C(a), P(a)\}$$
$$P_M = \{A(a), B(a), C(a), A(a) \supset P(a), A(a) \wedge B(a) \wedge C(a) \supset P(a)\}$$
$$N = \{A(a), B(a), C(a)\}$$
$$P_N = \{A(a), B(a), C(a), A(a) \wedge B(a) \supset \neg P(a)\}$$

By the fact:

$$A(a) \wedge B(a) \supset \neg P(a) < A(a) \wedge B(a) \wedge C(a) \supset P(a)$$

we know $M \prec N$. Furthermore, it can be also proved that $M$ is a least exceptional model of this conditional program.  ■

# 4 The Relationship Between Least Exceptional Model Semantics and Perfect Model Semantics

Negation with respect to perfect model semantics could be regarded as extended NAF rule, where all the predicates appearing in a general program are decomposed into several strata according to their priorities and a ground atom $A$ of predicate $p$ should be false, if $A$ could not be derived from its premises whose priorities are lower than $p$'s. For any ground atom $A$ of predicate $p$ occuring in a conditional program, however, its truth value may be logic true, logic false, or false according to NAF rule. It seems reasonable to consider that exceptions exist in a conditional program if one clause is contradictory to another. The goal of this section is to find out the programs in which the exceptions could be reasoned and logic false could be replaced by NAF rule.

The relationship between general programs and conditional programs could be regarded as

$$conditional\ program\ +\ tacit\ exception\ =\ general\ program.$$

A conditional program could be easily transformed into a general program if it is known how to reason about omitted tacit exceptions.

Firstly, let us try to define what is the omitted tacit exception of one clause.

**Definition 4.1** *tacit exception*

Let $P(P = L_1 \wedge \ldots \wedge L_n \supset L)$ be any conditional program clause in conditional program $D$, $\theta$ be any ground substitution of $P$, $B_L$ be Herbrand base of $D$, $M$ be any least exceptional model of $D$. Any $d$ satisfying the following condition is called tacit exception of $P$.

$$\forall \theta \forall M \{if\ M \not\models P\theta,\ then\ M \models d\theta,\ or\ if\ M \models (L_1 \wedge \ldots \wedge L_n \wedge L)\theta\ then\ M \not\models d\theta\} \ \blacksquare$$

On the equality of the least exceptional models of one conditional program with another, all clauses of a conditional program $D$ must hold in least exceptional models if for every conditional clause $P$, the negation of tacit exception $\neg d$ is added into the premises of $P$, and conditional program $D$ can be transformed into a general program.

**Definition 4.2** *Procedure transforming a conditional program into a general program*

**step1** :*For any conditional program clause $P$ of conditional program $D$, the negation $\neg d$ of the tacit exception of $P$ is put into the premises of $P$.*

$$P = L_1 \wedge \ldots \wedge L_n \supset L \implies L_1 \wedge \ldots \wedge L_n \wedge \neg d \supset L$$

*Let d be $d_1 \wedge \ldots \wedge d_n$, then all $d_i$ are decomposed into several groups according to internal variables which occur in $d_i$ but not in the head of P,*

$$\{d_{11}, d_{12}, \ldots\}, \{d_{21}, d_{22}, \ldots\}, \ldots, \{d_{k1}, d_{k2}, \ldots\},$$

*here all $d_{ij}$ occurring in the same group have common internal variables, and all $d_{ij}$ occurring in the different groups have no any common internal variables. $\vee$'s with respect to every group $j(j = 1, 2, ..., k)$ could be eliminated respectively as follows:*

$$L_1 \wedge \ldots \wedge L_n \wedge \neg AB_j(X_{j1}, X_{j2}, \ldots) \supset L$$
$$d_{j1} \wedge d_{j2} \wedge \ldots \supset AB_j(X_{j1}, X_{j2}, \ldots),$$

*where $AB_j$ are new predicate symbols introduced by us, and $X_{j1}, X_{j2}, \ldots$ are variables occurring in every group.*

**step2** *:All clauses with negative predicate in head are removed.* ∎

About this transformation, we have next result.

**Proposition 4.1** *Let D be a conditional program, S be the set of all predicates occurring in D, $D'$ be the conditional program transformed from D by step1 of definition 4.2, and $D''$ be the general program obtained by step2 of definition 4.2. Then*

(a) *the set of all least exceptional models of D is equal to the set of extensions of S in all least exceptional models of $D'$.*

(b) *$D'$ has an unique least exceptional model which is equal to the perfect model of $D''$.*

(c) *Therefore, D has an unique least exceptional model which is equal to the extension of S in the perfect model of $D''$.*

*Proposition 4.1 can be proved by the following two facts.*

(a) *Firstly, let $D^*$ be $D \cup D^+$, $D^+$ be the set of conditional program clauses of $D'$ whose predicates of heads do not occur in D. Then the set of all least exceptional models of D is equal to the set of extensions of S in all least exceptional models of $D^*$.*

(b) *For proving proposition 4.1, according to the first fact, we should only prove that $D^*$ has the same set of least exceptional models with $D'$. By the fact that $D^*$ has the same Herbrand base with $D'$, it is sufficient to prove that there must exist a correspondence of priority relations between clauses of $D^*$ with the priority relations between ground atoms illustrated by Fig.1. In Fig.2, M and N are two interpretations of conditional program $D^*$, P and $P'$ are ground conditional program clauses. L is the head of P and d the tacit exception of P. If P is preferable to $P'$ and P is true in M and $P'$ in N, then it must be that L is true in M, d in N and L is preferable to d. If L is preferable to d, L* is true in $M$ and $d$ in $N$, then $P$ is true in $M$, $P'$ in $N$ and $P$ is preferable to $P'$.

$$
\begin{array}{ccc}
P' & < & P \\
\Updownarrow & & \Updownarrow \\
d & < & L \\
\Updownarrow & & \Updownarrow \\
N & \succ & M
\end{array}
$$

*Fig.1   The correspondence of priority relations between clauses with the priority relations between ground literals*

The correctness of proposition 4.2 could be proved by the following fact: $D''$ has the same set of interpretations with $D'$ and the same set of priority relations $<$ with $D'$. ∎

If the priority $P <_P P'$ between conditional program clauses $P$ and $P'$ is known, then the premises of $P'$ can be viewed as the tacit exception of $P$. Generally, let $P_1, P_2, ..., P_n$ be all the conditional program clauses which priority is higher than $P$, then

$$d = ((L_{11} \wedge L_{12} \wedge \ldots) \vee \ldots \vee (L_{n1} \wedge L_{n2} \wedge \ldots))\theta$$

is said to be a possible tacit exception of $P$, here $\theta$ is the unifier of the heads of $P, P_1, P_2, ..., P_n$, $L_{i1} \wedge L_{i2} \wedge \ldots$ are the body of $P$.

About the possible tacit exception, we have following result.

**Proposition 4.2**    *Let $A$ be any atom occurring in conditional program $D$, $P^+$ be any clause with $A$ in head, $P^-$ be the one with $\neg A$ in head. If there must exist a priority relation between $P^+$ and $P^-$,*

$$P^+ <_P P^- \text{ or } P^- <_P P^+$$

*then for any conditional program clause $P$ of $D$ the possible tacit exception of $P$ is the tacit exception of $P$.* ∎

**Example 4.1**

$$
\begin{aligned}
D = \{ & A(a), A(b), B(a,b), \\
& A(X) \supset P(b, X), \\
& A(Y) \wedge \neg A(Z) \wedge B(Y, Z) \supset \neg P(Z, c)\}
\end{aligned}
$$

**step1** :Reasoning about tacit exceptions. According to

$$A(X) \supset P(b, X) <_P A(Y) \wedge \neg A(Z) \wedge B(Y, Z) \supset \neg P(Z, c)$$

the unifier of $P(b, X)$ and $P(Z, c)$ is $\theta$ $\{Z/b, X/c\}$. The tacit exception $d$ of $A(X) \supset P(b, X)$ is produced as follows:

$$
\begin{aligned}
d &= (A(Y) \wedge \neg A(Z) \wedge B(Y, Z))\theta \\
&= A(Y) \wedge \neg A(b) \wedge B(Y, b) .
\end{aligned}
$$

Therefore, the clause $A(X) \supset P(b, X)$ is transformed into

$$A(X) \wedge \neg(A(Y) \wedge \neg A(b) \wedge B(Y, b)) \supset P(b, X) .$$

∨'s are eliminated as following.

$$\neg A(b), \qquad A(Y) \wedge B(Y, b)$$

$$A(X) \wedge A(b) \supset P(b, X)$$
$$A(X) \wedge \neg AB(Y) \supset P(b, X)$$
$$A(Y) \wedge B(Y, b) \supset AB(Y) .$$

**step2** :Eliminating clauses whose heads are negative literals. Then the following general program is obtained.

$$\begin{aligned}
D" = \{ &A(a), A(b), B(a, b), \\
&A(X) \wedge A(b) \supset P(b, X), \\
&A(X) \wedge \neg AB(Y) \supset P(b, X), \\
&A(Y) \wedge B(Y, b) \supset AB(Y) \} .
\end{aligned}$$

Let us conform the relation between $D$ and $D"$. Firstly

$$P(b, a), \neg P(b, c)$$

are obtained from $D$. In the other way, $P(b, a)$ is obtained from $D"$, $AB(a)$ from $A(a)$ and $B(a, b)$, but $P(b, c)$ could not be obtained from $D"$. Therefore

$$\neg P(b, c)$$

is inferred from NAF rule. ∎

**Example 4.2** For the conditional program shown in example 3.2

$$\begin{aligned}
D &= \{p_1, p_2, p_3\}, \\
p_1 &= A(X) \supset P(X), \\
p_2 &= A(X) \wedge B(X) \supset \neg P(X), \\
p_3 &= A(X) \wedge B(X) \wedge C(X) \supset P(X),
\end{aligned}$$

according to the following priorities between clauses

$$p_1 <_P p_2, \quad p_2 <_P p_3 ,$$

the tacit exceptions with respect to every clause are

$$\begin{aligned}
d_{p_1} &= A(X) \wedge B(X), \\
d_{p_2} &= A(X) \wedge B(X) \wedge C(X), \\
d_{p_3} &= \{\}.
\end{aligned}$$

This conditional program is transformed into

$$D" = \{A(X) \wedge \neg B(X) \supset P(X), A(X) \wedge B(X) \wedge C(X) \supset P(X)\}. \quad ∎$$

**Theorem 4.1** *Let $D$ be any conditional program, $S$ be the set of all predicates occurring in $D$, $A$ be any atom occurring in $D$, $P^+$ be any clause with $A$ in head, $P^-$ be the one with $\neg A$ in head. If there must exist a priority relation between $P^+$ and $P^-$,*

$$P^+ <_P P^- \text{ or } P^- <_P P^+$$

*then the conditional program $D$ could be transformed into a general program $D''$ according to the definition 4.2 and $D$ has an unique least exceptional model which is equal to the extension of $S$ in the perfect model of $D''$.* ∎

# 5 The Relationship Between Least Exceptional Model Semantics and Nonmonotonic Logics

So far, several approaches for representing knowledge about defaults, such as default logic and circumscription, have been presented. This section will discuss the relationship between the least exceptional model semantics and these nonmonotonic formalisms.

## 5.1 The Relation with Default Logic

In default logic [Reit80], A default is any expression of the form

$$\frac{\alpha : \beta_1, \beta_2, \ldots, \beta_n}{\omega}.$$

A default theory $(D, W)$ consists of a set of defaults $D$ and a set of first-order formulae $W$. An extension $E$ of default theory $(D, W)$ is required to have the following properties:

(a) $W \subseteq E$

(b) $Th(E) = E$

(c) $\alpha : \beta_1, \beta_2, \ldots, \beta_n / \omega$ and if $\alpha \in E, \neg \beta_i \notin E (i = 1, \ldots, n)$, then $\omega \in E$.

The model-theoretic semantics for default logic [Ethe87] could be viewed as restricting the set of all models for real world $W$ by applying defaults one after another. The resulting set of models characterizes an extension if the application of each default does not violate the justifications of already-applied defaults.

Preference $\geq_\delta$ captures this intuition. It is said that $\delta$ prefers $\Gamma_1$ to $\Gamma_2$, written $\Gamma_1 \geq_\delta \Gamma_2$, if

(a) $\forall \gamma \in \Gamma_2, \gamma \models \alpha, \exists \gamma_1, \ldots, \gamma_n \in \Gamma_2, \gamma_i \models \beta_i$ and

(b) $\Gamma_1 = \Gamma_2 - \{\gamma \mid \gamma \models \neg \omega\}$

where $\delta = \alpha : \beta_1, \ldots, \beta_n/\omega$, $\Gamma$ is a set of models of $W$ and $\Gamma_1, \Gamma_2 \in 2^\Gamma$. According to preference $\geq_\delta$, all models in $\Gamma_1$ are also in $\Gamma_2$ and no justifications of $\delta$ are violated by the application of another default. In order to show the model-theoretic semantics for default logic, it is sufficient to consider the maximal elements of $2^{MOD(W)}$ with respect to $D$ and $\geq_\delta$.

It is said that $\Gamma$ is stable for $(D, W)$ if $\Gamma$ is a maximal element of $2^{MOD(W)}$ with respect to $D'$ and $\geq_\delta$ where $D' \subseteq D$ such that

$$\forall \frac{\alpha : \beta_1, \ldots, \beta_n}{\omega} \in D', \ \Gamma \geq_\delta MOD(W), \ and \ \exists \gamma_1, \ldots, \gamma_n \in \Gamma, \gamma_i \models \beta_i$$

The stable sets of models for a default theory provide a semantic interpretation for default logic. Let $\Delta$ be a default theory $(D, W)$, then $\Gamma$ is stable for $\Delta$ iff $\Gamma$ is the set of models for an extension $E$.

There exists a close relationship between this semantics and least exceptional model semantics. Generally, this relationship could be viewed as

$$minimal \ models \ + \ preference \ for \ models \ = \ least \ exceptional \ model.$$

Any conditional program clause of conditional program $D$

$$A_1 \wedge \ldots \wedge A_n \wedge \neg B_1 \wedge \ldots \wedge \neg B_m \supset L$$

could be viewed as a default as follows:

$$\frac{A_1 \wedge \ldots \wedge A_n : \neg B_1, \ldots, \neg B_m, \neg d}{L}$$

where $A$'s and $B$'s are atoms, $L$ is a literal and $d$ is the tacit exception of the corresponding clause. Other conditional program clauses whose tacit exception is empty and which have no negative premises can be viewed as an axioms.

It could be viewed that the preference $\geq_\delta$ correspondences to the priority between clauses, the stable set of models $\Gamma$ for a default theory $(D', W)$, which is generated from conditional program $D$, correspondences to the least exceptional model of conditional program $D$. This corresponding relation could be verified from the facts:

(a) For any conditional program clause, the interpretation in which its tacit exception $d$ fails as well as its negative premises $B$'s should be preferable to the one in which tacit exception $d$ holds.

(b) If the priorities between all contradictory clauses in conditional program $D$ are already known, denote by $D^*$ the set of all clauses which fail in the least exceptional model $M$ of $D$, then there must exist an extension $E$ for default theory $(D', W)$, which is generated from conditional program $D$, $\Gamma$ is a stable set of models of $E$ with respect to $\geq_\delta$ and $D^*$ such that the least exceptional model $M$ is one of the minimal models of $E$.

Least exceptional model semantics is different from the semantics for default logic at two points:

(a) Only the interpretations, which are minimized as much as possible while clauses remain true as much as possible, are considered; but not all of interpretations.

(b) The preference of one interpretation over another is also determined by the priorities between predicates.

## 5.2   The Relation with Circumscription

Circumscription is the most thoroughly investigated of all of the approaches to nonmonotonic reasoning. In this paper, we compare the procedure of transforming conditional programs into general programs with the approach of compiling circumscriptive theories into logic programs [Gelf88].

For any set of clauses $A$, the circumscription of $P^1, P^2, ..., P^k$ in A is represented as

$$CIRCUM.(A; P^1, P^2, ..., P^k; Z) ,$$

where $k$ disjoint lists of predicates $P^1, P^2, ..., P^k$ are minimized: those included in $P^1$ with the highest priority and those included in $P^k$ with the lowest priority, $Z$ is a list of predicates allowed to vary.

Gelfond's approach could shown as follows:

(a) A new clause

$$A_1 \wedge ... \wedge A_N \wedge \neg B_1 \wedge ... \wedge \neg B_{i-1} \wedge \neg B_{i+1} \wedge ... \wedge \neg B_M \supset B_i$$

is generated from a pair of clauses as below whose predicates of heads have the same predicate symbol occurring in $Z$.

$$A_1 \wedge ... \wedge A_n \wedge \neg B_1 \wedge ... \wedge \neg B_m \supset C$$
$$A_{n+1} \wedge ... \wedge A_N \wedge \neg B_{m+1} \wedge ... \wedge \neg B_M \supset \neg C$$

$B_i$ is the predicate having the lowest priority in all $B$'s.

(b) Any clause whose predicate symbol of head $C$ is included in $Z$

$$A_1 \wedge ... \wedge A_n \wedge \neg B_1 \wedge ... \wedge \neg B_m \supset \neg C(t_1, ..., t_n)$$

is replaced by a clause with a new predicate $\bar{C}$ in head.

$$A_1 \wedge ... \wedge A_n \wedge \neg B_1 \wedge ... \wedge \neg B_m \supset \bar{C}(t_1, ..., t_n)$$

(c) Let $C$ be the program compiled by this approach, then the relation of program $C$ with circumscription is as follows:

$$CIRCUM.(A; P; Z) \models \begin{cases} p(c) & C \models p(c) \\ \neg p(c) & C \not\models p(c), p \in P \\ undecidable & C \not\models p(c), p \in Z. \end{cases}$$

Our procedure introduced in the section 4 is different from Gelfond's approach at twofold:

(a) Firstly, only the clauses whose predicates of heads occur in $Z$ could be complied into a general program by Gelfond's approach. However, there are no any restrictions in our approach at this point.

(b) Let $D^*$ be a set of formulae transformed from all conditional program clauses of $D$. For any conditional program clause $P$, if the tacit exception of $P$ is empty then $P$ is formula of $D^*$, else a new negative predicate $\neg AB_i$ is added into the premises of $P$ and this new clause is a formula of $D^*$ where $AB_i$ is a new predicate which does not occur in $D$. Then we have the following results.

$$CIRCUM.(D^*; P) \models \left\{ \begin{array}{ll} p(c) & C \models p(c) \\ \neg p(c) & C \not\models p(c) \end{array} \right.$$

where $C$ is the general program transformed from $D$.

# 6   Conclusion

This paper has presented the least exceptional model semantics of conditional programs, introduced an approach for transforming a conditional program into a general program, and discussed the relationship between least exceptional model semantics and non-monotonic logics. The least exceptional model semantics could be regarded as an extension of perfect model semantics and has some common characteristics with nonmonotonic logics, such as minimality of exceptions and preference for models. A better understanding about the relationship between forms of non-monotonic formalisms can be achieved by least exceptional model semantics of conditonal programs.

In this paper, only conditional programs without functions are considered. For the programs with functions, it is necessary to show priorities between literals according to local stratified programs. The semantics of those programs remains to be discussed.

# References

[Delg88] Delgrande,P. : An Approach to Default Reasoning Based on a First-Order Conditional Logic:Revised Report, Artifi. Intell.36(1988), pp.63-90

[Delg87] Delgrande,P. : A First-Order Conditional Logic for Protypical Properties, Artifi. Intell.33(1987), pp.105-130

[Ethe87] Etherington,D,W. : A Semantics for Default Logic, IJCAI-87,pp.495-498

[Geff88] Geffner,H. : On the Logic of Defaults, AAAI-88,pp.449-454

[Gelf88] Gelfond,M. and Lifschitz,V. : Compiling Circumscriptive Theories into Logic Programs:Preliminary Report, AAAI-88,pp.455-459

[Lloy84] Lloyd,J,W. : Foundations of Logic Programming, Springer, Berlin(1984).

[Przy88a] Przymusinski,C. : On the Declarative Semantics of Deductive Databases and Logic Programs, Minker,J.:"Foundations of Deductive Databases and Logic Programming",chapter 5,pp.193-216

[Przy88b] Przymusinski,C. : On the Relationship Between Logic Programming and Non-monotonic Reasoning, AAAI-88,pp.444-448

[Reit80] Reiter,R. : A Logic for Default Reasoning, Artifi. Intell.13(1980),pp.81-132

# Time-Bounded Reasoning
# in First Order Knowledge Base Systems

Yihua Shi*    Setsuo Arikawa*

Department of Information Systems Kyushu University 39

Kasuga, Fukuoka 816, Japan

E-mail: shi@rifis.sci.kyushu-u.ac.jp

### Abstract

In first order predicate logic, it is undecidable whether a formula is deducible from a set of axioms. In order to realize a practical knowledge base system in the framework of the first order logic, we must overcome this problem.

In this paper, we propose a time-bounded reasoning and investigate the properties of the knowledge base management system based on our time-bounded reasoning. We also show that the time-bounded reasoning is sound and valid. Furthermore, we discuss the selection of time functions and give three parameters of time functions. We also outline a prototype system we have realized in K-prolog on a Sun-3.

## 1    Introduction

Many reasoning methods including default reasoning[11], inductive inference[13, 14], analogical reasoning [4] as well as deductive inference have been proposed and used in Artificial Intelligence. A derivation procedure to decide whether $KB \vdash \alpha$ is commonly used in all of the reasoning methods above, where $KB$ is a knowledge base, i.e., a set of axioms and $\alpha$ is a formula. This decision problem, however, is known to be unsolvable in case of first order predicate logic. In order to realize a practical reasoning system, it is necessary to discuss whether the basic derivations terminate.

In this paper we present a new method called a time-bounded reasoning that forces the derivation procedure to terminate within a limited time $n$. That is, we use $KB \vdash_n \alpha$ instead of $KB \vdash \alpha$. Thus we can escape the undecidability. With this restriction, however, our method may infer a false result such that $KB \not\vdash_n \alpha$, but $KB \vdash \alpha$. Hence, it is

---

*Mailing address: Research Institute of Fundamental Information Science Kyushu University 33, Fukuoka 812, JAPAN

important that there be a discussion of the reliability of conclusions thus derived from a knowledge base and of the knowledge base itself.

In this paper, we first give definitions of time-bounded reasoning and other concepts necessary for our discussion. Then, we design a special inference system which makes use of our time-bounded reasoning. In Section 3, we show this inference system is sound and valid in some sense. In Section 4, we discuss problems about truth maintenance of knowledge base, reliability and capability of our time-bounded reasoning system. In Section 5, we consider time functions for some subclasses of first order predicate logic. In Section 6, we briefly describe the implemented system.

## 2   Time-Bounded Reasoning

This section defines a time-bounded reasoning, and designs an inference system that uses it. The basic logic programming terminology and concepts not defined in this paper may be found in [8].

First we show the concepts of *BF-derivation* (BF stands for *Breadth-First*), *derivation tree*, and the *depth of derivation tree* as in Figure 1, where $B \leftarrow A_1, \ldots, A_m$ is a clause, and $A$ is an atom.

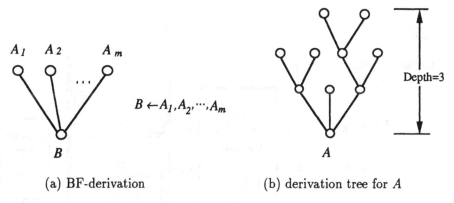

(a) BF-derivation                    (b) derivation tree for $A$

**Figure 1.**   BF-derivation and BF derivation tree

The derivation tree of Figure 1(b) is constructed by BF-derivation of Figure 1(a). We denote the depth of the derivation tree by the length of its longest branch, e.g. the depth of $A$'s derivation tree is 3 in Figure 1(b). Now, we define that the derivation of an atom, say $A$ in Figure 1(b), is rank $n$ if the depth of its derivation tree is $n$.

In the above notions, $n$ corresponds to that in $T_p \uparrow n$ [8], as proved in [18].

**Proposition 2.1 (Wolfram, Maher and Lasezz[18])** Let $P$ be a program and $A \in B(P)$ be an atom. $A \in Tp \uparrow k$ $(k > 0)$ iff there is a BF-refutation of $P \cup \{\leftarrow A\}$ of length at most $k$.

**Definition 2.1** Let $KB$ be a knowledge base and $\alpha$ be a positive ground literal called a query.

(1)   $\alpha$ is derived in depth $n$ from $KB$, denoted by $KB \vdash_n \alpha$, if it has a successful derivation tree of depth less than or equal to $n$.

(2)   $\alpha$ is failed in depth $n$ from $KB$, denoted by $KB \nvdash_n^F \alpha$, if all of its derivation trees are failures and their depths are less than or equal to $n$.

(3)   The other case is denoted by $KB \nvdash_n^I \alpha$.

Notice that (1) and (2) correspond to the concepts of success and failure in the theory of logic programming [8]. (3) is a specific feature of our time-bounded reasoning, that is, the derivation is forced to terminate at depth $n$.

If $\alpha$ has no successful derivation tree whose depth is less than or equal to $n$, we denote it as $KB \nvdash_n \alpha$. Then, clearly

$$KB \nvdash_n \alpha \iff (KB \nvdash_n^F \alpha \text{, or } KB \nvdash_n^I \alpha).$$

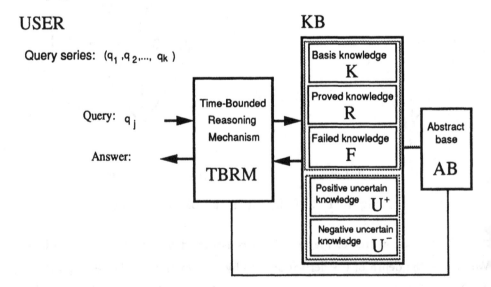

**Figure 2.**   Organization of Time-Bounded Reasoning System

**Definition 2.2** Let $\alpha$ be a positive ground literal called a query. *Time-bounded reasoning*(TBR for short) is an inference and an addition, defined in the following way:

(1)  Infer $\alpha$, and add it to $KB$, if $KB \vdash_n \alpha$.

(2)  Infer $\neg\alpha$, and add it to $KB$, if $KB \not\vdash_n^F \alpha$.

(3)  Infer $\neg\alpha$, and add it to $KB$, if $KB \not\vdash_n^I \alpha$.

Since the above three kinds of derivations are different from each other in their meaning and reliability, it is necessary to classify them. In order to use TBR effectively, we design a TBR system of three parts as in Figure 2, where

(1)  *TBRM* is a mechanism to infer queries within bounded time,

(2)  *KB* is a knowledge base to store the basic knowledge supplied by users and inferred results, and

(3)  *AB* is an abstract base to store the relations just among the predicate symbols in *KB*.

In this paper, we consider the following problem solving:

*In order to solve a problem, a user puts a query to the system. TBRM infers it by using the knowledge in KB within a bounded time, and then returns inferred results to the user, and adds it to KB at the same time. Depending on the answer from the system, the user can put another query to repeat the above process.*

For simplicity, we assume users are sufficiently intelligent to put no queries unnecessary to solve the problem.

We divide a *knowledge base KB* into five parts:

$$KB = K \cup R \cup F \cup U^+ \cup U^-$$

and denote it also by

$$KB = < K, R, F, U^+, U^- >,$$

where

$K$ is the finite set of normal clauses given by users, called *basic knowledge set*.

$R$ is the set of positive ground literals, called *proved knowledge set*.

$F$ is the set of negative ground literals, called *failed knowledge set.*

$U^+$ is the set of positive ground literals, called *positive uncertain knowledge set.*

$U^-$ is the set of negative ground literals, called *negative uncertain knowledge set.*

$K$ works as a basis of the knowledge base $KB$. A change of $K$ will propagate through the whole of the knowledge base.

A *query series* $(q_1, \ldots, q_i, \ldots)$ is a list of queries successively put to the system by a user, where $q_i (i \geq 1)$ is a positive ground literal.

In the following sections, we will consider a sequence of knowledge bases $KB_0, \ldots,$ $KB_i, \ldots$ which corresponds to $(q_1, \ldots, q_i, \ldots)$, where $KB_0 = < K, \phi, \phi, \phi, \phi >$ is called an *initial knowledge base*, and $KB_i = < K, R_i, F_i, U_i^+, U_i^- >$ is successively constructed by the method defined below.

# 3 Properties of the System

This section describes the operations of the TBR system, and discuss its properties. By the definition of the TBR, when receiving a query, the TBR system will infer it, and add the derived results to $KB$. Now we give the way of adding.

**Definition 3.1** Let $KB = < K, R, F, U^+, U^- >$ be a knowledge base, and $q$ be a query. the TBR constructs $KB' = < K, R', F', U^{+'}, U^{-'} >$ by adding derived results to $KB$ in the following way.

$$R' = R \cup \{q \mid K \cup R \cup F \vdash_n q, q \notin K\}$$

$$F' = F \cup \{\neg q \mid K \cup R \cup F \not\vdash_n^F q\}$$

$$U^{+'} = U^+ \cup \{q \mid KB \vdash_n q, q \notin K, q \notin R'\}$$

$$U^{-'} = U^- \cup \{\neg q \mid KB \not\vdash_n q, \neg q \notin F'\}$$

Now we will show that this system has many good properties. Since the TBR system may derive even a false result such as $KB \not\vdash_n q$ but $K \vdash q$, it is necessary to consider reliability and properties of this system.

In the previous section we have designed a TBR system with an organization as in Figure 2 from which we can easily obtain the following results.

**Proposition 3.1** In the knowledge base $KB$, any knowledge in parts $R$ and $F$ is not deleted if $K$ is not changed.

**Proof:** By the definition of $R$, clearly we have

$$\alpha \in R_i \Rightarrow K \vdash_{n \cdot i} \alpha \ (i \geq 1).$$

That is, every knowledge $\alpha$ in $R$ is a consequence of $K$. Thus, if $K$ is not changed, $\alpha$ cannot be deleted. Similarly we can prove it for $F$. $\square$

By Proposition 3.1, it is obvious that the more queries that are put to the TBR system, the stronger the proof power of the TBR system becomes. Clearly, the false knowledge is only in $U^+$ and $U^-$.

**Definition 3.2** Let $K$ be a set of basic knowledge. Then, we define three sets:

(1)  $C(K) = \{\alpha \mid K \vdash \alpha\}$: a set of successful knowledge from $K$.

(2)  $NAF(K) = \{\neg \alpha \mid K \not\vdash \alpha\}$: a set of failure knowledge from $K$.

(3)  $DKB = K \cup R \cup F$: a definite portion of $KB$.

**Corollary 3.2** If $K$ is not changed, the set of proved knowledge $R$ and the set of failed knowledge $F$ monotonically increases. That is,

$$R_0 \subseteq \ldots \subseteq R_i \subseteq R_{i+1} \subseteq \ldots \subseteq C(K)$$
$$F_0 \subseteq \ldots \subseteq F_i \subseteq F_{i+1} \subseteq \ldots \subseteq NAF(K),$$

where $R_0, \ldots, R_i, \ldots$ is a sequence of sets of proved knowledge, and $F_0, \ldots, F_i, \ldots$ is a sequence of sets of failed knowledge that respond to $(q_1, \ldots, q_i, \ldots)$.

By the assumption that a user is intelligent enough to organize a series of queries to derive the result about $\alpha$ in a finite time if $K \vdash \alpha$, we have the following proposition.

**Proposition 3.3**

(1)  $\bigcup_{i=0}^{\infty} R_i = C(K)$.

(2)  $\bigcup_{i=0}^{\infty} F_i = NAF(K)$.

Since $KB$ may have some false knowledge, it is not sound in general. By the discussion above, however, we can prove $DKB$, a part of $KB$, is sound and valid.

**Theorem 3.4 (Soundness)** Let $\alpha$ be a positive ground atom. Then

$$DKB \vdash_n \alpha \ \Rightarrow \ \alpha \in C(K).$$

**Theorem 3.5 (Validness)** Let $\alpha$ be a positive ground atom. Then under the NF rule (NF stands for negation as failure) in the TBR,

$$K \vdash \alpha \quad \Leftrightarrow \quad \text{there is a series of queries } q_1, \ldots, q_i(= \alpha) \text{ such that}$$
$$DKB_i \vdash_2 \alpha.$$

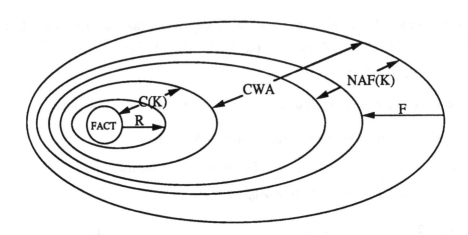

**Figure 3.** The power of inferences

From these discussions, we can summarize the relations between our the TBR and the usual time-unbounded reasoning as in Figure 3.

# 4  Truth Maintenance and Reliability of the System

## 4.1  Truth Maintenance

In our system, there are two kinds of truth maintenance problems. One is, as in Doyle [2], the contradiction that users want to avoid. We use a special predicate symbol *nogood* to express that a rule with "nogood" as its head and some bodies leads to a contradiction. In our TBR, three situations may arise:

$$K \vdash_n nogood, \qquad K \not\vdash_n^F nogood, \qquad K \not\vdash_n^I nogood.$$

In this paper, we say $K$ is consistent if $K \not\vdash_n nogood$. More detailed discussion about them is in Shi[16]. The other is the logical contradiction such as $KB \vdash_n \alpha$ and $KB \vdash_n \neg\alpha$, when a newly derived result is added as in Definition 3.1. In this section, we will mainly discuss this case.

With the TBR, the results of a derivation are frequently added to $KB$. Hence, to maintain the consistency of $KB$, it is necessary to delete some knowledge from $KB$ which may cause a contradiction of the second case above.

**Definition 4.1** We define a binary relation $Rel$ on the set of predicate symbols of $K$ by

$$Rel = \{(p,q) \mid p(\ldots) \leftarrow L_1(\ldots),\ldots,L_m(\ldots) \in K\},$$

where $q$ is a predicate symbol that occurs in a literal of $L_1,\ldots,L_m$.

**Definition 4.2** An influence of predicate symbol $q$, denoted $connect(q)$, is defined by

$$connect(q) = \{p \mid (p,q) \in Rel^+\},$$

where $Rel^+$ is a transitive closure of $Rel$.

After the adding of $q$ or $\neg q$(a derived result), the derivation of $q$ becomes of rank 1. Thus, the rank of the derivation of $p(\in connect(q))$ will become smaller than before. That is, some knowledge that were derived within greater ranks than $n$ may now be derived within rank $n$. We give the definition of truth maintenance.

**Definition 4.3** Let $KB' =< K, R', F', U^{+'}, U^{-'} >$ be a knowledge base that is defined by Definition 3.1, and $q$ be a query. A knowledge base $KB''$ is defined as follows:

$$KB'' =< K, R', F', U^{+''}, U^{-''} >,$$

where

$U^{+''} = U^{+'} - \Delta$

$U^{-''} = U^{-'} - \Delta$

$\Delta = \{p \mid p \in U^{+'}, p \in connect(q)\} \cup \{\neg p \mid \neg p \in U^{-'}, p \in connect(q)\}$.

$KB''$ is thus obtained by correcting $KB'$.

**Theorem 4.1** Let $KB'$ be a knowledge base constructed by Definitions 3.1 and 4.3 from $KB$. If $KB$ is consistent, then so is $KB'$.

**Proof:** It is clear from Definitions 3.1, 4.2, 4.3, and Proposition 3.1. $\square$

**Proposition 4.2** The sets $K$, $R_k$, $F_k$, $U_k^+$ and $U_k^-$ are mutually disjoint, if $KB_k =< K, R_k, F_k, U_k^+, U_k^- >$ is constructed by Definitions 3.1 and 4.3.

Although the additions and rechecks of knowledge are carried out very frequently in the TBR system, we can see they only have influence on a small portion of knowledge base.

## 4.2 Abstract Base

By the TBR, the derived results are frequently added to $KB$. In order to maintain the consistency of $KB$, the system has to recheck the knowledge stored in $KB$. This operation may cost a huge amount of time. To save time, we introduce an abstraction procedure[19].

**Definition 4.4** Let $KB$ be a knowledge base. An *abstract base $AB$* is defined by

$$AB = \{ab(id, p, n, Fp, Bp, connect(p)) \mid p \text{ is an n-ary predicate symbol in } KB\},$$

is a set of atoms that express the relations among the predicate symbols in $KB$, where

$id$ is a natural number, called an identifier of the knowledge,

$p$ is a predicate symbol,

$n$ is the arity of predicate symbol $p$,

$Fp = \{q \mid q(\ldots) \leftarrow \ldots, p(x_1, \ldots, x_n), \ldots \in KB\}$,

$Bp = \{r \mid p(x_1, \ldots, x_n) \leftarrow \ldots, r(\ldots), \ldots \in KB\}$,

$connect(p)$ is a set of predicate symbols (Definition 4.2), called the influence of $p$.

The TBR system uses $AB$ to simplify the relations in $KB$ in this way:

"$p(\ldots)$ is related to $q(\ldots)$ in $KB$" $\implies$ "$p$ is related to $q$ in $AB$".

As is easily seen, any literal which is not derived in $AB$ is not derived even in $KB$. The calculations and operations on $AB$ are much simpler than those on the original $KB$. Furthermore, the TBR system suffices to calculate $AB$ only when $K$ is changed by users. Thus, the abstraction technique contributes to making the TBR system efficient.

## 4.3 Reliability of System

From the discussions in Sections 2 and 3, we can now briefly summarize the reliability of our inference and knowledge in $KB$ itself.

(1) Knowledge base $KB$: As defined in Section 2, $KB$ in the TBR system has three parts, of different reliabilities:

(a) Since $K$ is the basic knowledge base given by the user at the starting point of inference, its reliability should be the highest among the three.

(b) $R$ and $F$ are sets of knowledge that can be asserted from $DKB$ under NF. Their reliability is medium.

(c) $U^+$ and $U^-$ are sets of derived knowledge under the TBR. Since there may be some false knowledge in it, their reliability is the lowest.

(4) Result of inference: the TBR system gives one of the following answers for a user's query in limited time.

(a) $< yes >$ : the query can be derived from $K$ by NF.

(b) $< no >$ : the query cannot be derived from $K$ by NF.

(c) $< yes, uncertain >$ : the query can be derived from $KB$ by the current TBR. It may be an uncertain result.

(d) $< no, uncertain >$ : the query cannot be derived from $KB$ by the current TBR. It may also be an uncertain result.

# 5 Time Functions of the TBR

When we put some queries to an inference system for solving a problem, we consciously or unconsciously require the system to return answers in a finite time. In general, there are two methods which meet the requirement: to find some safe subclasses, and to select a suitable compromise between time and reliability.

First we will discuss several subclasses which are constructed by imposing some syntactic restrictions on $KB$. For any $KB$ in such classes, there is a computable time function $f(KB)$ which satisfies "$KB \vdash_{f(KB)} q \iff KB \vdash q$". Hence the TBR can cut derivations at depth $f(KB)$. In this meaning we say these classes are safe to the TBR. We also pay attention to the relation between the time function, reliability, query, and $KB$. We use the following notations:

$S(KB) = max\{m \mid (\alpha \leftarrow \beta_1, \ldots, \beta_m) \in KB\}$, denotes the size of $KB$.

$D(KB)$: the depth of $KB$, i.e., the number of rules with different heads.

## 5.1 Time Functions of Propositional Logic

**Proposition 5.1** Let $A$ be an atom and $KB$ be a knowledge base in propositional logic. If $KB \vdash A$, there is a successful derivation tree of depth less than or equal to $D(KB)$.

**Proof:** By $KB \vdash A$, there is a finite successful derivation tree for $A$. First we suppose its depth is greater than $D(KB)$. Then there is a branch in the tree whose length is longer than $D(KB)$, that is,

$$p_1, p_2, \cdots, p_m \ (m > D(KB)),$$

where $p_1 = A$ is a root and $p_m$ is a leaf. In propositional logic, by the definition of $D(KB)$, there are $i$ and $j$ $(1 \le i < j \le m)$ such that $p_i = p_j$. We can replace the subtree with a root $p_i$ by the subtree with a root $p_j$. The depth of new tree is less than that of the old one. By repeating this process for every branch of length longer than $D(KB)$, a successful derivation tree of depth less than $D(KB)$ can be constructed. $\square$

By this proposition, we show that $D(KB)$ relates to a time function which guarantees the correctness of results of the TBR. From the relations between the BF-derivation and the binary derivation, we can easily see that $S(KB)$ is related to the actual time for processing, i.e., deriving a query.

## 5.2 Time Functions of Deductive Knowledge Bases

In first order knowledge base $KB$, there is no computable function $f$, hierarchical $KB$ and strongly stratified $KB$, for which there exist time functions $f$ which satisfy the above equivalence. By $pred(L)$ we denote the predicate symbol in the literal $L$.

**Definition 5.1 (Lloyd[8])** *A level mapping* of a knowledge base $KB$, denoted by $V_{level}$, is a mapping from the set of predicate symbols in $KB$ to non-negative integers. We refer to the value of a predicate symbol under this mapping as the *level* of the predicate symbol.

**Definition 5.2 (Lloyd[8])** A knowledge base $KB$ is *hierarchical* if it has a level mapping $V_{level}$ such that

$$V_{level}(p) > V_{level}(pred(L_i))$$

for any rule $p(t_1, \ldots, t_n) \leftarrow L_1, \ldots, L_m \in KB$ and any $i$ $(1 \le i \le m)$.

A hierarchical $KB$ has several good properties. For example, there is no recursive relation in $KB$, and any one step of BF-derivation will decrease the level of each subgoal by at least one. Since the number of predicate symbols in $KB$ is finite, so are the levels of predicate symbols in $KB$.

**Proposition 5.2** Let $KB$ be a hierarchical knowledge base, and $g(KB) = max\{V_{level}(p) \mid p \in KB\}$. Then, for any atom $A$,

$$KB \vdash A \; \Rightarrow \; KB \vdash_{g(KB)} A.$$

**Definition 5.3** A knowledge base $KB$ is *strongly stratified* if it has a *one-to-one level mapping* $V_{level}$ such that

$$V_{level}(p) \geq V_{level}(pred(L_i))$$
$$V_{level}(p) > V_{level}(pred(L_j))$$

for any rule $p(t_1, \ldots, t_n) \leftarrow L_1, \ldots, L_m \in KB$, any positive literal $L_i$ $(1 \leq i \leq m)$ and any negative literal $L_j$ $(1 \leq j \leq m)$.

From the definition we can see that the recursive relations are only on the same predicate symbols in the strongly stratified $KB$. We use the following notations:

$l(p) = max\{n \mid q(t_1, \ldots, t_n), \text{ and } (p, q) \in Rel^*\}$, the maximum length of predicate symbol $p$.

$U_{KB}$ : the domain of $KB$, the Herbrand universe of $KB$.

$\mid U_{KB} \mid$: the size of $U_{KB}$, the number of elements in $U_{KB}$.

**Proposition 5.3** Let $KB$ be a function-free strongly stratified knowledge base, and $L$ be a literal. Then

$$KB \vdash L \Leftarrow KB \vdash_{f(KB,L)} L,$$

where $f(KB, L) = V_{level}(L) * (\mid U_{KB} \mid^{l(L)} + 1)$.

**Proof** In a function-free knowledge base $KB$, the number of constant symbols is finite, i.e., $\mid U_{KB} \mid$ is finite. Thus, we can enumerate all ground atoms of an n-ary predicate, and it is clear that the number of them is less than or equal to $\mid U_{KB} \mid^n$. Furthermore, the number of predicate symbols in any branch of a derivation tree is less than or equal to $V_{level}(L)$, and the arity of each predicate in them is less than or equal to $l(L)$. So, by the same method as in the proof of Proposition 5.1, we can prove that the depth of any successful derivation tree is less than or equal to $V_{level}(L) * (\mid U_{KB} \mid^{l(L)} + 1)$. $\square$

## 5.3  Parameters in Time Functions

There may be, however, some unsafe $KB$'s which have no such $f(KB)$ as in Sections 5.1 and 5.2. In such a case, we usually take account of a tradeoff between time and reliability. By the discussions in Sections 5.1 and 5.2, we can intuitively see that the time is related to the following parameters:

(1)  $S(KB)$, $D(KB)$ (the size and depth of $KB$),

(2)  $l(p)$ (the maximum length of predicate symbol $p$),

(3)  $\mid U_{KB} \mid$ (the size of domain of $KB$).

Further, a user may have much knowledge and experience in the problem domain, so his/her decision will be very important in selecting the time bound. The detailed discussion of this will go beyond the scope of this paper. Finally we want to emphasize that the validness of the TBR system is guaranteed by Theorem 3.5 independently of the selected time bound.

# 6  Implementation of the TBR System

From the discussions in Sections 3 and 4, the configuration in Figure 2 can easily be implemented as a TBR system. Now we briefly describe the implemented system.

In the previous sections, we have discussed a TBR system under the assumption that $K$ is not changed and is consistent. In realizing the TBR as a practical system, however, we must supply an approach to check and maintain the consistency of $K$. In our TBR system implemented on a Sun-3 in K-prolog, we consider $DKB \vdash_n nogood$, $DKB \nvdash_n^F nogood$, and $DKB \nvdash_n^I nogood$. When a contradiction has been found, we can search for the suspects with the contradiction backtracking algorithm (CBA for short) [13, 14].

First, we divide a knowledge base $KB$ into five parts: $K$, $R$, $F$, $U^+$, and $U^-$. For simplifying the operation of rechecking for truth maintenance, we have introduced an abstract base $AB$ as in Definition 4.4. For dealing with queries and truth maintenance of $KB$, we have built in a time-bounded reasoning mechanism $TBRM$. It has four main functions:

(1)  *Query Treatment Function.*

For a query, $TBRM$ can return the best answer that is inferred within a limited time, and store the result in the corresponding part of $KB$.

(2) *Addition and Deletion of Knowledge.*

On demand of users, $TBRM$ can add or delete knowledge to or from $K$.

(3) *Truth Maintenance Function.*

Since (1) and (2) may destroy the consistency of $KB$, $TBRM$ has been designed to recheck and maintain the consistency of $KB$ by using the techniques of $AB$ and CBA.

(4) *Calculation and Modification of AB.*

When $K$ is changed, $TBRM$ can automatically correct $AB$.

Shi[16, 17] has given algorithms for these operations and the implementation principles.

Now we show an example to illustrate the operation of our TBR system. Let a set of basic knowledge $K$ be given as follow:

```
sunday(731).
student(shi).
student(ito).
student(arimura).
worker(sato).
worker(kawa).
holiday(101).
holiday(115).
holiday(321).
holiday(505).
climb(X,D):-nothing(X,D),noschool(X,D),asked(X,Y,D),weather(D).
nothing(X,D):-student(X),sw(D).
noschool(X,D):-holiday(D);sunday(D);(sw(D),student(X)).
asked(X,li,D):-student(X),D>=801,D=<826.
weather(D):-not(raining(D)).
raining(D):-D>=806,D=<808.
sw(D):-summer(D);winter(D).
sw(D):-D==312.
summer(D):-D>=720,D=<910.
winter(D):-D>=101,D=<120.
nogood:-climb(ayumi,820).
nogood:-student(X),worker(X).
```

The interaction 74 below shows that the set of basic knowledge $K$ is given as an input *ex1*, and $TBRM$ calculates its abstract base at the same time.

```
74: ?- input_kb(ex1).
*** the number of predicate symbols is 14
*** the number of facts and rules is 22
*** the length of K is  4
*** the depth of K is  10
```

In order to treat queries from users, we supply a predicate $query(G, D)$ as an operation of $TBRM$, where $G$ is a query and $D$ is a value of time function. Its role is to decide whether $KB \vdash_D G$ as in Definition 3.1. From the following interactions 75–77, we can see that the proof power of the TBR system gradually becomes stronger.

```
75: ?- query(climb(shi,820),4).
*** <no, uncertain>
76: ?- query(sw(820),4).
*** yes
77: ?- query(climb(shi,820),4).
*** yes
```

In order to permit users to change $K$, we supply two more predicates, $addpro(G)$ and $delpro(G)$. The $addpro(G)$ adds a new fact or rule $G$ to $K$, maintains the consistency of $KB$, and automatically corrects $AB$. The $delpro(G)$ deletes a fact or rule $G$ from $K$, maintains the consistency of $KB$, and automatically corrects $AB$.

In a Prolog program, the order of the knowledge(facts and rules) is very important. For example, if its order is as in interactions 78 and 79 below, the derivation from the query, e.g. $query(nothing(X, 311), 40)$, will fall into an infinite loop. Our TBR system, however, can find all answers independently of the order of the knowledge such that interaction 80. And this system can prevent derivation from infinite loop as in interaction 81.

```
78: ?- addpro(nothing(X,Y):-nothing(X,Z)).
yes
79: ?- addpro(nothing(shi,311)).
yes
80: ?- query(nothing(X,311),40).
X=shi
*** yes
81: ?- query(nothing(ito,X),40).
*** <no, uncertain>
```

The kernel of this TBR system is a meta-interpreter $solve(M, G, D, W)$, where $M$ is a value to express the property of the result ($M = 0$ means "success", $M = 1$ means "failure", and $M = 2$ means "the result is uncertain"), $G$ is a query, $D$ is a value of the time function, and $W$ is the information about derivation, e.g. the derivation tree. $W$ is important in debugging and constructing of a query series from the user.

For truth maintenance, we also supply a predicate $cba(X, W, E)$. According to the interaction with users, it can find a reason which causes a contradiction. The interactions 82 and 83 below show how to backtrack a contradiction by using predicates *solve* and *cba*.

```
82: ?- solve(M,climb(shi,819),7,W),M==0,cba(Y,W,S).
[(nothing(shi,819) , 0)] ? t/f  t.
[(noschool(shi,819) , 0)]?t/f  f.
[(holiday(819) , 1)]?t/f  t.
[(sunday(819) , 1)]?t/f  t.
[(sw(819) , 0)]?t/f  f.
[(summer(819) , 0)]?t/f  t.
[(sw(819):-summer(819) ; winter(819))] is an error.
83: ?- solve(M,climb(shi,819),7,W),M==0,cba(Y,W,S).
[(nothing(shi,819) , 0)]?t/f  t.
[(noschool(shi,819) , 0)]?t/f  f.
[(holiday(819) , 1)]?t/f  t.
[(sunday(819) , 1)]?t/f  t.
[(sw(819) , 0)]?t/f  t.
[(student(shi) , 0)]?t/f  f.
[(student(shi) , 0)] is an error.
```

When $K$ is changed, the following contradictions may also be created. They may be corrected in the following way.

```
84: ?- addpro(worker(shi)).
A contradiction has been found
***CBA starts***
[(student(shi), 0)]?t/f  f.
[(student(shi), 0)] is an error
85: ?- delpro(student(shi)).
Do you want to delete it from K-base?  yes
86: ?- addpro(student(ayumi)).
A contradiction has been found
***CBA starts***
[(climb(ayumi), 0)]?t/f  f.
[(nothing(ayumi,820), 0)]?t/f  t.
[(noschool(ayumi,820), 0)]?t/f  t.
[(asked(ayumi,li,820), 0)]?t/f  f.
[(student(ayumi), 0)]?t/f  t.
[(820>=801, 0)]?t/f  t.
[(820=<826)]?t/f  t.
[asked(ayumi,li,820):-student(ayumi),820>=801,820=<826] is an error
yes
```

```
87: ?- delpro((asked(X,li,D):-student(X),D>=801,D=<826)).
Do you want to delete it from K-base?  yes
```

To supply a better environment to users, we have made many other predicates [16].

# 7  Conclusion

This paper has discussed the problem of terminating derivations like $KB \vdash \alpha$. To escape the undecidability of first order predicate logic, we have proposed a time-bounded reasoning, and designed a special system for it. Then we have discussed the properties, truth maintenance, and reliability of the TBR system. Although there may be some false knowledge in $KB$, it is only in $U^+$ and $U^-$, special parts of $KB$. $DKB$, the other part of $KB$, monotonically increases, and is sound and valid in some sense. We can see that the power of proof and the reliability of the TBR system will gradually become stronger and higher.

Also by using $AB$, we have shown our system can work effectively, although it has to recheck and modify the stored knowledge of $KB$. Furthermore, we have implemented a prototype system of the TBR, and with it we have also made sure of the properties above.

Our system stores the derived results in $KB$, and hence it has a learning function. The TBR is similar to our problem solving activities, so we can say that it is a natural reasoning method.

Further discussions on the query series and time function are left for future problems.

# Acknowledgment

We would like to thank S. Miyano, A. Yamamoto, and A. Arimura for their helpful discussions.

# References

[1] Blum, L., Blum, M.,  Towards a Mathematical Theory of Inductive Inference, *Information and Control 28*, 1975.

[2] Doyle, J., A Truth Maintenance System, *Artificial Intelligence*, Vol.12, pp.231-272, 1979.

[3] Golfesddrt, S., Micali, S. and Rackoff, C., The Knowledge Complexity of Interactive Proof-System, *Proceedings of the 17th STOC ACM*, pp. 291-303, 1985.

[4] Haraguchi, M., Arikawa, S., A Foundation of Reasoning by Analogy– Analogical Union of Logic Programs, *LNCS 264*, pp.58-69, 1987.

[5] Kitakami, H., Kunifuji, S., Miyachi, T., and Furukawa, K., Knowledge Base Management System Implemented in Logic Programming Language Prolog, *Information processing*, Vol. 26, No. 11, pp.1283-1295, in Japanese, 1985.

[6] Lloyd, J.W., Topor, R.W., A Basis for Deductive Database Systems, *J. Logic Programming*, Vol.2, No.2, pp.93-109, 1985.

[7] Lloyd, J.W., Topor, R.W., A Basis for Deductive Database Systems, *J. Logic Programming*, Vol.3, No.1, pp.55-67, 1986.

[8] Lloyd, J.W., *Foundations of Logic Programming*, (Second, Extended Edition), Springer-Verlag, 1987.

[9] Matsuda, T., Ishizuka, M., Knowledge Assimilation and Management Mechanism for Frame Knowledge-Base Including Hypothesis Knowledge, *The Transactions of the Institute of Electronics Information and Communication Engineers*, J71D,5,pp.902-908, in Japanese, 1988.

[10] Reiter, R., On Closed World Data Bases, *Logic and Data Bases*, pp. 55-76, viii+458, 1978.

[11] Reiter, R., The Default Logic, *Artificial Intelligence*, Vol.13, pp.231-272, 1979.

[12] Reiter, R., de Kleer, J., Foundations of Truth Maintenance: Preliminary Report, *Proceedings of AAAI-87 the 6th National Conference on Artificial Intelligence*, pp. 183-188, 1987.

[13] Shapiro, E.Y., Inductive Inference of Theories from Facts, *Technical Report 192*, Yale University 1981.

[14] Shapiro, E.Y., *Algorithmic Program Debugging*, MIT Press, Cambridge, Mass., 1983.

[15] Shapiro, E.Y., Alternation and the Computational Complexity of Logic Programs, *J. Logic Programming*, Vol.1, No.1, 1984.

[16] Shi, Y., *Studies on Knowledge Base Management Systems by Time-Bounded Reasoning and Contradiction Backtracking Algorithm*, The Dissertation of D. M., Interdisciplinary Graduate School of Engineering Sciences, Kyushu University, in Japanese, 1989.

[17] Shi, Y., The Principles of Time-Bounded Knowledge Base Management Systems, *Engineering Sciences Reports, Kyushu University*, Vol.11, No.1, pp.77-84, in Japanese, 1989.

[18] Wikfram, D.A., Maher, M.J., and Lasezz, J.-L., A Unified Treatment of Resolution Strategies for Logic Program, *Proceedings of the Second International Conference of Logic Programming*, pp. 263-276, 1984.

[19] Yamamoto, A., An Anatomy of Abstraction, *Bulletin of Informatics and Cybernetics*, Vol.22, No.3-4, pp.179-188, 1987.

# Elementary Formal System
## as
# a Logic Programming Language

### Akihiro YAMAMOTO
Department of Information Systems
Kyushu University 39, Kasuga 816, JAPAN

Mailing address : Research Institute of Fundamental Information Science
Kyushu University 33, Fukuoka 812, JAPAN

### Abstract

In this paper, we give a theoretical foundation of EFS (elementary formal system) as a logic programming language. We show that the set of all the unifiers of two atoms is finite and computable by restricting the form of axioms and goals without losing generality. The restriction makes the negation as failure rule complete. We give two conditions of EFS's such that the negation as failure rule is identical to the closed world assumption. We also give a subclass of EFS's where a procedure of CWA is given as bounding the length of derivations We compare these classes with the Chomsky hierarchy.

## 1. Introduction

In this paper we give a theoretical foundation of EFS (elementary formal system) as a logic programming language.

EFS was first introduced by Smullyan [13] to develop his recursive function theory. Both EFS and logic programming use definite clauses as axioms, but the structures of their terms are different. Logic programming uses the first order terms, but the terms of EFS are patterns in $(\Sigma \cup X)^+$ as terms. Arikawa [1] showed EFS is suitable to generate languages.

We formalize a derivation procedure for EFS, and give the same semantics to EFS as that of logic programming. Our motivation for this is to give a unifying framework of inductive inference of languages by combining MIS [12] with EFS. The framework is given as MIEFS [2]. Thus we need a complete refutation procedure to accept languages defined by EFS's, nearly in the same way as that of logic programming.

Our theory is based on that of *logic programming schema* given by Jaffar et al. [7]. In order to show the completeness of refutation for EFS, we give the declarative semantics of EFS's by introducing the associative law as an equational theory to represent the unification of patterns. It would seem that our theory is an instance of the schema such that the Herbrand universe is $\Sigma^+$. However, there still remains a big problem in the operational semantics, that is, there are infinitely many maximally general unifiers of two atoms. No method for avoiding this problem was given in the schema, and so the NF(negation as failure rule) is incomplete in general.

We give a solution of the problem by simply assuming that EFS's are variable-bounded and goals are ground. The assumption does not lose generality, because it is known that every recursively enumerable language is definable by a variable-bounded EFS [2]. We show that the set of all unifiers of two atoms is finite and computable when we use variable-bounded EFS's and ground goals. Thus NF is complete under the assumption.

Moreover, we give two procedures of the CWA (closed world assumption) for variable-bounded EFS's. One is to make use of NF by giving some restrictions to the axioms. We show that NF is identical to CWA for hierarchical EFS's and reducing EFS's. The other is to bound the length of derivations with the size of atoms in the goal. We show that this procedure realizes CWA for weakly reducing EFS's. Since EFS combines logic programming and formal language theory, we can compare these classes with Chomsky hierarchy. We show that every context-free language is definable by a reducing EFS. It is shown in [2] that every context-sensitive language is definable by a weakly reducing EFS.

The paper is organized as follows. In Section 2 we give the fundamental definitions of EFS and introduce the variable-bounded EFS. In Section 3, we give the derivation procedure for EFS and show that all unifiers can be effectively computed for variable-bounded EFS's and ground goals. In Section 4 we give the same semantics to EFS as that of logic programming. In Section 5 we prove the completeness of NF for variable-bounded EFS. In Section 6 we discuss CWA mainly for weakly reducing EFS.

## 2. Elementary Formal System

We start with recalling the definitions of EFS.

Let $\Sigma$, $X$, and $\Pi$ be mutually disjoint sets. We assume that $\Sigma$ and $\Pi$ are finite. We refer to $\Sigma$ as the *alphabet*, to each element of it as a *symbol*, which will be denoted by $a, b, c, \ldots$, to each element of $X$ as a *variable*, denoted by $x, y, z, x_1, x_2, \ldots$, and to each element of $\Pi$ as a *predicate symbol*, denoted by $p, q, \ldots$, where each of them has an *arity*.

**Definition.** A *word* over a set $A$ is a finite sequence of elements of $A$. $A^+$ denotes the set of all non-empty words over the set $A$, and $A^* = A^+ \cup \{\lambda\}$ where $\lambda$ is the empty word.

**Definition.** A *term* of $S$ is an element of $(\Sigma \cup X)^+$. Each term is denoted by, $\pi, \tau, \pi_1, \pi_2, \ldots$, $\tau_1, \tau_2, \ldots$. A *ground term* of $S$ is an element of $\Sigma^+$. Terms are also called *patterns*.

**Definition.** An *atomic formula* (or *atom* for short) of $S$ is an expression of the form $p(\tau_1, \ldots, \tau_n)$, where $p$ is a predicate symbol in $\Pi$ with arity $n$ and $\tau_1, \ldots, \tau_n$ are terms of $S$. The atom is *ground* if $\tau_1, \ldots, \tau_n$ are all ground.

**Notation.**

(1) For a term $\pi$, $|\pi|$ denotes the length of $\pi$, that is, the number of all occurrences of symbols and variables in $\pi$. For an atom $p(\pi_1, \ldots, \pi_n)$, let

$$|p(\pi_1, \ldots, \pi_n)| = |\pi_1| + \cdots + |\pi_n|.$$

(2) For a term $\pi$ and variable $x$, $o(x, \pi)$ is the number of all occurrences of $x$ in $\pi$. For an atom $p(\pi_1, \ldots, \pi_n)$, let

$$o(x, p(\pi_1, \ldots, \pi_n)) = o(x, \pi_1) + \cdots + o(x, \pi_n).$$

(3) $v(\alpha)$ denotes the set of all variables in a term or an atom $\alpha$.

**Example 1.** Let $A = p(ax, bycx)$. Then $|A| = 6$, $o(x, A) = 2$, and $v(A) = \{x, y\}$.

A *well-formed formula* is defined in the same way as in first-order predicate logic.

**Definition.** A *clause* is a well-formed formula of the form

$$\forall(A_1 \vee \ldots \vee A_n \vee (\neg B_1) \vee \ldots \vee (\neg B_m)),$$

where $A_1, \ldots, A_n, B_1, \ldots, B_m$ are atoms of $S$ and $n, m \geq 0$. The formula with $n = m = 0$ is assumed to denote $\square$, and called *the empty clause*. We denote the above clause by

$$A_1, \ldots, A_n \leftarrow B_1, \ldots, B_m.$$

The clause is *ground* if the atoms $A_1, \ldots, A_n, B_1, \ldots, B_m$ are all ground.

**Definition.** A *definite clause* is a clause of the form

$$A \leftarrow B_1, \ldots, B_n \qquad (n \geq 0).$$

**Definition (Smullyan [13]) .** An *elementary formal system* (*EFS* for short) $S$ is a triplet $(\Sigma, \Pi, \Gamma)$, where $\Gamma$ is a finite set of definite clauses. The definite clauses in $\Gamma$ are called *axioms* of $S$.

Now we explain the provability of atoms in the theory of EFS. Arikawa [1] gave his theory of formal languages using this provability.

**Definition.** A *substitution* $\theta$ is a (semi-group) homomorphism from $(\Sigma \cup X)^+$ to itself such that $a\theta = a$ for every $a \in \Sigma$ and the set $\{x \in X | x\theta \neq x\}$, denoted by $D(\theta)$, is finite. The substitution is *ground* if $x\theta$ is ground for every $x \in D(\theta)$.

Let $\theta$ be a substitution. If $D(\theta) = \{x_1, \ldots, x_n\}$ and $x_i\theta = \tau_i$, then $\theta$ is denoted by

$$\{x_1 := \tau_1, \ldots, x_n := \tau_n\}.$$

We also define

$$p(\tau_1, \ldots, \tau_n)\theta = p(\tau_1\theta, \ldots, \tau_n\theta)$$

and

$$(A \leftarrow B_1, \ldots, B_m)\theta = A\theta \leftarrow B_1\theta, \ldots, B_m\theta.$$

for a substitution $\theta$, an atom $p(\tau_1, \ldots, \tau_n)$ and a clause $A \leftarrow B_1, \ldots, B_m$.

**Definition.** Let $S = (\Sigma, \Pi, \Gamma)$ be an EFS. We define the relation $\Gamma \vdash C$ for a clause $C$ of $S$ inductively as follows:

(2.1) If $\Gamma \ni C$, then $\Gamma \vdash C$.

(2.2) If $\Gamma \vdash C$, then $\Gamma \vdash C\theta$ for any substitution $\theta$.

(2.3) If $\Gamma \vdash A \leftarrow B_1, \ldots, B_n$ and $\Gamma \vdash B_n \leftarrow$, then $\Gamma \vdash A \leftarrow B_1, \ldots, B_{n-1}$.

$C$ is *provable from* $\Gamma$ if $\Gamma \vdash C$.

**Definition.** For an EFS $S = (\Sigma, \Pi, \Gamma)$ and $p \in \Pi$ with arity $n$, we define

$$L(S, p) = \{(\alpha_1, \ldots, \alpha_n) \in (\Sigma^+)^n \,|\, \Gamma \vdash p(\alpha_1, \ldots, \alpha_n) \leftarrow\}.$$

In case $n = 1$, $L(S, p)$ is a language over $\Sigma$. A language $L \subseteq \Sigma^+$ is *definable by an EFS* or an *EFS language* if such $S$ and $p$ exist.

We introduce an important subclass of EFS's.

**Definition.** A definite clause $A \leftarrow B_1, \ldots, B_n$ is *variable-bounded* if $v(A) \supset v(B_i)$ $(i = 1, \ldots, n)$. An EFS is *variable-bounded* if its axioms are all variable-bounded.

**Example 2.** An EFS $S = (\{a, b, c\}, \{p, q\}, \Gamma)$ with

$$\Gamma = \left\{ \begin{array}{l} p(a, b, c) \leftarrow, \\ p(ax, by, cz) \leftarrow p(x, y, z), \\ q(xyz) \leftarrow p(x, y, z) \end{array} \right\}$$

is variable-bounded and defines a language

$$L(S, q) = \{a^n b^n c^n \,|\, n \geq 1\}.$$

# 3. Derivation Procedure

First we give a derivation procedure for an EFS with unification defined as follows:

**Definition.** Let $\alpha$ and $\beta$ be a pair of terms or atoms. Then a substitution $\theta$ is a *unifier* of $\alpha$ and $\beta$, or $\theta$ *unifies* $\alpha$ and $\beta$ if $\alpha\theta = \beta\theta$. $\alpha$ and $\beta$ are *unifiable* if there exists a unifier of $\alpha$ and $\beta$. $U(\alpha, \beta)$ denotes the set of all unifiers $\theta$ of $\alpha$ and $\beta$ such that $D(\theta) \subset v(\alpha) \cup v(\beta)$.

It is often the case that there are infinitely many maximally general unifiers.

**Example 3 (Plotkin[10]).** Let $S = (\{a, b\}, \{p\}, \Gamma)$. Then $\{x := a^i\}$ for every $i$ is the unifier of $p(ax)$ and $p(xa)$. All the unifiers are maximally general.

We overcome the problem with the following proposition.

**Lemma 1.** *Let $\alpha$ and $\beta$ be a pair of terms or atoms. If one of them is ground, then every unifier of $\alpha$ and $\beta$ is ground and $U(\alpha, \beta)$ is finite and computable.*

**Proof.** First we show that the result holds in case $\alpha$ and $\beta$ are terms. Assume that $\alpha$ is ground, $v(\beta) = \{x_1, \ldots, x_n\}$ and $\theta = \{x_1 := \pi_1, \ldots, x_k := \pi_k\}$ unifies $\alpha$ and $\beta$ where $k \leq n$. Then $k = n$ and $\pi_1, \ldots, \pi_k$ are all ground; that is, $\theta$ is ground by the definitions of ground terms and substitutions. By comparing $|\alpha|$ with $|\beta\theta|$, it holds that $|\pi_i| \leq |\alpha|$. Since the number of ground terms $\pi$ with $|\pi| \leq |\alpha|$ is finite, and the set

$$T(\alpha, \beta) = \{\sigma \mid D(\sigma) = v(\beta) \text{ and } |x\sigma| \leq |\alpha| \text{ for every } x \in D(\sigma)\}$$

is finite and computable, we can compute $U(\alpha, \beta)$ by testing every element $\sigma$ of $T(\alpha, \beta)$ to see whether $\alpha = \beta\sigma$ or not.

Now let $\alpha$ be a ground atom and $\beta$ be an atom. If the predicate symbols of $\alpha$ and $\beta$ are different, it is clear that $\alpha$ and $\beta$ are not unifiable. Thus we assume $\alpha = p(\tau_1, \ldots, \tau_n)$ and $\beta = p(\pi_1, \ldots, \pi_n)$. A unifier of $\alpha$ and $\beta$ is also a unier of $\tau_i$ and $\pi_i$ for $i = 1, \ldots, n$. Then $U(\alpha, \beta)$ can be computed by testing every tuple of $(\sigma_1, \ldots, \sigma_n)$ where $\sigma_i \in U(\tau_i, \pi_i)$ $(i = 1, \ldots, n)$ to see whether $\alpha = \beta\sigma_1 \cdots \sigma_n$ or not.

Next, we formalize the derivation for an EFS with no requirement that every unifier should be most general.

**Definition.** A *goal clause* (or *goal* for short) of $S$ is a clause of the form

$$\leftarrow B_1, \ldots, B_n \qquad (n \geq 0).$$

**Definition.** Let $C$ and $D$ be two clauses. Then $C$ is a *variant* of $D$ if $C = D\theta$ and $C\theta' = D$ for some substitutions $\theta$ and $\theta'$. Similarly we define variants of a clause.

**Definition.** A *computation rule* is a rule which selects an atom from every goal clause.

**Definition.** Let $S$ be an EFS, $G$ be a goal of $S$, and $R$ be a computation rule. A *derivation from* $G$ is a (finite or infinite) sequence of triplets $(G_i, \theta_i, C_i)$ $(i = 0, 1, \ldots)$ which satisfies the following conditions:

(3.1) $G_i$ is a goal, $\theta_i$ is a substitution, $C_i$ is a variant of an axiom of $S$, and $G_0 = G$.

(3.2) $v(C_i) \cap v(C_j) = \phi$ $(i \neq j)$, and $v(C_i) \cap v(G) = \phi$ for every $i$.

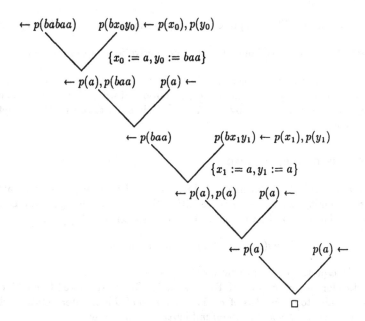

Figure 1: A refutation

(3.3) If $G_i =\leftarrow A_1,\ldots, A_k$ and $A_m$ is the atom selected by $R$, then $C_i = A \leftarrow B_1,\ldots, B_q$, $\theta_i$ is a unifier of $A$ and $A_m$, and

$$G_{i+1} = (\leftarrow A_1,\ldots, A_{m-1}, B_1,\ldots, B_q, A_{m+1},\ldots, A_k)\theta_i.$$

$A_m$ is a *selected atom* of $G_i$, and $G_{i+1}$ is a *resolvent* of $G_i$ and $C_i$ by $\theta_i$.

**Definition.** For a finite derivation $(G_i, \theta_i, C_i)\,(i = 0,\ldots n)$, we define its *length* as $n$.

**Definition.** A *refutation* is a finite derivation ending with the empty goal $\Box$.

**Example 4.** Let EFS $S = (\{a, b\}, \{p\}, \Gamma)$ with

$$\Gamma = \left\{ \begin{array}{l} p(a) \leftarrow, \\ p(bxy) \leftarrow p(x), p(y) \end{array} \right\}.$$

Then a refutation from $\leftarrow p(babaa)$ is illustrated in Figure 1, where the computation rule selects the leftmost atom from every goal.

The aim of our formalization of derivation is to give a procedure accepting languages definable by EFS's. Thus we assume every derivation starts from a ground goal. Then we get the following lemma by Lemma 1 and the definition of variable-bounded clauses.

**Lemma 2.** *Let $S$ be a variable-bounded EFS, and $G$ be a ground goal. Then every resolvent of $G$ is ground, and the set of all the resolvents of $G$ is finite and computable.*

The power of variable-bounded EFS's is shown by using the derivation procedure in [2].

**Theorem 1 ([2]).** *Let $\Sigma$ be an alphabet with at least two symbols. Then a language $L \subset \Sigma^+$ is definable by a variable-bounded EFS if and only if $L$ is recursively enumerable.*

Thus the variable-bounded EFS's are powerful enough, and we make the following assumption.

**Assumption.** Every EFS is variable-bounded and every derivation starts from a ground goal.

Moreover, by Lemma 2, we can implement the derivation in nearly the same way as for the traditional logic programming languages under the assumption. If we don't have the assumption, we need another formalization, such as given by Yamamoto[14], in order to control the nondeterministic algorithm of unification.

## 4. Completeness of Refutation

We describe the semantics of EFS's according to Jaffar, et al.[7]. They have given a general framework of various logic programming languages by representing their unification algorithm as an equality theory. To represent unification in derivations for EFS's we use the equality theory

$$E = \{cons(cons(x,y),z) = cons(x, cons(y,z))\},$$

where $cons$ is to be interpreted as the catenation of terms.

The first semantics for an EFS $S = (\Sigma, \Pi, \Gamma)$ is its model. To interpret well-formed formulas of $S$ we can restrict the domains to the models of $E$. Then a model of $S$ is an interpretation which makes every axiom in $\Gamma$ true. We use $\Sigma^+$ as the *Herbrand universe* and the set

$$B(S) = \{p(\tau_1, \ldots, \tau_n) \mid p \in \Pi \text{ and } \tau_1, \ldots, \tau_n \in \Sigma^+ \}$$

as the *Herbrand base*. A subset $I$ of $B(S)$ is called an *Herbrand interpretation* in the sense that $A \in I$ means $A$ is true and $A \notin I$ means $A$ is false for $A \in B(S)$. Then

$$M(S) = \cap\{M \mid M \text{ is an Herbrand model of } S \}$$

is an Herbrand model of $S$, and every ground atom in $M(S)$ is true in any model of $S$.

The second semantics is the least fixpoint $lfp(T_S)$ of the function $T_S : 2^{B(S)} \longrightarrow 2^{B(S)}$ defined by

$$T_S(I) = \left\{ A \in B(S) \left| \begin{array}{c} \text{there is a ground instance} \\ A \leftarrow B_1, \ldots, B_n \\ \text{of an axiom in } \Gamma \text{ such that } B_k \in I \text{ for } k = 1, \ldots, n. \end{array} \right. \right\}.$$

$T_S$ is shown to be continuous in [7]. We use the following sets defined by $T_S$:

$$
\begin{aligned}
T_S \uparrow 0 &= \phi, \\
T_S \uparrow \alpha &= T_S(T_S \uparrow (\alpha - 1)), && \text{if } \alpha \text{ is a successor ordinal,} \\
T_S \uparrow \alpha &= \cup\{T_S \uparrow \beta \mid \beta < \alpha\}, && \text{if } \alpha \text{ is a limit ordinal,}
\end{aligned}
$$

$$
\begin{aligned}
T_S \downarrow 0 &= B(S), \\
T_S \downarrow \alpha &= T_S(T_S \downarrow (\alpha - 1)), && \text{if } \alpha \text{ is a successor ordinal,} \\
T_S \downarrow \alpha &= \cap\{T_S \downarrow \beta \mid \beta < \alpha\}, && \text{if } \alpha \text{ is a limit ordinal.}
\end{aligned}
$$

$lfp(T_S)$ is characterized by the fact that

$$lfp(T_S) = T_S \uparrow \omega.$$

The third semantics, using refutation, is defined by

$$SS(S) = \{A \in B(S) \mid \text{there exists a refutation from } \leftarrow A\}.$$

These three semantics were shown to be identical:

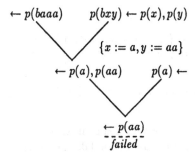

Figure 2: A derivation finitely failed with length 2

**Theorem 2 (Jaffar et al.[7]).** *For any EFS $S$,*

$$M(S) = lfp(T_S) = SS(S).$$

Now we give another semantics of EFS using the provability as the set

$$PS(S) = \{A \in B(S) \mid \Gamma \vdash A\}.$$

**Theorem 3.** *For any EFS $S$,*

$$PS(S) = SS(S).$$

This theorem is important from the viewpoint of language theory because the refutation is complete as *accepting* EFS languages. The proof of the theorem is clear from the definition.

## 5. Negation as Failure Rule

Now we discuss the inference of negation.

**Definition.** A derivation is *finitely failed with length $n$* if its length is $n$ and there is no axiom which satisfies the condition (3.3) for the selected atom of the last goal.

**Example 5.** Let $S$ be the EFS in Example 4. Then the derivation illustrated in Figure 2 is finitely failed with length 2.

**Definition.** A derivation $(G_i, \theta_i, C_i)$ $(i = 0, 1, \ldots)$ is *fair* if it is finitely failed or, for each atom $A$ in $G_i$, there is a $k \geq i$ such that $A\theta_i \cdots \theta_{k-1}$ is the selected atom of $G_k$. A computation rule is *fair* if it makes all derivations *fair*.

The *negation as failure rule* (NF for short) is the rule that infers $\neg A$ when a ground atom $A$ is in the set

$$FF(S) = \left\{ A \in B(S) \, \middle| \, \begin{array}{l} \text{for any fair computation rule, there is an } n \text{ such that} \\ \text{all derivations from } \leftarrow A \text{ are finitely failed within length } n \end{array} \right\}.$$

$FF(S)$ is characterized by the fact that

$$FF(S) = T_S \downarrow \omega.$$

Note that $FF(S)$ is not always identical to the set

$$GF(S) = \left\{ A \in B(S) \, \middle| \, \begin{array}{l} \text{for any fair computation rule, all derivations} \\ \text{from } \leftarrow A \text{ are finitely failed} \end{array} \right\}.$$

The following example was pointed out in [7].

**Example 6.** Let an EFS $S = (\{a, b\}, \{p, q, r\}, \Gamma)$ with

$$\Gamma = \left\{ \begin{array}{l} p(a) \leftarrow q(ax, xa), \\ q(x, x) \leftarrow r(x), \\ r(ax) \leftarrow r(x) \end{array} \right\}.$$

Then $p(a) \in GF(S)$ but $p(a) \notin FF(S)$ because there are infinitely many unifiers of $ax$ and $xa$, as was shown in Example 3.

We put $ecj(\theta) = (x_1 = \tau_1 \wedge \ldots \wedge x_n = \tau_n)$ for a substitution $\theta = \{x_1 := \tau_1, \ldots, x_n := \tau_n\}$, and $ecj(\theta) = true$ for an empty $\theta$. From the discussions in Jaffar, et al. [7], NF for EFS is complete if the following two conditions are satisfied:

(5.1) There is a theory $E^*$ that logically implies

$$(\pi = \tau) \rightarrow \vee_{i=1}^{k} ecj(\theta_i)$$

for every two terms $\pi$ and $\tau$, where $\theta_1, \ldots, \theta_k$ are all the unifiers of $\pi$ and $\tau$.

(5.2) $FF(S) = GF(S)$.

In general, NF for EFS is not complete, by Example 6, and there is no $E^*$ of (5.1) for an EFS, because there are infinitely many maximal unifiers.

Now we prove that NF for variable-bounded EFS's is complete. We prove that $FF(S)$ is also identical to the set

$$GGF(S) = \left\{ A \in B(S) \; \middle| \; \begin{array}{l} \text{for any fair computation rule, all derivations} \\ \text{from} \leftarrow A \text{ such that all goals in them} \\ \text{are ground are finitely failed} \end{array} \right\}.$$

The inference rule that infers $\neg A$ for a ground atom $A$ if $A$ is in $GGF(S)$ is called the *Herbrand rule*[8].

**Theorem 4.** *For any variable-bounded EFS $S$,*

$$FF(S) = GF(S) = GGF(S).$$

**Proof.** Since $S$ is variable-bounded, $GF(S) = GGF(S)$ by Lemma 2. It is also shown that $FF(S) = GF(S)$ by Lemma 2 and König's Lemma.

By Lemma 2 we use the following equational theory for a variable-bounded EFS instead of (5.1):

$$E^* = \left\{ \tau = \pi \rightarrow \vee_{i=1}^{k} ecj(\theta_i) \; \middle| \; \begin{array}{l} \tau \text{ is a term, } \pi \text{ is a ground term,} \\ \text{and } \theta_1, \ldots, \theta_k \text{ are all the unifiers of } \pi \text{ and } \tau \end{array} \right\}.$$

This $E^*$ exists by Lemma 1. Thus NF is complete and identical to the Herbrand rule for variable-bounded EFS's.

## 6. Closed World Assumption

In this section we discuss the *closed world assumption* (CWA for short) for EFS. For an EFS $S = (\Sigma, \Pi, \Gamma)$ and $A \in B(S)$, CWA infers $\neg A$ if $A$ is not a logical consequence of $\Gamma$[11]. When we use the refutation procedure to show that $A$ is a logical consequence of $\Gamma$, CWA infers $\neg A$ if $A \notin SS(S)$. When we treat the refutation as a procedure to accept languages, CWA is very natural because $w \notin L(S, p)$ if $p(w) \notin SS(S)$.

However, since the complement of a recursively enumerable set is not always recursively enumerable, there is no general procedure of CWA by Theorem 1. Moreover, $w \notin L(S, p)$ does not always imply $p(w) \in FF(S)$ even if $L(S, p)$ is recursive, as shown in the following example.

**Example 7.** Let $S = (\{a, b\}, \{p\}, \Gamma)$ with

$$\Gamma = \left\{ \begin{array}{l} p(a) \leftarrow, \\ p(b) \leftarrow p(b) \end{array} \right\}.$$

Then $SS(S) = \{p(a)\}$, $L(S, p) = \{a\}$ and $b \notin L(S, p)$, but $FF(S) = GGF(S) = \phi$.

In the following, we give two procedures of CWA and introduce some subclasses of EFS's.

## 6.1. Termination property of EFS

First we give some conditions for variable-bounded EFS's so that CWA is equivalent to NF, that is, $SS(S) = B(S) - FF(S)$. By Theorem 4 and the definition of $GF(S)$ it suffices to show that there are no infinite derivations from $\leftarrow A$ for every $A \in B(S)$. Noting that every derivation from $\leftarrow A$ is ground, we treat only ground goals. From now on we identify every ground goal $\leftarrow A_1, \ldots A_k$ with a sequence of ground atoms $A_1, \ldots A_k$. Then we consider the partial order $\succ$ of $B(S)^*$.

**Definition.** Let $D$ be a set with a partial order $\succ_D$. Then $\succ_D$ is *well-founded* if there is no infinite sequence $d_1, d_2, d_3 \ldots$ in $D$ such that

$$d_1 \succ_D d_2 \succ_D d_3 \succ_D \cdots.$$

**Proposition 1.** *Let $S = (\Sigma, \Pi, \Gamma)$ be a variable bounded EFS. Then there is no infinite derivation from $\leftarrow A$ for every $A \in B(S)$ if there is a well-founded partial order $\succ$ of $B(S)^*$ which satisfies the following two conditions:*

(6.1) For every two sequences $A_1, \ldots, A_k$ and $B_1, \ldots, B_q$ such that $q \geq 0, k > 0$,

$$A_m \succ B_1, \ldots, B_q$$
$$\Rightarrow \quad A_1, \ldots, A_k \succ A_1, \ldots, A_{m-1}, B_1, \ldots, B_q, A_{m+1}, \ldots, A_k.$$

(6.2) For every ground instance $A \leftarrow B_1, \ldots, B_q$ of an axiom in $\Gamma$,

$$A \succ B_1, \ldots, B_q.$$

**Proof.** Let $G_1$ and $G_2$ be two goals. Suppose $G_2$ is a resolvent of $G_1$ and the selected atom is $A_m$. Then there is a ground instance $A_m \leftarrow B_1, \ldots, B_q$ of an axiom. By the condition (6.2), $A_m \succ B_1, \ldots, B_q$ and thus $G_1 \succ G_2$ by the condition (6.1).

Now we show two examples of the order $\succ$. In the first example we use the method introduced into traditional logic programming by Lloyd [8]. We write $pred(p(\pi_1, \ldots, \pi_n)) = p$ for every atom $p(\pi_1, \ldots, \pi_n)$.

**Definition.** An EFS $S = (\Sigma, \Pi, \Gamma)$ is *hierarchical* if there is a mapping $\varphi$ from $\Pi$ to a set of natural numbers such that $\varphi(pred(A)) > \varphi(pred(B_i))$ for every axiom $A \leftarrow B_1, \ldots, B_n$ and $i = 1, \ldots, n$.

**Proposition 2.** *If a variable-bounded EFS $S$ is hierarchical, then*

$$B(S) - FF(S) = SS(S).$$

**Proof.** By Proposition 1, it is sufficient to show that there is a well-founded partial order $\succ$ of $B(S)^*$. Let $\varphi$ be a mapping given in the definition of hierarchical EFS. Then we define $\succ$ as follows:

$$A_1, \ldots, A_n \succ B_1, \ldots, B_k$$
$$\Leftrightarrow$$

there is an atom $A_m$ and a sequence $C_1, \ldots, C_q$ of atoms such that

$$B_1, \ldots, B_k = A_1, \ldots, A_{m-1}, C_1, \ldots, C_q, A_{m+1}, \ldots, A_n$$

and

$$\varphi(pred(A_m)) > \varphi(pred(C_i))$$

for every $i = 1, \ldots, q$.

It is easily shown that this order satisfies the conditions (6.1) and (6.2). Moreover the order is well-founded because it is subsumed by the multiset-ordering, which was shown to be well-founded by Dershowitz and Manna [4].

**Example 8.** An EFS $S = (\{a, b\}, \{p, q\}, \Gamma)$ with

$$\Gamma = \left\{ \begin{array}{l} p(x) \leftarrow q(abx, xab) \\ q(y, y) \leftarrow \end{array} \right\}$$

is hierarchical and it defines a language $L(S, p) = \{(ab)^n, | n \geq 1\}$.

We define an important class of EFS to give the second example of $\succ$ making use of the length of atoms.

**Definition.** A clause $A \leftarrow B_1, \ldots, B_n$ is *reducing* if

$$|A\theta| > |B_i\theta|$$

for any substitution $\theta$ and $i = 1, \ldots, n$. An EFS $S = (\Sigma, \Pi, \Gamma)$ is *reducing* if axioms in $\Gamma$ are all reducing.

The following lemma, which is a modification of a lemma in [2], is useful to characterize the concepts we are introducing.

**Lemma 3.** *Let $A, B_1, \ldots, B_n$ be atoms. Then*

$$|A\theta| > |B_1\theta| + \cdots + |B_n\theta| \qquad (|A\theta| \geq |B_1\theta| + \cdots + |B_n\theta|)$$

*for any substitution $\theta$ if and only if*

$$|A| > |B_1| + \cdots + |B_n| \qquad (|A| \geq |B_1| + \cdots + |B_n|)$$

*and*

$$o(x, A) \geq o(x, B_1) + \cdots + o(x, B_n)$$

*for any variable $x$.*

For example the concept of reducing is characterized as follows:

**Proposition 3.** *A clause $A \leftarrow B_1, \ldots, B_n$ is reducing if and only if*

$$\begin{aligned} |A| &> |B_i|, \\ o(x, A) &\geq o(x, B_i) \end{aligned}$$

*for any variable $x$ and $i = 1, \ldots, n$.*

The EFS in Example 4 is reducing.

**Theorem 5.** *For every reducing EFS S,*

$$B(S) - FF(S) = SS(S).$$

**Proof.** The order $\succ$ defined in the same way as Proposition 2 satisfies the conditions (6.1) and (6.2).

**Theorem 6.** *Every context-free language $L \subseteq \Sigma^+$ is definable by a reducing EFS.*

**Proof.** Let $G$ be a context-free grammar in Chomsky's normal form representing $L$. Then we can construct a reducing EFS $S$ by using every non-terminal symbol of $G$ as a predicate symbol of $S$, and by transforming the rule in $G$ of the form $A \rightarrow B, C$ into a clause

$$A(xy) \leftarrow B(x), C(y)$$

and the rule of the form $A \rightarrow a$ into

$$A(a) \leftarrow .$$

The following example shows that the converse of Theorem 6 does not hold.

**Example 9.** An EFS $S = (\{a, b, c\}, \{p, q\}, \Gamma)$ with

$$\Gamma = \left\{ \begin{array}{l} p(a, bb, cc) \leftarrow, \\ p(ax, by, cz) \leftarrow p(x, y, z), \\ q(abc) \leftarrow, \\ q(axyz) \leftarrow p(x, y, z) \end{array} \right\}$$

is reducing and defines a language $L(S, q) = \{a^n b^n c^n \mid n \geq 1\}$, which is not context-free.

## 6.2. Bounding the length of derivations

We give a class of EFS's where we give another procedure of CWA. Roughly speaking, the procedure we are introducing is to bound the length of derivations even if $SS(S) \neq B(S) - FF(S)$.

**Definition.** A clause $A \leftarrow B_1, \ldots, B_n$ is *weakly reducing* if

$$|A\theta| \geq |B_i\theta|$$

for any substitution $\theta$ and $i = 1, \ldots, n$. An EFS $S = (\Sigma, \Pi, \Gamma)$ is *weakly reducing* if axioms in $\Gamma$ are all weakly reducing.

The concept of weakly reducing is also characterized by Lemma 3.

**Proposition 4.** *A clause $A \leftarrow B_1, \ldots, B_n$ is weakly reducing if and only if*

$$\begin{aligned} |A| &\geq |B_i|, \\ o(x, A) &\geq o(x, B_i) \end{aligned}$$

*for any variable $x$ and $i = 1, \ldots, n$.*

For every subset $U$ of $B(S)$, we put $U|_n = \{A \in U \mid |A| \leq n\}$. Note that $U|_n$ is a finite set for every $U$.

The following is the main theorem to get the procedure.

**Theorem 7.** *Let $S = (\Sigma, \Pi, \Gamma)$ be a weakly reducing EFS. Then*

$$A \in T_S \uparrow \omega \quad \Leftrightarrow \quad A \in T_S \uparrow \sharp(B(S)|_{|A|}).$$

**Proof.** It suffices to prove the $\Rightarrow$ part. First we show

$$(6.3) \qquad T_S((T_S \uparrow k)|_n)|_n = (T_S \uparrow k+1)|_n \qquad (k \geq 0).$$

The $\subset$ part is proved directly from the definition. Thus we prove the $\supset$ part. Let $B \in (T_S \uparrow k+1)|_n$. Then there is a ground instance $B \leftarrow B_1, \ldots, B_q$ of an axiom. Since $S$ is weakly reducing,

$$\{B_1, \ldots, B_q\} \subset (T_S \uparrow k)|_n,$$

and thus

$$B \in T_S((T_S \uparrow k)|_n)|_n.$$

By (6.3) and the monotonicity of $T_S$,

$$(6.4) \qquad (T_S \uparrow k)|_n \subset (T_S \uparrow k+1)|_n \qquad (k \geq 0).$$

Moreover, if $(T_S \uparrow K)|_n = (T_S \uparrow K+1)|_n$ for some $K$ then

$$(T_S \uparrow K)|_n = (T_S \uparrow k)|_n \qquad (k \geq K).$$

Since $(T_S \uparrow k)|_n \subset B(S)|_n$ and $B(S)|_n$ is finite,

$$(6.5) \qquad (T_S \uparrow k)|_n = (T_S \uparrow \#(B(S)|_n))|_n \qquad (k \geq \#(B(S)|_n)).$$

From (6.4) and (6.5) we get

$$(6.6) \qquad (T_S \uparrow k)|_n \subset (T_S \uparrow \#(B(S)|_n))|_n \qquad (k \geq 0)$$

Now let $A \in T_S \uparrow \omega$. Then $A \in T_S \uparrow k$ for some $k$. By (6.6) we get

$$A \in (T_S \uparrow k)|_{|A|} \subset (T_S \uparrow \#(B(S)|_{|A|}))|_{|A|} \subset T_S \uparrow \#(B(S)|_{|A|}).$$

We define $lob(A \leftarrow B_1, \ldots, B_m) = m$ for a definite clause $A \leftarrow B_1, \ldots, B_m$. $lob$ means the length of the body. The following lemma gives the upper-bound of the length of the shortest refutation from $\leftarrow A$ such that $A \in T_S \uparrow n$.

**Lemma 4.** *Let $S = (\Sigma, \Pi, \Gamma)$ be an EFS, and $m = \max_{C \in \Gamma}(lob(C))$. If $A \in T_S \uparrow n$ then there is a refutation with length less than or equal to $f(m)$ where*

$$f(m, n) = \begin{cases} 1 & \text{if } m = 0 \\ \displaystyle\sum_{i=0}^{n-1} m^i & \text{otherwise.} \end{cases}$$

**Proof.** The result is clear in case $m = 0$. In case $m > 0$, we prove the result by induction on $n$.

First suppose $n = 1$. Then there exists an axiom of the form $A' \leftarrow$ in $\Gamma$. Thus the results holds because there is a refutation from $\leftarrow A$ with length 1.

Now we suppose the result holds for $n$ and $A \in T_S \uparrow (n+1)$. Then there is a ground instance $A \leftarrow B_1, \ldots, B_k$ $(k \leq m)$ of the axiom where $\{B_1, \ldots, B_k\} \subset T_S \uparrow n$. By induction hypothesis there is a refutation from each $B_i$ with length less than or equal to $\displaystyle\sum_{i=0}^{n-1} m^i$. Then a refutation can be constructed by combining these refutations, and its length is less than or equal to $1 + m \displaystyle\sum_{i=0}^{n-1} m^i = \sum_{i=0}^{n} m^i$.

By combining Theorem 7 and Lemma 4 we get the following theorem.

**Theorem 8.** *Let $S = (\Sigma, \Pi, \Gamma)$ be a weakly reducing EFS, and $m = \max_{C \in \Gamma}(lob(C))$. If $A \in SS(S)$ then there is a refutation from $\leftarrow A$ with length less than or equal to $f(m, \#(B(S)|_{|A|}))$.*

Now we get a procedure of CWA. For a weakly reducing EFS $S$, we can conclude $A \notin SS(S)$ if there is no refutation from $\leftarrow A$ with length less than or equal to $f(m, \sharp(B(S)|_{|A|}))$. Arimura [3] pointed out the same procedure for traditional logic programming by observing derivation trees.

**Example 10.** Let $S$ be the EFS in Example 7. There is no refutation from $\leftarrow p(b)$ with length less than or equal to $f(1,2) = \sum_{i=0}^{1} 1^i = 1 + 1 = 2$. Thus we can decide $p(b) \notin SS(S)$.

Now we compare the class of weakly reducing EFS's and Chomsky hierarchy. We use the following class of EFS's.

**Definition.** A variable-bounded EFS $S = (\Sigma, \Pi, \Gamma)$ is *length-bounded* if

$$|A\theta| \geq |B_1\theta| + \cdots + |B_n\theta|$$

for every axiom $A \leftarrow B_1, \ldots, B_n$ $(n \geq 1)$ in $\Gamma$.

Clearly any length-bounded EFS is weakly reducing. The concept of length-boundness is also characterized by Lemma 3 [2].

Every EFS $S$ in Examples 2, 4, and 7 is length-bounded. The relation between EFS and CSG is shown as follows in [2].

**Theorem 9 ([2]).**

1) *Any length-bounded EFS language is context-sensitive.*

2) *For every context-sensitive language $L \subseteq \Sigma^+$, there exist a superset $\Sigma_0$ of $\Sigma$, a length-bounded EFS $S = (\Sigma_0, \Pi, \Gamma)$ and $p \in \Pi$ such that $L = L(S, p) \cap \Sigma^+$.*

## 7. Concluding Remarks

The main problem of derivation procedure for EFS is unification. We have got an algorithm of unification because our aim is to get a procedure to accept languages and apply it to MIEFS. The computational complexity of the algorithm is described in [2].

There are other formalizations of derivations for EFS. A famous one is CLP(X) [6]. CLP($\Sigma^+$) could be got if we could give an algorithm to test the unifiability of two patterns. Makanin [9] showed the existence of the algorithm.

Fitting [5] also formalized EFS as a logic programming language. In the formalization, terms are elements of $\Sigma^+ \cup X$, not $(\Sigma \cup X)^+$, and the procedural semantics is out of consideration.

The original theory of EFS given by Smullyan [13] uses the elements of $(\Sigma \cup X)^*$ as terms. The derivation procedure and semantics as logic programming for the original EFS can be given in the same way as that of this paper by putting

$$E = \left\{ \begin{array}{l} cons(cons(x, y), z) = cons(x, cons(y, z)), \\ cons(\lambda, x) = cons(x, \lambda) = x \end{array} \right\}.$$

However, the results about CWA do not always hold because the empty word may be substituted for variables, and thus Lemma 3 does not hold.

The discussions on CWA can be applied to traditional logic programming (which is based on first order terms), if we introduce a proper size function of first order terms so that Lemma 3 holds [3].

## Acknowledgements

The author would like to express his thanks to the reviewers for many helpful comments and suggestions on the original version of this paper.

# References

[1] Arikawa, S. , Elementary Formal Systems and Formal Languages - Simple Formal Systems. *Memoirs of Fac. Sci., Kyushu University Ser. A*. Math. 24:47–75 (1970).

[2] Arikawa, S. , Shinohara, T. , and Yamamoto, A. , Elementary Formal System as a Unifying Framework for Language Learning, in Rivest, R. , Haussler, D. , and Warmuth, M. K. (eds.), *Proc. COLT'89*, 312–327, Morgan-Kaufmann, 1989.

[3] Arimura, H. , Completeness of Depth-Bounded Resolution in Logic Programming, Internal report, Research Institute of Fundamental Information Science, Kyushu University, 1989, to appear in 6th Conf. Proc. of JSSST.

[4] Dershowitz, N. and Manna, Z. , Proving Termination with Multiset Orderings. *CACM* 8(22):465–476 (1979).

[5] Fitting, M. , *Computability Theory, Semantics, and Logic Programming*, Oxford University Press, 1987.

[6] Jaffar, J. and Lassez, J.-L. , Constraint Logic Programming, in *Proc. Conference on Principle of Programming Languages*, 1987.

[7] Jaffar, J. , Lassez, J.-L. , and Maher, M. J. , Logic Programming Scheme, in DeGroot, D. and Lindstrom, G. (eds.), *Logic Programming: Functions, Relations, and Equations*, 211–233, Prentice-Hall, 1986.

[8] Lloyd, J. W. , *Foundations of Logic Programming Second, Extended Edition*, Springer - Verlag, 1987.

[9] Makanin, G. S. , The Problem of Solvability of Equations in a Free Semigroup. *Soviet Math. Dokl.* 18(2):330–335 (1977).

[10] Plotkin, G. D. , Building in Equational Theories, in *Machine Intelligence 7*, 132–147, Edinburgh University Press, 1972.

[11] Reiter, R. , On Closed World Data Bases, in Gallaire, H. and Minker, J. (eds.), *Logic and Data Bases*, 55–76, Plenum Press, 1978.

[12] Shapiro, E. Y. . Inductive Inference of Theories From Facts. Research Report 192, Yale University, 1981.

[13] Smullyan, R. M. , *Theory of Formal Systems*, Princeton Univ. Press, 1961.

[14] Yamamoto, A. , A Theoretical Combination of SLD-Resolution and Narrowing, in Lassez, J.-L. (ed.), *Proc. 4th ICLP*, 470–487, The MIT Press, 1987.

# Debugger for a Parallel Logic Programing Language Fleng

Junichi Tatemura and Hidehiko Tanaka
Dept. of Electrical Engineering, Univ. of Tokyo

For the programming environment of a parallel logic programming language, it is an important problem to develop a debugger. However it is difficult to debug parallel programs by observing their execution traces. Using the characteristics of logic programming languages, one solution to this problem is debugging using declarative semantics programs. However parallel logic programming languages (Concurrent Prolog, GHC, etc.) are not pure logic programming languages because of their new primitives for synchronization. We must consider the causality relation between input and output because some operational meaning must be added to the declarative semantics for parallel logic programs. Hence, in this paper, we introduce a communicating process model to represent execution of parallel logic programs. And we present extended algorithmic debugging using this model.

## 1 Introduction

During the last few years, several parallel programming languages based on horn logic, such as PAR-LOG [Clark86], Concurrent Prolog [Shapiro83a], and GHC [Ueda85a], have been investigated. Now their programming environments must be developed. A debugger is an important part of the environment. However it is difficult to debug parallel programs because concurrent execution is more complex for tracing than sequential execution.

The role of a debugger is to show users an execution model which is abstracted from the execution of a program. A programmer compares the model shown by the debugger and an intended model, and finds bugs from the difference between them. Therefore to develop a debugger for parallel logic programs, we must introduce an execution model for parallel logic programs.

It is difficult to find a bug in a parallel program in the conventional way of tracing. Although declarative debugging is applicable to logic programs, the declarative semantics for pure logic is insufficient for parallel logic programs. So the execution model should be created by adding operational aspects to the declarative model. In this paper, we present an execution model based on several works related to the semantics of parallel programming languages. It represents execution of parallel logic programs by processes and their input/output. We use this model for debugging.

## 2 A Committed-Choice Language Fleng

Some parallel logic programming languages, such as GHC and Concurrent Prolog, are called Committed-Choice Languages. Instead of the back-tracking mechanism in Prolog, a control primitive "guard" is introduced for synchronization. They are designed as general purpose parallel languages.

Fleng is a committed-choice language that was designed in our laboratory [Nilsson86]. It is a language simplified from GHC and made easier to implement. GHC is also simple, but its implementation is complicated because a logical truth value of a goal affects execution of other goals. In execution of a Fleng program, execution of a goal is not associated with any logical truth values. So it doesn't affect the execution of another goals. If a logical truth value is needed, it is realized as the variable parameter of the goal. A clause of Fleng is committed when the head matches with the goal successfully, so it has no guard goal. The guard is realized with only its head.

## 3 Debugging of Parallel Logic Programs

A logic program has two different aspects; it has declarative semantics and operational semantics. So it can be read declaratively and/or operationally. While a tracer shows programmers the operational model, there are debuggers using the declarative model. Shapiro proposed an algorithmic debugger based on the declarative model [Shapiro83b]. The debugger has been implemented for Prolog. However it is not directly applicable to a parallel logic programming language which has been added the meaning of guard for synchronization because it is for a pure logic programming language. .

Many works about sequential Prolog have been applied to parallel programming languages. For instance, several tracers which are the same as tracers of Prolog have been developed for parallel logic programs. They are implemented on sequential systems [Ueda85b]. New models like the box model on Prolog have been applied for a tracer of parallel logic programs. However they trace execution sequentially.

An algorithmic debugger for GHC is also developed [Takeuchi86]. But it uses a model similar to the model for Prolog which is not sufficient for parallel programs.

Most of these debuggers are extensions of debuggers on Prolog which run sequentially. Although a parallel logic programming language is the same as Prolog with respect to logic programming, it is obviously different with respect to its parallelism. The problem of developing a debugger applicable to parallel programs still remains.

The problem on the semantics is discussed in several works. There are some problems which the pure logic programming language doesn't have.

The notion of "input-output" is discussed for the semantics of parallel logic programs. For instance, a Fleng program 'append / 3' is:

```
append([A|X], Y, Z) :-
        Z = [A|Z1], append(X, Y, Z1).
append([], Y, Z) :- Z = Y.
```

If given a goal, say append([1],[2],X), the result is append([1],[2],[1,2]). It can be said of the predicate append(X,Y,Z) that X and Y are for inputs and Z is for outputs. In the above example, inputs are {X = [1], Y = [2]}, and the output is {Z = [1,2]}.

However, it is known that there are cases where it is not sufficient to show only the result of input-output to determine for the meaning of a parallel logic program. For example, we shall compare the following two programs, p1/2 and p2/2.

```
p1([A|In],O) :-
        O = [A|Out], p11(In, Out).
p11([A|In], O) :- O = [A].

p2([A,B|In], O) :- O = [A,B].
```

In both programs, the input-output is like this :

```
p1(X,Y) [or p2(X,Y)]

Input  = {X = [A,B|_]}
Output = {Y = [A,B]}
```

We cannot distinguish these two programs while p1 and p2 are different in the causality relation between input and output. When these programs run with other nondeterministic programs in parallel, the results may be different [Brock81]. In several works about the semantics of GHC, the causality relation between input and output is shown to be necessary for the semantics of parallel logic programs [Takeuchi87] [Murakami88b].

In this paper, accordingly, the input-output of a program will be defined with the clauses committed when the program is executed. And we use this to represent the execution of a parallel logic program.

## 4　The Process Model

### 4.1　The Notion of the Process

Generally, the notion of a process is used to represent the execution of a parallel logic program. But the conventional 'process' for GHC is associated with one goal. When a goal is reduced, new goals are generated. It is very hard to trace many processes generating and terminating concurrently.

The process model proposed in this paper is equivalent not only to a goal but to all of its subgoals generated by reduction. The substance of the process is a set of goals that are derived from a goal. Even if goals are generated or terminated by reductions, they can be treated as one process. From outside, the execution of the process is looked upon as the input-output of the process.

Since a goal is reduced to sub-goals, a process can be divided into sub-processes. It corresponds to an execution tree which represents a computation of a logic program. The tree has subtrees whose roots are nodes of the tree. The tree corresponding to the process can be divided into subtrees, and each subtree corresponds to the sub-process of the process.

In the process model described above, the definition clause is considered to be defining a relation between a process and its sub-processes.

### 4.2　Model for Execution of Programs

Using the process described in the previous section, we model the execution of parallel logic programs. The debugger shows programmers this model.

Let $G$ be a goal which is computed in a Fleng program and $Q$ be a set of goals which are derived from $G$. We call the process whose substance is $Q$

the process with respect to $G$.

For example, when a goal $g_1$ is reduced to goals, $g_2$ and $g_3$, the process with respect to $g_2$ and the process with respect to $g_3$ are sub-processes of the process with respect to $g_1$.

The process $P$ with respect to $G$ is represented as follows from outside.

$$\langle G_{skel}, I, O, S, G_{ins} \rangle$$

$G_{skel}$ is the skeletal predicate of $G$ whose arguments are replaced by distinct variables like this :

$$p(v_1, \ldots, v_i)$$

$v_1, \ldots, v_i$ are distinct variables which are the ports for communication with outer processes.

$I, O$ are *Input* and *Output* respectively which represent the communication of the process $P$. They show how the variables of $G_{skel}$ are bound by unification from outside and inside. Their detail will be described in the next section.

$S$ is the *Status* which indicates the termination status of $P$. There exists the following statuses :

- *terminate*
  This indicates that all of the goals in $P$ have terminated.

- *suspend (deadlock)*
  This indicates that there are no active goals in $P$ and that there are some suspended goals. When one of the suspended goals is activated by *Input* from outside, the status turns into *active*. If no possible input from outside can activate the suspended goals of $P$, the status can be called *deadlock*.

- *active*
  This indicates that some active goals exist in $P$ and that $P$ can be executed.

Given this definition of status, the model is suitable for running program or a program which runs infinitely.

$G_{ins}$ is the *instance* of $G$. It is regarded as the result of the bindings to $G_{skel}$ of *Input / Output*.

## 4.3 Input/Output of the Process

In this section, we will define the *Input/Output* of the process.

Let $G_{skel}$ with respect to a goal $P$ be

$$p(V_1, \cdots, V_n)$$

Because $V_1, \cdots, V_n$ are regarded as the ports for communication, there is a pair of input/output corresponding to each port. Therefore the input-output $I_P, O_P$ of the process with respect to $P$ can be represented as follows.

$$\begin{cases} I_P = I_{PV_1}, \cdots, I_{PV_n} \\ O_P = O_{PV_1}, \cdots, I_{PV_n} \end{cases}$$

where $I_{PV_i}, O_{PV_i}$ is the input-output of $P$ through $V_i$.

Since a definition clause defines the relation between a process and its sub-processes, it also defines the relation between I/O of the process and I/O of the sub-processes. I/O of the process is defined recursively by the clauses committed in the execution of the program.

The committed clause defines the output of the process and the input of the sub-processes if the input of the process and the output of the sub-processes are given. At first, the input of the initial top goal $P$ is given. Let $P$ be

$$P = p(t_1, \cdots, t_k, V_{k+1}, \cdots, V_m)$$

where

$$t_i = t_i(X_{i1}, \cdots, X_{in_i}).$$

Then $G_{skel}$ and $I_P$ which are the input of $P$ are as follows.

$$G_{skel} = p(V_1, \cdots, V_m)$$

$$I_P = \{I_{PV_1}, \cdots, I_{PV_m}\}$$

$$I_{PV_i} = \begin{cases} [V_i = t_i(X_{i1}, \cdots, X_{in_i})] & i \leq k \\ nil & k < i \leq m \end{cases}$$

$t_i(X_{i1}, \cdots, X_{in_i})$ is a term which is not an undefined variable. $X_{ij}$ is an undefined variable in the term $t_i$.

Next, assume that the following clause is committed.

$$H :- B_1, \cdots, B_i, S_1, \cdots, S_j.$$

$$\begin{cases} H(t_1, \cdots, t_k, V_1, \cdots, V_m) \\ B_i(t_{i1}, \cdots, t_{ik_i}, V_{i1}, \cdots V_{im_i}) \end{cases}$$

$$\begin{cases} t_i = t_i(X_{i1}, \cdots, X_{in_i}) \\ t_{ij} = t_{ij}(X_{ij1}, \cdots, X_{ijn_{ij}}) \end{cases}$$

where $S_i$ is a system builtin predicate, and $B_i$ is a body predicate. At first we consider a system predicate as '= / 2' :

$$s_i(Z_{i1}, \cdots, Z_{im_i}) = s_i'(Z_{i1}', \cdots, Z_{im_i'}')$$

where $s_i$ is a term which may be a variable. The head and the body goals of the clause are translated as follows.

$$\begin{cases} H(W_1, \cdots, W_k, V_1, \cdots, V_m) \\ W_1 = t_1, \cdots, W_k = t_k \end{cases}$$

$$\begin{cases} B_i(U_{i1}, \cdots, U_{ik_i}, V_{i1}, \cdots, V_{im_i}) \\ U_{i1} = t_{i1}, \cdots, U_{ik_i} = t_{ik_i} \end{cases}$$

Now, Assume that the input of the process with respect to $H$ and the output of the process with respect to $B_i$ are given :

$$I_H = I_{HW_1}, \cdots, I_{HW_k}, I_{HV_1}, \cdots, I_{HV_m} \quad (1)$$

$$O_{B_i} = O_{B_iU_{i1}}, \cdots, O_{B_iU_{ik_i}}, O_{B_iV_{i1}}, \cdots, O_{B_iV_{im}} (2)$$

Then the output of the process with respect to $H$ is defined as

$$O_{HW_i} = Cond \mid [W_i = t_i, \sum_j O_{X_{ij}}] \qquad (3)$$

$$O_{HV_i} = Cond \mid O_{V_i} \qquad (4)$$

where

$$Cond = \sum_j (W_j = t_j \Leftarrow I_{HW_j})$$

The summation represents the concatenation of lists. $\sum_i A_i$ is the list $[A_1, \cdots, A_n]$. $Cond \mid O$ shows that the output $O$ exists with a clause committed if there is an input such as $Cond$. This is associated with the input-output causality relation. $(C \Leftarrow IO)$ is the element of the list $Cond$. $C$ is a condition and $IO$ is the actual input. $[V = t, IO]$ shows that there is output (or input) $V = t$ and output ( or input) $IO$ through the variables in $t$.

$$O_{X_{ij}} = \sum_{X_{ij} \equiv V_{kl}, k, l} O_{B_k V_{kl}}$$
$$+ \sum_{X_{ij} \equiv X_{klm}, k, l, m} [t_{kl} = U_{kl}, O_{B_k U_{kl}}]$$
$$+ \sum_{X_{ij} \equiv Z_{kl}, k, l} [s_k = s'_k, \sum_m IO_{Z'_{km}}]$$
$$+ \sum_{X_{ij} \equiv Z'_{kl}, k, l} [s'_k = s_k, \sum_m IO_{Z_{km}}]$$

$$O_{V_i} = \sum_{V_i \equiv V_{kl}, k, l} O_{B_k V_{kl}}$$
$$+ \sum_{V_i \equiv X_{klm}, k, l, m} [t_{kl} = U_{kl}, O_{B_k U_{kl}}]$$
$$+ \sum_{V_i \equiv Z_{kl}, k, l} [s_k = s'_k, \sum_m IO_{Z'_{km}}]$$
$$+ \sum_{V_i \equiv Z'_{kl}, k, l} [s'_k = s_k, \sum_m IO_{Z_{km}}]$$

$X \equiv Y$ shows that $X$ and $Y$ are defined as the same variable in the clause.

$$IO_{Z_{km}} = I_{HZ_{km}} + \sum_i O_{B_i Z_{km}}$$

$$I_{HZ_{km}} = \sum_{Z_{km} \equiv X_{ij}, i, j} [t_i = W_i, I_{HW_i}] + \sum_{Z_{km} \equiv V_i, i} I_{HV_i}$$

$$O_{B_i Z_{km}} = \sum_{Z_{km} \equiv X_{ijl}, i, j, l} [t_{ij} = U_{ij}, O_{B_i U_{ij}}]$$
$$+ \sum_{Z_{km} \equiv V_{ij}, i, j} O_{B_i V_{ij}}$$

Similarly the input of the sub-process can be defined.

$$I_{BU_{ij}} = Cond \mid [U_{ij} = t_{ij}, \sum_k I_{ijk}] \qquad (5)$$

$$I_{BV_{ij}} = Cond \mid I_{V_{ij}} \qquad (6)$$

Next, we have to think about the system predicates except '= / 2' such as

$$f(Z_1, \cdots, Z_n)$$

It is necessary to add the following term to $O_{X_{ij}}$ and $O_{V_i}$.

$$\sum_{X_{ij} \equiv Z_k, k} [Z_k \leftarrow f, \sum_{m \neq k} IO_{Z_{km}}]$$

# 5 The Debugger's Display

## 5.1 Rules for Display

Before presenting examples, we shall discuss how the debugger represents the input-output of the process. Though the debugger gets the construction which is defined in section 4.3, it is too complex to read. So the debugger displays the construction as a kind of tree.

$$\sum A_i = [A_1, \cdots, A_n]$$

is displayed as

```
|-A1
|-A2
 .
 .
|-An .
```

This shows that the sub-goals share the same variable and that the path of I/O forks.

$$[V = t, \sum O_{Z_i}]$$

is displayed as

```
V = t
|-Oz1
 .
```

,

$$\begin{cases} Cond \mid X \\ Cond = [(V_1 = t_1 \Leftarrow I_1), \cdots, (V_n = t_n \Leftarrow I_n)] \end{cases}$$

is displayed as

```
cond(V1 = t1,...,Vn = tn)
|    <- I1
 .
 .
|    <- In
|-X
```

and,

$$[Z \leftarrow f, IO]$$

is displayed as

```
f -> Z
|-IO
```

## 5.2 Examples

For example, we shall discuss about the Brock and Ackermann's program which is described in the chapter 3.

```
p1([A|In],0) :- 0 = [A|Out], p11(In, Out).
p11([A|In], 0) :- 0 = [A].

p2([A,B|In], 0) :- 0 = [A,B].

dup([A|I], 0) :- 0 = [A,A].

merge([A | Ix], Iy, 0) :-
    0 = [A|Out], merge(Ix, Iy, Out).
merge(Ix, [A | Iy], 0) :-
    0 = [A|Out], merge(Ix, Iy, Out).
merge(Ix, [], 0) :- 0 = Ix.
merge([], Iy, 0) :- 0 = Iy.

s1(Ix, Iy, Out) :-
    dup(Ix, Ox), dup(Iy, Oy),
    merge(Ox, Oy, Oz), p1(Oz, Out).
s2(Ix, Iy, Out) :-
    dup(Ix, Ox), dup(Iy, Oy),
    merge(Ox, Oy, Oz), p2(Oz, Out).

t1(In, Out) :- s1(In, Mid, Out),plus1(Out, Mid).
t2(In, Out) :- s2(In, Mid, Out),plus1(Out, Mid).

plus1([A|In], 0) :- add(A, 1, A1), 0 = [A1].
```

p1(X,Y) and p2(X,Y) have the same output Y = [A,B] if the input is X = [A,B|_]. At this point, they cannot be distinguished. However if they are used with merge / 3 which is a nondeterministic program, the results of the two programs can be different. If t1(In,Out) and t2(In,Out) are given the input In = [5], the output of t2 must be Out = [5,5], but the output of t1 may be Out = [5,5] or Out = [5,6]. Therefore we must describe the causality relation between input and output to model the execution of programs.

First the execution of t2 is described. The processes are divided as follows (they are displayed as a execution tree).

```
t2([5],[5,5])
 |-s2([5],[6],[5,5])
 | |-dup([5],[5,5])
 | |-dup([6],[6,6])
 | |-merge([5,5],[6,6],[5,5,6,6])
 | |-p2([5,5,6,6],[5,5])
 |-plus1([5,5],[6])
```

Here s2 and plus1 are the sub-processes of t2 and they communicate with each other. Our interest is in s2(X,Y,Z). There are inputs to X and Y and output from Z. The ports used for communication with plus1 are Y and Z.

```
Goal : s2(_1,_2,_3)
Ins  : s2([5],[6],[5,5])
OUTPUT OF _3 :
cond{_4 = [_5,_6|_7]}
```

```
|                    <-cond{_8 = [_9|_10]}
|                       |        <-cond{_1 = [_11|_12] / [5]}
|                       |        |-_8 = [_11,_11]
|                    |-_4 = [_9|_12]
|                    |-cond{_10 = [_13|_14]}
|                       |-_12 = [_13|_15]
|                       |-cond{_14 = nil}
|                          |-_15 = _16
|                          |-cond{_2 = [_17|_18] / [6]}
|                             |-_16 = [_17,_17]
|-_3 = [_5,_6]
```

```
INPUT OF _2 :
cond{_3 = [_19|_20] / [5,5]}
 |-_2 = [_21]
    |-add(_19,_22,_21) -> _21 = 6
       |-_22 = 1
```

Goal is $G_{skel}$ and Ins is $G_{ins}$. Status is *terminate* for all processes in the example, so it is omitted. Although there are as many pairs of $I/O$ as the number of variables in $G_{skel}$, only the remarkable ones are shown in this paper. There are some additional rules for display to the ones discussed in the previous section :

1. If $I$ of $\{V = t, I\}$ in $Cond$ includes the input from outside, $I$ is omitted and the instance of the variable in $G_{skel}$ is added instead.

    Ex. cond{_1 = [_11|_12] / [5]}

2. If one of the elements of $[IO_1, \cdots, IO_n]$ has no output, it is not displayed (this is the case when the process shares a variable with others but does not bind it).

3. The instance of $Z$ in $\{Z \leftarrow f, IO\}$ is displayed.

    Ex. add(_19,_22,_21) -> _21 = 6

The output of the sub-process p2 is like this :

```
Goal : p2(_4,_3)
Ins  : p2([5,5,6,6],[5,5])

OUTPUT OF _3 :
cond{_4 = [_5,_6|_7]}
 |-_3 = [_5,_6]
```

Next let us look at the execution of t1. In the case where the instance of the top goal is t1([5],[5,5]), the process and its sub-processes are as follows.

```
t1([5],[5,5])
 |-s1([5],[6],[5,5])
 | |-dup([5],[5,5])
 | |-dup([6],[6,6])
 | |-merge([5,5],[6,6],[5,5,6,6])
 | |-p1([5,5,6,6],[5,5])
 |-plus1([5,5],[6])
```

The sub-process s1 and its sub-process p1 are displayed as follows.

```
Goal: s1(_1,_2,_3)
Ins : s1([5],[6],[5,5])

OUTPUT OF _3 :
cond{_4 = [_5|_6]}
 |      <-cond{_7 = [_8|_9]}
 |      |      <-cond{_1 = [_10|_11] / [5]}
 |      |      |-_7 = [_10,_10]
 |      |-_4 = [_8|_12]
 |      |-cond{_9 = [_13|_14]}
 |            |-_12 = [_13|_15]
 |            |-cond{_14 = nil}
 |                  |-_15 = _16
 |                  |-cond{_2 = [_17|_18] / [6]}
 |                        |-_16 = [_17,_17]
 |-_3 = [_5|_19]
   |-cond{_6 = [_20|_21]}
        |-_19 = [_20]

INPUT OF _2 :
cond{_3 = [_22|_23] / [5,5]}
 |-_2 = [_24]
   |-add(_22,_25,_24) ->_24 = 6
      |-_25 = 1

Goal : p1(_4,_3)
Ins : p1([5,5,6,6],[5,5])

OUTPUT OF _3 :
cond{_4 = [_5|_6] / [5,5,6,6]}
 |-_3 = [_5|_19]
   |-cond{_6 = [_20|_21]}
 ''    |-_19 = [_20]
```

The difference between s1 and s2 is whether the output cannot be obtained before the input becomes _4 = [_5,_6|_7] or it can be obtained after the input becomes _4 = [_5|_6]. If there is output _3 = [_5|_9], there can be input at _2. If the input _2 = [_17|_18] comes from outside, _16 = [_17,_17] can be obtained, and the second element of the list _4 may be _17. In that case, the second element of the list _3 is _17 and the instance of the top goal becomes t1([5],[5,6]). Its process is described as follows.

```
Goal: s1(_1,_2,_3)
Ins: s1([5],[6],[5,6])

OUTPUT OF _3 :
cond{_4 = [_5|_6]}
 |      <-cond{_7 = [_8|_9]}
 |      |      <-cond{_1 = [_10|_11] / [5]}
 |      |      |-_7 = [_10,_10]
 |      |-_4 = [_8|_12]
 |      |-cond{_13 = [_14|_15]}
 |            |      <-cond{_2 = [_16|_17] / [6]}
 |            |      |-_13 = [_16,_16]
 |            |-_12 = [_14|_18]
 |            |-cond{_15 = [_19|_20]}
 |                  |-_18 = [_19|_21]
 |                  |-cond{_20 = nil}
 |                        |-_21 = _9
 |-_3 = [_5|_22]
   |-cond{_6 = [_23|_24]}
        |-_22 = [_23]

INPUT OF _2 :
cond{_3 = [_25|_26] / [5,6]}
 |-_2 = [_27]
   |-add(_25,_28,_27) -> _27 = 6
```

|-_28 = 1

Such a difference between t1 and t2 is due to the difference in meaning between p1/2 and p2/2.

# 6  Debugging Using the Process Model

## 6.1  Algorithmic Debugging

We applied the model proposed in this paper to algorithmic debugging. It is based on the 'Divide and Query' algorithm proposed by Shapiro which has been applied to the debugging of Prolog. It shows a programmer an instance which is a node of an execution tree and asks him if it is correct. Repeating the query, it searches the erroneous clause.

Correctness means that the instance is included in the set of instances which is the logical meaning of the predicate intended by the programmer. Therefore it is applicable only to a *pure* logic program. As already discussed, parallel logic programs are not pure. Accordingly this is not sufficient for a parallel logic program.

The debugger we developed shows the process model instead of the instance. If it is correct, it can be said that there is no bug in the execution tree with respect to this process. If it is not an intended result of a process, the programmer has to answer its correctness carefully. There are the following cases.

1. the case that there is an incorrect output while the input is correct

2. the case that there is an incorrect input

In case 1, there is a bug in the tree with respect to the process. It is similar to the case of answering 'no' to Shapiro's 'Divide and Query' debugger. In case 2, however, there are some bugs out of the process. The process is correct if the causality relation between the input and the output is correct. Then the programmer has to answer 'yes'. So, to this debugger, the programmer answers 'out' in case 1, and answer 'in' in case of 2.

As a result, the algorithm for this debugger is :

1. Let $P$ be a process. The debugger asks about the sub-processes of $P$.

2. According to the answer of the programmer in step 1,

   (a) If all of the sub-processes are correct, return the clause with respect to $P$.

   (b) If there is an incorrect sub-process, go to step 1 with this sub-process as $P$.

where the clause with respect to $P$ is the clause that defines the relation between $P$ and its subprocesses, in other words, the clause that is committed when the root goal of $P$ is reduced.

## 6.2 Analysis and Abstraction of I/O

The construction of I/O described in this paper becomes complex in proportion to program size. To display such a complex construction makes it difficult for a programmer to understand and decreases the efficiency of debugging. To solve this problem, the debugger analyses the I/O construction and abstracts it partially. The details can be displayed only when needed. There are several levels of abstraction.

1. summarize the part which includes no 'cond'

2. summarize the part which includes no 'cond' that cannot be observed from the outside.

3. summarize all

An example of level 1 is like this :

```
cond{A = t(X)}          cond{A = t(X)}
 |-B = [X|C]      -->     |-B = [X,X|D]
 |-C = [X|D]              |-cond ...
 |-cond ...
```

At level 2, the debugger gets rid of the inner information which has no relation to other processes. It is equivalent to the execution of the process observed from outside. In the following example, the variable C cannot be observed from the outside of p(A,B).

```
Goal:p(A,B)

cond{C = [D]}
 |         <-cond{A = [X|A1]}
 |          |-C = [X]
 |-B = D

    -->

cond{A = [X|A1]}
 |-B = X
```

At level 3, the input-output causality relation is disregarded and only the result of I/O is described.

There are other types of analysis : watching one of the variables and tracing how it is bound, tracing the causality relation to check whether there is a loop, and so on. By adding the name of the reduced goal to the data, we can know whose goal (or process) binds a variable which is attended to. The following representation (of the example in 5.2)is also possible.

```
cond{_4 = [_4|_6]}
 |   <-merge(_7,_16,_4) : _4 = [5,6,6,5]
 |        <-cond{_1 = [_10|_11] / [5]}
 |            |-_7 = [_10,_10]
 |        <-cond{_2 = [_17|_18] / [6]}
 |            |-_16 = [_17,_17]
 |-_3 = [_5|_19]
    |-cond{_6 = [_20|_21]}
        |-_19 = [_20]
```

## 6.3 Examples of Debugging

We implemented the debugger on a UNIX workstation. Though the system runs sequentially, the debugger can run on a parallel inference machine for the debugger is written in Fleng itself. Here, we show some examples of algorithmic debugging.

### 6.3.1 Bugs due to I/O mode

The following is the example program 'Quick Sort'. If X in qsort(X,Y) is given a list of integers, the sorted list is returned in Y.

```
qsort(X,Y) :- qsort(X,Y,[]).
qsort([X | L], R, R0) :-
    partition(L, X, L1, L2),
    qsort(L2, R1, R0), qsort(L1, R, [X | R1]).
qsort([], R1, R2) :-
    R1 = R2.
partition([X | L], Y, L1, L2) :-
    gt(X, Y, Z), p10(Z, [X | L], Y, L1, L2).
partition([], X, L1, L2) :-
    L1 = [], L2 = [].
p10(false, [X | L], Y,  L1, L2) :-
%    L1 = [X | L3], partition(L, Y, L3, L2). %right
    L1 = [X | L3], partition(L, Y, L1, L3). %buggy
p10(true, [X | L], Y, L1, L2) :-
    L2 = [X | L3], partition(L, Y, L1, L3).
```

If qsort([2,1,3],X) is given as a goal, deadlock occurs. The result should be X = [1,2,3] if the program is correct. Let us apply algorithmic debugging to this program.

The debugger shows the following model of execution which is abstracted and displayed only the result of I/O (it is equivalent to the level 3 in section 6.2). Though it is not sufficient for the semantics of parallel programs, it is sufficient for many cases. For efficiency, such abstraction is useful. The detail can be displayed when it is needed.

```
Goal: qsort(_2,_3,_4)
Ins:  qsort([2,1,3],[1,3,2|_0],nil)
Stat: suspend
[_2]    IN = [2,1,3]      ((no output))
[_3]    ((no input))      OUT =[1,3,2|_0]
[_4]    IN = nil          ((no output))
query>
```

I/O of each variable in $G_{skel}$ is displayed. The output of the variable _3 which must be [1,2,3] is incorrect. Since there is an incorrect output, the programmer answers 'out'. After this, the queries of the debugger are repeated as follows.

```
Goal: partition(_6,_7,_8,_9)
Ins:  partition([1,3],2,[1,3],_1)
Stat: terminate
[_6]    IN = [1,3]        ((no output))
[_7]    IN = 2           ((no output))
[_8]    ((no input))     OUT =[1,3], OUT =nil
[_9]    ((no input))     ((no output))
query>out.
Goal: p10(_10,_11,_7,_8,_9)
Ins:  p10(false,[1,3],2,[1,3],_1)
Stat: terminate
[_10]   IN = false       ((no output))
[_11]   IN = [1,3]       ((no output))
[_7]    IN = 2           ((no output))
[_8]    ((no input))     OUT =[1,3], OUT =nil
[_9]    ((no input))     ((no output))
query>out.
Goal: partition(_12,_7,_8,_13)
Ins:  partition([3],2,[1,3],[3])
Stat: terminate
[_12]   IN = [3]         ((no output))
[_7]    IN = 2           ((no output))
[_8]    IN = [1,3]       OUT =nil
[_13]   ((no input))     OUT =[3]
```

The process partition/4 has input which is not intended in the third argument (variable) of $G_{skel}$ and the input binds the variable to [1,3]. In that case, the programmer answers 'in'.

```
query>in.
Buggy clause:
p10(false,[1,3],2,[1,3],_1) :-
    [1,3] = [1,3],
    partition([3],2,[1,3],[3]).

p10(false,[_0|_1],_2,_3,_4) :-
    _3 = [_0|_5],
    partition(_1,_2,_3,_5).
```

Then the debugger detects an erroneous clause, and shows the clause instance and the definition clause.

If the debugger shows only the instance partition([3],2,[1,3],[3]) the programmer answers 'no' and the debugger cannot detect a bug.

### 6.3.2  Bugs due to I/O causality relation

For the example in the previous section, the level 3 in the section 6.2 is sufficient since the bugs of the program can be detected by checking its input-output mode. The next example is similar to Brock and Ackermann's example for which level 3 is not sufficient. In this case, we must examine the input-output causality relation.

In the program in Figure 1, several processes communicate with each other. The outputs of all the processes are merged and received by all the processes. A message transmitted by a process is broadcasted to all processes. Figure 2 shows how the streams of the program in Figure 1 flow.

```
term1(I,O):- merge(I, Proc, 0), proc1(0,Proc).
term2(I,O):- merge(I, Proc, 0), proc2(0,Proc).
```

```
proc1([getstr,X|_], 0) :- 0 = [string,Y], string(X,Y).
proc1([getsym,X|_], 0) :- 0 = [symbol,Y], symbol(X,Y).

proc2([getstr|I], 0) :-
    0 = [string|01], proc2_str(I,01).
proc2([getsym|I], 0) :-
    0 = [symbol|01], proc2_sym(I,01).
proc2_str([X|_],0) :- 0 = [Y], string(X,Y).
proc2_sym([X|_],0) :- 0 = [Y], symbol(X,Y).

merge([A|X],Y,Z) :- Z = [A|Z1], merge(X,Y,Z1).
merge(X,[A|Y],Z) :- Z = [A|Z1], merge(X,Y,Z1).
merge([],Y,Z) :- Z = Y.
merge(X,[],Z) :- Z = X.
```

Figure 1: The example erroneous program

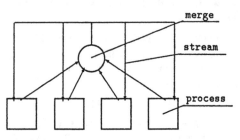

Figure 2: Streams of the example program of Fig. 1

In this example, there are two processes. One of them sends an instruction to the other and monitors the replies. The latter process gets the instruction and executes it. The instruction consists of two elements in a list. For example, the latter process replies [string,[97,98]] for the instruction [getstr,ab] and replies [symbol,xyz] for the instruction [getsym,[120,121,122]].

If the goal term2([getstr,abc],X) is given in this program, the intended result is

X = [getstr,abc,string,[97,98,99]].

The results of term2 in the above program, however, can be different as follows.

```
term2([getstr,abc],
      [getstr,string,[115,116,114,105,110,103],abc])
|-merge([getstr,abc],
        [string,[115,116,114,105,110,103]],
        [getstr,string,[115,116,114,105,110,103],abc])
|-proc2([getstr,string,[115,116,114,105,110,103],abc],
        [string,[115,116,114,105,110,103]])
```

Though the two sub-processes merge and proc2 are correct with respect to I/O sets, proc2 is not an intended process. This bug cannot be detected on level 3 in section 6.2. In this case, the causality relation must be displayed as follows.

```
Goal: term2(_1,_2)
Ins : term2([getstr,abc],
      [getstr,string,[115,116,114,105,110,103],abc])
Stat: terminate
[_1]IN = [getstr,abc]
```

```
((no output))
[_2]((no input))
    OUT = [getstr,string,[115,116,114,105,110,103],abc]
```

We must examine the output of _2 and will get it as follows.

```
query>output(2).
OUTPUT OF _2 :
cond{_1 = [_3|_4] / [getstr,abc]}
|-_2 = [_3|_5]}
  |-cond{_6 = [_7|_8]}
  |  <-cond{_2 = [getstr|_9]}
  |     |-_6 = [string|_10]
  |     |-cond{_9 = [_11|_12]}
  |          |-_10 = [_13]
  |          |-string(_11,_13)
  |               |-> _13 = [115,116,114,
  |-_5 = [_7|_15]                 105,110,103]
     |-cond{_8 = [_16|_17]}
        |-_15 = [_16|_18]
        |-cond{_17 = nil}
             |-_18 = _4
query>out.
```

While the second element of the list _2 is intended to be abc, it is, in fact, string and computed by 'string/2'. The reason it is string is that _6 can be bound when the first element of _2 is bound. The erroneous causality relation is

$$\text{cond}\{\_2 = [\text{getstr}|\_9]\}$$
$$|-\_6 = [\text{string}|\_10].$$

Next, the debugger shows the following process and the programmer examines the output of _6 and input of _2.

```
Goal: proc2(_2,_6)
Ins:proc2([getstr,string,[115,116,114,105,110,103],abc],
          [string,[115,116,114,105,110,103]])
Stat: terminate
[_2] IN = [getstr,string,[115,116,114,105,110,103],abc]
     ((no output))
[_6] ((no input))
     OUT = [string,[115,116,114,105,110,103]]
query>output(2).
OUTPUT OF _6 :
cond{_2 = [getstr|_9]
     / [getstr,string,[115,116,114,105,110,103],abc]}
|-_6 = [string|_10]
  |-cond{_9 = [_11|_12]}
     |-_10 = [_13]
     |-string(_11,_13)
          |-> _13 = [115,116,114,105,110,103]
query>input(1).
INPUT OF _2 :
cond{_1 = [_3|_4]}
|  <-_1 = [getstr,abc]
|-_2 = [_3|_5]
  |-cond{_6 = [_7|_8]
         / [string,[115,116,114,105,110,103]]}
     |-_5 = [_7|_15]
     |-cond{_8 = [_16|_17]}
        |-_15 = [_16|_18]
        |-cond{_17 = nil}
             |-_18 = _4
query>out.
```

The programmer must answer 'out' since it contains the erroneous causality relation which is the same as before.

Then the debugger shows the following process. Since it is correct, the programmer answers 'yes'.

```
Goal : proc2_str(_9,_10)
Ins: proc2_str([string,[115,116,114,105,110,103],abc],
               [[115,116,114,105,110,103]])
Stat: terminate
[_9]  IN = [string,[115,116,114,105,110,103],abc]
      ((no output))
[_10]  ((no input))
      OUT = [[115,116,114,105,110,103]]
query>yes.
```

The debugger detects the erroneous clause and shows it as follows.

```
Buggy clause:
proc2([getstr,string,[115,116,114,105,110,103],abc],
      [string,[115,116,114,105,110,103]]) :-
    [string,[115,116,114,105,110,103]]
       = [string,[115,116,114,105,110,103]],
    proc2_str([string,[115,116,114,105,110,103],abc],
              [[115,116,114,105,110,103]]).

proc2([getstr|_1],_2) :-
    _1 = [string|_3],
    proc2_str(_2,_3).
```

## 7  Related Works

[Takeuchi86] proposes an algorithmic debugger for GHC, the instances are divided into three sets which are success, suspend, and failure set. Since this model does not use the input-output relation, it is not sufficient for the meaning of GHC programs [Takeuchi87].

[Lichtenstein88] proposes an algorithmic debugger for Concurrent Prolog. Though it can detect an erroneous I/O mode because it shows I/O history, it does not show causality relation.

[Takeuchi87] proposes semantics which introduce the causality relation, and suggests debugging using it. In our paper, we fulfilled it.

## 8  Conclusion

In this paper, we proposed the communicating process model to represent the execution of the parallel logic programming language Fleng and applied it to debugging. It is able to represent the input-output causality relation which is necessary for the meaning of a parallel logic program.

Unlike verification, we think that there is no need for debugging to deal with bugs which do not appear in execution. Therefore, in this paper, we discussed a debugger that searches for bugs from one execution of a program. If all cases of committing clauses are traced, our model is applicable to verification. However it is too complex to compute in practice. We think it is a moderate extension to add *Cond* with respect to all clauses which may be committed and to continue one of them corresponding to the committed clause. Using it, we can analyze alternative execution.

We are planning to develop the debugger analyzing the loop of causality relation and detecting causes of deadlocks.

Concerning algorithmic debugging, we will investigate the technique to detect a bug efficiently using the information where the erroneous part of the construction of I/O is. We will also investigate techniques to enable the debugger to answer not only which clause is erroneous but also where in the clause the erroneous part is.

Our model is applicable to GHC and other parallel logic programming languages. In this case, the execution of guard goals is added to *Cond*.

## Acknowledgement

We would like to thank Hiroaki Nakamura (IBM) and Shinji Kono (SONY CSL) for their helpful advice.

## References

[Brock81] Brock, J. D. and Ackermann, W. B. : *Scenarios: A Model of Nondeterminate Computation*, Lecture Notes in Computer Science, No. 107, 1981.

[Clark86] Clark, K. and Gregory, S. : *PARLOG: Parallel Programming in Logic*, In ACM Transactions on Programming Language and Systems, Vol. 8, No. 1, 1986.

[Lichtenstein88] Lichtenstein, Y. and Shapiro E. : *Abstract Algorithmic Debugging*, Logic programming: proceedings of the fifth international conference and symposium, 1988.

[Murakami88a] Murakami, M. : *An Axiomatic Verification Method for Synchronization of Guarded Horn Clauses Programs*, Technical Report TR-339, 1988.

[Murakami88b] Murakami, M. : *A Declarative Semantics of Parallel Logic Programs with Perpetual Processes*, Technical Report TR-406, ICOT, 1988.

[Nilsson86] Nilsson, M. and Tanaka, H. : *Fleng Prolog - The Language which turns Supercomputers into Prolog Machines*, In Wada, E. (Ed. ): Logic Programming '86, LNCS 264, Springer-Verlag, 1986.

[Shapiro83a] Shapiro, E. : *A Subset of Concurrent Prolog and Its Interpreter*, Technical Report TR-003, ICOT, 1983.

[Shapiro83b] Shapiro, E. : *Algorithmic Program Debugging*, MIT Press, 1983.

[Takeuchi86] Takeuchi, A. : *Algorithmic Debugging of GHC Programs and Its Implementation in GHC*, Technical Report TR-185, ICOT, 1986.

[Takeuchi87] Takeuchi, A. : *A Semantic Model of Guarded Horn Clauses* Technical Report, ICOT, 1987.

[Ueda85a] Ueda, K. : *Guarded Horn Clauses*, Technical Report, TR-103, ICOT, 1985.

[Ueda85b] Ueda, K. : *GHC Compiler User's Guide*, NEC Corporation, 1985.

# Parallel Generalized LR Parser
# based on Logic Programming

Hiroaki NUMAZAKI                    Naoyoshi TAMURA
Tokyo Institute of Technology      Yokohama National University

Hozumi TANAKA
Tokyo Institute of Technology
2-12-1 Oookayama Megro-Ku, Tokyo 152, Japan

### Abstract

Tomita's algorithm [Tomita 85] which treats context free grammars makes use of the breadth-first strategy to handle conflicts occurring in a LR parsing table. Considering the compatibility of a breadth-first strategy with parallel processing, we developed a parallel generalized LR parser called PLR, whose algorithm is based on Tomita's algorithm. PLR is implemented in GHC[Ueda 85] that is a concurrent logic programming language developed by the Japanese 5th generation computer project. We made two kinds of implementations of PLR. One implementation does not uses the Graph Structured Stacks (GSSs) developed by Tomita, and the other implementation uses them. In this paper, we describe two implementations of PLR. Then to evaluate the ability of PLR, we compare the parsing time of PLR with that of PAX[Matsumoto 87] which is an efficient parallel parser implemented in GHC. The experiment revealed that PLR with no GSSs runs faster than PAX.

## 1  Introduction

In order to get fast parser for natural languages, we should look for a parallel parsing method based on efficient and general parsing algorithms. It is well known that LR parser is a very efficient parser, but unfortunately LR grammar is too weak to parse sentences of natural language. When we apply the LR parsing algorithm to context free grammars, it is common that conflicts appear in the LR parsing table. So we need to generalize the LR parsing algorithm in order to handle these conflicts. There are two kinds of strategies to handle them, namely a depth-first strategy and a breadth-first strategy. Tomita[Tomita 85] has adopted a breadth-first strategy. As it is easy for us to simulate the breadth-first strategy by parallel processing, we have developed a parallel generalized LR parser called PLR whose algorithm is based on Tomita's algorithm. PLR is implemented in a concurrent logic programming language GHC[Ueda 85] developed by the Japanese 5th generation computer project. We have two kinds of implementations of PLR. One implementation does not uses the Graph Structured Stacks (GSSs) developed by Tomita, and the other implementation uses them. In the first implementation, there is no need to make processes synchronize. Each parsing process has its own stack and parses a sentence with no communications. On the other hand, the second implementation has a synchronization mechanism. There is one process which manages GSSs. The process communicates with many parsing processes and controls them to synchronize one another on a shift action. The most significant feature of PLR is to describe each entry of a LR parsing table as a process which conducts shift and reduce operations. If a parsing process encounters a conflict in a LR table, it creates and activates subprocesses in order to conduct shift and reduce operations in the conflict.

The rest of this paper is as follows. Section 2 and 3 briefly introduce the LR parsing algorithm and a concurrent logic programming language GHC. Section 4 and 5 give the implementation of PLR. Section 6 explains how to handle DCG rules[Pereira 80] in PLR. Section 7 shows the results of experiments in which we compared the parse time of PLR and PAX that is an efficient parallel parser implemented in GHC. The experiment revealed that PLR with no GSSs runs faster than PAX.

$$
\begin{array}{lll}
(1) & S & \rightarrow \text{NP, VP.} \\
(2) & S & \rightarrow \text{S, PP.} \\
(3) & NP & \rightarrow \text{NP, RELC.} \\
(4) & NP & \rightarrow \text{NP, PP.} \\
(5) & NP & \rightarrow \text{det, noun.} \\
(6) & NP & \rightarrow \text{noun.} \\
(7) & NP & \rightarrow \text{pron.} \\
(8) & VP & \rightarrow \text{v, NP.} \\
(9) & RELC & \rightarrow \text{relp, VP.} \\
(10) & PP & \rightarrow \text{p, NP.}
\end{array}
$$

Figure 1: An Ambiguous English grammar

| | det | noun | pron | v | p | relp | $ | NP | PP | VP | RELC | S |
|---|---|---|---|---|---|---|---|---|---|---|---|---|
| 0 | sh1 | sh2 | sh3 | | | | | 5 | | | | 4 |
| 1 | | sh6 | | | | | | | | | | |
| 2 | | | | re6 | re6 | re6 | re6 | | | | | |
| 3 | | | | re7 | re7 | re7 | re7 | | | | | |
| 4 | | | | | sh7 | | acc | 8 | | | | |
| 5 | | | | sh10 | sh7 | sh9 | | | 12 | 11 | 13 | |
| 6 | | | | re5 | re5 | re5 | re5 | | | | | |
| 7 | sh1 | sh2 | sh3 | | | | | 14 | | | | |
| 8 | | | | | re2 | | re2 | | | | | |
| 9 | | | | sh10 | | | | | | 15 | | |
| 10 | sh1 | sh2 | sh3 | | | | | 16 | | | | |
| 11 | | | | | re1 | | re1 | | | | | |
| 12 | | | | re4 | re4 | re4 | re4 | | | | | |
| 13 | | | | re3 | re3 | re3 | re3 | | | | | |
| 14 | | | | re10 | sh7/re10 | sh9/re10 | re10 | | 12 | | 13 | |
| 15 | | | | re9 | re9 | re9 | re9 | | | | | |
| 16 | | | | re8 | sh7/re8 | sh9/re8 | re8 | | 12 | | 13 | |

Figure 2: LR parsing table obtained from Fig.1 grammar

## 2  Generalized LR Parsing algorithm

The generalized LR parser uses one or more stacks to parse a sentence. There are two kinds of stack operations, a shift and a reduce operations, that are specified by a LR parsing table generated from given grammar rules. Fig.1 shows an ambiguous English grammar. Fig.2 shows a LR parsing table generated from the English grammar.

The left-hand side of the table is called 'action part', the entry of which is determined by a pair of parser state (the row of the table) and a look-ahead preterminal (the column of the table) of an input sentence.

The symbol 'sh N' in some entries means that the LR parser has to push a Look-ahead preterminal on the LR stack and go to 'state N'. The symbol 're N' means that the LR parser has to reduce several topmost elements on the stack using a rule numbered 'N'. The symbol 'acc' means that the generalized LR parser ends with success of parsing. If an entry doesn't contain any operation, the LR parser recognizes an error. The right-hand side of the table is called a 'goto part' that decides which state the parser should enter after a reduce operation.

Some entries of the LR table specify more than two operations, that is called a conflict. All operations in the conflict are conducted by the generalized LR parser. The LR table shown in Fig.2 has four 'shift-reduce' conflicts at state 14 (row number 14) and state 16 for the column of 'p' and 'relp'. In PLR explained in section 4 and 5, conflicts are processed in parallel. So the order of the operations in a conflict does not matter.

```
(1) a:- true | b(X),c(X).
(2) b(X):- true | X=[a|Y], b(Y).
(3) c([a|Y]):- true | c(Y).
```

Figure 3: Typical Statement of GHC

# 3  A Brief Introduction to GHC

In this section, we give a brief introduction to GHC. Typical GHC statements are given in Fig.3. The vertical bar in a GHC statement of Fig.3 is a commit operator that works like a cut operator in Prolog. When a goal 'a' is executed, a process corresponding to the statement (1) is activated and the body becomes a new goal in which 'b(X)' and 'c(X)' are activated concurrently. Note that the definition of process 'c' in statement (3) requires the first element of the input list to be an atom 'a'. When the process 'c(X)' with an unbound variable 'X' is called, the unification of 'c(X)' and 'c([a|Y])' is suspended by a synchronization mechanism of GHC until X is bound with an list '[a|Y]' by the process 'b(X)'. In general, If the unification on the left-hand side of the commit operator tries to instantiate the variable in the process like 'c(X)', it will be suspended until the variable is instantiated by other processes.

# 4  Implementation of PLR with no GSSs

In this section, we give an implementation of PLR with no GSSs. The feature of the implementation is that each entry in an LR parsing table is described as a process in GHC which handles shift and reduce operations. A parsing process has its own stack and list of input words. If the process encounters a conflict, it activates two or more subprocesses in order to conduct shift or reduce operations in the conflict. These subprocesses run in parallel with no communications. So there is no need to make subprocesses synchronize during parsing.

## 4.1  Description of the PLR Algorithm

There are three kinds of processes in PLR.

- action process:
  An action process carries out shift and reduce operations. In case of a shift operation, the action process pushes a look-ahead preterminal on a stack and activates a subprocess which corresponds to the entry corresponding to the new state and the next preterminal. In case of a reduce operation, the action process activates a reduce process and send it the input stack. When an action process encounters a conflict, more than two subprocesses are activated, each of which performs a shift or a reduce operation specified in the entry. When an action process encounters an 'acc' entry, the action process gets the result of the parsing and ends with success. By contrast, if all of the above conditions are not satisfied, an action process ends with no information of parsing.

- reduce process:
  Using a grammar rule specified by a reduce operation, the reduce process reduces a stack and activates a goto process to enter a new state.

- goto process:
  Accordig to the state on the top of the stack given by a reduce process, a goto process activates an action process to conduct the next shift or reduce operation.

In the following subsections, we give the definition of PLR processes obtained by the LR table shown in Fig.2.

## 4.2 Definition of Action Process

Following are examples of definitions of an action process.

1. Suppose an action process 'i0' that corresponds to the entry in Fig.2 whose row and column are 0 and 'noun' respectively. The entry that contains 'sh 1' operation is described below.

```
i0(noun, Stack, [noun,NextCat|List], Info):- true|
    i1(NextCat, [[1,noun]|Stack], [NextCat|List], Info).
```

In the above definition, the predicate 'i0' is a process name, and its first argument is a look-ahead preterminal 'noun'. The second argument 'Stack' has states and grammatical symbols. The third is a list of preterminals of an input sentence. The fourth 'Infor' outputs the results of parsing. The subprocess 'i1' receives a new stack which consists of 'Stack', state '1' and a preterminal 'noun' and the list of preterminals.

2. Consider an entry of state '2' and a look-ahead preterminal 'v' in Fig.2. The definition of action process 'i2' is given below :

```
i2(v, Stack, List, Info):- true|
    re6(v, Stack, List, Info).
```

In the body of an action process 'i2', a subprocess 're6' is activated in order to conduct a reduce operation. The subprocess 're6' receives the same stack information and a preterminal list as those of the parent process 'i2'. The detail of the reduce process will be explained later.

3. Look at an entry of state '14' and a look-ahead preterminal 'p' in Fig.2. There is a shift-reduce conflict, 'sh 7/re 10'. The definition of an action process 'i14' is as follows.

```
i14(p, Stack, [p,NextCat|List], Info):- true|
    i7(NextCat, [[7,p]|Stack], [NextCat|List], Info1),
    re10(p, Stack, [p,NextCat|List], Info2),
    merge(Info1, Info2, Info).
```

In the body of the process 'i14', both subprocesses 'i7' and 're10' carry out a shift and a reduce operation simultaneously. The 'merge' process is a built-in process which merges the output produced by the subprocesses 'i7' and 're10'.

4. The entry of state '4' and a look-ahead preterminal '$' in Fig.2 is an 'acc' entry, which indicates success of parsing. The definition of the action process 'i4' for this entry is as follows.

```
i4($, [[_,Result]|_], _, Info):- true|
    Info=[Result].
```

In the body of the action process 'i4','[Result]' is sent to the fourth argument 'Info', and finally the action process 'i4' terminates with success.

5. If no operation is specified in an entry, an error handling process is activated. The following is a definition of the process for state '0' which should be placed at the end of definitions of the process 'i0'.

```
otherwise.
i0(_, _, _, Info):- true|
    Info=[].
```

The statement 'otherwise' is a built-in statement which declares that GHC statements below 'otherwise' should be executed after all GHC statements over 'otherwise' fails.

### 4.3 Definition of Reduce Process

The following definition of a process 're10' is an example of reduce process corresponding to the grammar rule numbered 10 in Fig.1 ( (10) PP→p,NP ).

```
re10(NextCat, OldStack, List, Info):-
    OldStack=[[_,T1],[_,T2],[State,T3]|Tail]|
    pp(State, NextCat, [pp,T2,T1], [[State,T3]|Tail], List, Info).
```

In the second argument of 're10', the topmost two elements of 'OldStack' are popped and they are sent to a goto process 'pp' in which the third argument '[pp,T2,T1]' is a syntactic tree whose root is 'pp' in accordance with the grammar rule 10. The name of the goto process 'pp' is the same as the name of the nonterminal symbol on the left-hand side of the grammar rule 10. The first argument 'State' is a state number on the top of reduced stack.

### 4.4 Definition of Goto Process

After a reduce operation is carried out, a goto process is activated in order to enter a new state in which a new action process will be activated. At that time, the goto process uses both an incoming nonterminal symbol and a state number on the top of the stack.

There is a sample definition of goto processes.

```
s(0, NextCat, Tree, Stack, List, Info):- true|
    i4(NextCat, [[4,Tree]|Stack], List, Info).
```

The process 's' is activated after 's' is constructed by a reduce process in state '0'. As the entry of row '0' and column 's' in the LR table of Fig.2 includes '4', the goto process 's' activates an action process 'i4' pushing state '4' and tree information onto the stack.

## 5 Implementation of PLR with GSSs

In the implementation shown in section 4, the stack information is assigned to each parsing process which parses a sentence independently. Tomita noticed that two or more processes may sometimes have the same state due to 'shift' actions. And after that, the processes behave in the same way until the state is removed from the stack by 'reduce' actions. So he devised a mechanism which merges the stacks at the point where they have the same state. The stack is called Graph Structured Stack (GSS) which enables us to avoid the duplication of parsing processes. In this section, we introduce GSSs into our implementation of PLR. The features of the implementation are as follows :

- We make a GSS Manage Process (GMP) which handles a shift or reduce operation of GSSs and controls every parsing processes to synchronize in the 'shift' action.

- Each parsing process has a pointer to the top of GSS and requests GMP to operate the 'shift' or 'reduce' operation.

- If GMP receives the same 'shift' request from two or more parsing processes, it terminates all parsing processes except one and merges all GSSs pointed to by their processes into one GSS.

In the following subsections, we explain the GMP and parsing processes.

### 5.1 Implementation of GSSs

In our PLR, the Graph Structured Stack devised by Tomita[Tomita 85] is described as a set of following data structures :

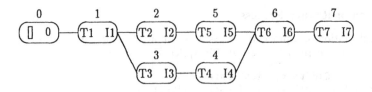

Figure 4: Graph Structured Stack

$$N : (T, I, L)$$

where 'N' is a node number assigned to each node, 'T' is a preterminal or a subtree, 'I' is a state which is held in the node, and 'L' is a connection list, the elements of which indicate the node number connecting behind with the node numbered N.

For example, a GSS shown in Fig.4 is described as follows.

$$0 : ([], 0, [])\qquad 1 : (T1, I1, [0])$$
$$2 : (T2, I2, [1])\qquad 3 : (T3, I3, [1])$$
$$4 : (T4, I4, [3])\qquad 5 : (T5, I5, [2])$$
$$6 : (T6, I6, [4, 5])\qquad 7 : (T7, I7, [6])$$

PLR has one process called GMP which manages GSS like the above. The action of GMP is determined by the following requests which are sent from parsing processes.

- shift(N, Top, NextTop↑, NextCat↑)
  When a parsing process shifts a look-ahead on the top of a GSS and goto state 'N', this request is sent to GMP. In this request, 'Top' is a pointer indicating the place on which a look-ahead is shifted, 'NextTop' is a new pointer and 'NextCat' is a next look-ahead preterminal, the value of which will be returned from GMP. GMP postpones assigning the next look-ahead to the variable 'NextCat' until all parsing processes send 'shift' messages to it. With this function, all parsing processes synchronize on the shift actions.

- pop(Top, N, Poplist↑)
  Before a parsing process executes a 'reduce' action, the process sends this request to GMP. Here, 'Top' is a pointer to the element of the stack, 'N' is the number of the elements needed by the 'reduce' action, 'Poplist' is a list of elements which are poped from a GSS.

- goto(N, Tree, Top, NextTop↑)
  This request is sent to GMP when a 'goto' process is called by a 'reduce' process. In this request, 'N' is a state number to which a parsing process will go, 'Tree' is a subtree constructed by a 'reduce' process, 'Top' is a pointer indicating where the subtree should be put, and 'NextTop' is a new pointer the value of which will be assigned by GMP.

- accept(Top, Info↑)
  When a parsing process encounters a 'acc' entry, the process sends this request. GMP will pick a parse tree out of a node numbered 'Top' and bind it with 'Info'.

- create
  This message is sent to GMP when a parsing process encounters a conflict and a new process is created.

- terminate
  This message shows that a parsing process was terminated because it detected an 'error' or it was merged into other process.

Details of an implementation of GMP are omitted in this paper. We show implementations of parsing processes in the following subsections.

## 5.2 Definition of Action Process

Following are examples of definitions of an action process which communicates with GMP.

1. A 'shift' entry

The definition of an action process corresponding to 'sh 1' entry shown in 4.2 is changed as follows :

```
i0(noun, Top, Stream, Info):- true|
    Stream=[shift(1, Top, NextTop, NextCat) | Rst],
    i1(NextCat, NextTop, Rst, Info).
```

By putting a 'shift(1, Top,...)' request on the 'Stream', the action process 'i0' communicates with GMP and gets a 'NextCat' and 'NextTop' needed to activate the next action process 'i1'.

2. A 'reduce' entry

The definition of an action process corresponding to 're 6' entry shown in 4.2 is changed as follows :

```
i2(v, Top, Stream, Info):- true|
    Stream=[pop(Top, 2, Poplist) | Rst],
    reduce(6, v, Poplist, Rst, Info).
```

By sending a 'pop' request through 'Stream', the action process 'i2' receives 'Poplist'. The information in 'Poplist' will be used by the 'reduce' process.

3. A 'shift-reduce' conflict

The definition of an action process corresponding to 'sh 7/re10' entry is changed as follows :

```
i14(p, Top, Stream, Info):- true|
    Stream=[create, pop(Top, 3, Poplist),
            shift(7, Top, Ntop, Ncat) | Rst],
    reduce(10, p, Poplist, St1, Inf1),
    i7(Ncat, Ntop, St2, Inf2),
    merge(St1, St2, Rst),
    merge(Inf1, Inf2, Info).
```

The process 'i14' activates two parsing processes: 'reduce' and 'i7' process which run in parallel, and send a 'create' message to GMP.

4. An accept entry

The definition of an action process corresponding to an 'acc' entry is changed as follows :

```
i4($, Top, Stream, Info):- true|
    Stream=[accept(Top, Info)]
```

5. An 'error' entry

```
otherwise.
i0(_, _, Stream, Info):- true~|
    Stream=[terminate], Info=[].
```

After sending a 'terminate' massage to GMP, this process terminates with no information of parsing.

## 5.3 Definition of Reduce Process

The reduce process is activated by an action process with a list of popped stack elements 'Poplist' on the third argument of the definitions below.

```
reduce(N, NextCat, [List], Stream, Info):- true|
    re(N, NextCat, List, Stream, Info).
reduce(N, NextCat, [List | Rest], Stream, Info):- true|
    Stream=[create | Rst],
    re(N, NextCat, List, St1, Inf1),
    reduce(N, NextCat, Rest, St2, Inf2),
    merge(St1, St2, Rst),
    merge(Inf1, Inf2, Info).
```

If 'Poplist' contains two or more lists of elements like '[[...],[...], ...  ]', the process 'reduce' activates the process 're' as many times as the number of lists. Each of the lists is assigned to each process 're' running in parallel.

The following example definition of a process 're' corresponds to the grammar rule numbered 1 in Fig.1 ((1) S→NP,VP).

```
re(1, NextCat, [A1, A2, A3], Stream, Info):- true|
    A1=[_, _, T1],
    A2=[_, _, T2],
    A3=[Top, State, _],
    s(State, Top, NextCat, [s,T2,T1], Stream, Info).
```

This process activates a goto process 's' to put a syntactic tree '[s,T2,T1]' on the top of GSS and to go to the next state.

## 5.4 Definition of Goto Process

The definition of goto processes is changed as follows.

```
s(0, Top, NextCat, Tree, Stream, Info):- true|
    Stream=[goto(5, Tree, Top, NextTop) | Rst],
    i4(NextCat, NextTop, Rst, Info).
```

This process sends a request 'goto' to GMP and calls the next action process 'i4'.

# 6  Handling DCGs in PLR

PLR can handle the grammar rule written in DCG form. An example of a DCG rule is as follows.

(1) S(A_A, A_S) → NP(NP_A, NP_S), VP(VP_A, VP_S), { Augmentations }.

In this rule, each grammatical symbol has two arguments. We give syntactic information to the first argument and semantic information to the second argument. The 'Augmentations' checks the appropriateness of applying this rule. In order to handle DCGs, the data structure of a node of GSSs like N : (T, I, L) explained in 5.1 is changed into the following form.

N : ([ First-Argument, Second-Argument, T ], I, L)

The process in the augmentations is called from the process 're' as follows.

```
re(1, NextCat, [A1, A2, A3], Stream, Info):- true|
    A1=[_, _, [VP_A, VP_S, VP_T]],
    A2=[_, _, [NP_A, NP_S, NP_T]],
    A3=[Top, State, _],
    ' Augmentations ',
    s(State, Top, NextCat,
        [S_A,S_S,[s,NP_T,VP_T]], Stream, Info).
```

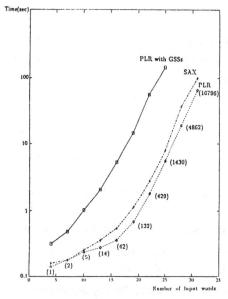

Figure 5: The result of Parsing time

# 7  The Results of A Experiment

We conducted an experiment to parse many English sentences with many PP attachments such as:

$$NP,v,NP$$
$$NP,v,NP,PP$$
$$NP,v,NP,PP,PP$$
$$\ldots\ldots$$

In the experiment, we compared the parse time of PLR and PAX. The number enclosed in parentheses in Fig.5 indicates the number of parsing trees. PLR with no GSSs runs 1.4 times faster than PAX that is known as an efficient parallel parser implemented in parallel logic programming language. To get all parsing trees of a sentence with 9 PP attachments, PLR takes about 65 sec. on a Sun-3/260 work-station. Note that the PLR with GSSs runs 10 times slower than PLR with no GSSs. We can consider two reasons for why PLR with GSSs is so inefficient. One reason is that PLR with GSSs makes use of side-effects to implement the data structure of GSSs. Another reason is that many parsing processes are suspended to synchronize with 'shift' actions during parsing. We should develop the more efficient implementation of GSS and the algorithm that decreases the number of suspended processes.

# 8  Conclusion

We described two implementations of the PLR algorithm in GHC where each entry of the LR table is described as a process which handles shift and reduce operations. When a conflict occurs in an entry of the LR table, the corresponding parsing process activates two or more subprocesses which run in parallel and simulate breadth-first strategy of the generalized LR parsing.

The experiment has revealed that PLR with no GSSs runs faster than PAX that has been known as an efficient parallel parser. PLR runs so fast that it is a promising parser for processing many complex natural language sentences. We are now considering how we can implement the Graph Structured Stacks without using side-effects. If we can do this, we will get a more efficient implementation of PLR.

# References

[Aho 72]     Aho,A.V.and Ulman,J.D.: *The Theory of Parsing,Translation,and Compiling,* Prentice-Hall,Englewood Cliffs,New Jersey (1972)

[Aho 85]     Aho,A.V.,Senthi,R.and Ulman,J.D.: *Compilers Principles,Techniques,and Tools,*Addison-Wesley (1985)

[Fuchi 87]    Fuch,K. Furukawa,K. Mizoguchi,F.:*Heiretu Ronri Gata Gengo GHC To Sono Ouyou,* Kyoritsu Syuppan (1987) in Japanese

[Knuth 65]    Knuth,D.E.: *On the translation of languages from left to right,*Information and Control 8:6,pp.607-639

[Konno 86]    Konno,A. Tanaka,H.:*Hidari Gaichi Wo Kouryo Shita Bottom Up Koubun Kaiseki,* Computer Softwear,Vol.3, No.2, pp.115-125 (1986) in Japanese

[Nakata 81]    Nakata,I.:*Compiler,* Sangyo Tosyo (1981) in Japanese

[Matsumoto 86]    Matsumoto,Y. Sugimura,R.:*Ronri Gata Gengo Ni Motodsuku Koubun Kaiseki System SAX,* Computer Softwear,Vol.3, No.4, pp.4-11 (1986) in Japanese

[Matsumoto 87]    Matsumoto,Y.:*A Parallel Parsing System for Natural Language Analysis,* New Generation Computing, Vol.5, No. 1, pp.63-78 (1987)

[Matsumoto 89]    Matsumoto,Y.:*Natural Language Parsing Systems based on Logic Programming,* Ph.D thesis of Kyoto University, (June 1989)

[Mellish 85]    Mellish,C.S.:*Computer Interpretation of Natural Language Descriptions,* Ellis Horwood Limited (1985)

[Nilsson 86]    Nilsson,U.: *AID:An Alternative Implementation of DCGs,* New Generation Computing, 4, pp.383-399 (1986)

[Okumura 89]    Okumura,M.:*Sizengengo Kaiseki Ni Okeru Imiteki Aimaisei Wo Zoushinteki Ni Kaisyou Suru Keisan Model,* Natural Language Analysis Working Group,Information Processing Society of Japan,NL71-1 (1989) in Japanese

[Pereira 80]    Pereira,F.and Warren,D.: Definite Clause Grammar for Language Analysis-A Survey of the Formalism and a Comparison with Augmented Transition Networks, *Artif. Intell,* Vol.13, No.3, pp.231-278 (1980)

[Tokunaga 88]    Tokunaga,T. Iwayama,M. Kamiwaki,T. Tanaka,H.:*Natural Language Analysis System LangLAB,* Transactions of Information Processing Society of Japan,Vol.29, No.7, pp.703-711 (1988) in Japanese

[Tomita 85]    Tomita,M.:*Efficient Parsing for Natural Language,* Kluwer Academic Publishers (1985)

[Tomita 87]    Tomita,M.: *An Efficient Augmented-Context-Free Parsing Algorithm,* Computational Linguistics, Vol.13, Numbers 1-2, pp.31-46 (1987)

[Ueda 85]    Ueda,K.:*Guarded Horn Clauses,* Proc. The Logic Programming Conference, Lecture Notes in Computer Science, 221 (1985)

[Uehara 83]    Uehara,K. Toyoda,J.: *Sakiyomi To Yosokukinou Wo Motsu Jutugo Ronri Gata Koubun Kaiseki Program : PAMPS,* Transactions of Information Processing Society of Japan, Vol.24, No.4, pp.496-504 (1983) in Japanese

# Knowledge Media Station

Y. Hosono, H. Kumagai, H. Shimizu, M. Sumida,
A. Takeuchi, N. Takiguchi, T. Wake, T. Yamaoka

Central Research Laboratory
Mitsubishi Electric Corp.
1-1,Tsukaguchi Honmachi,8 Chome,Amagasaki,Hyogo,661,Japan

Knowledge Media Station aims at an active medium which not only stores and utilizes knowledge represented by a well-formulated language, but also enables users to incorporate and organize this knowledge together with various types of knowledge using a hypermedia framework. Knowledge Media Station consists of a Knowledge Processor, Inference Engine and Hypermedia. In the Inference Engine, we have developed a constraint logic programming language $\tau$ for knowledge representation and as a problem solving language. In the Knowledge Processor, an interactive environment for $\tau$ was designed from the "constraint centered" view. It integrates several smart ideas invented so far in the logic programming community. These include query-the-user, qualified answer, incremental query and interactive query revision. It will be shown that these ideas nicely match the concept of constraint, and they promote and encourage incremental and interactive characteristics of constraint-based computation. The hypermedia part of Knowledge Media Station is knowledge-base with the function of so-called hypermedia. We will claim that, from the viewpoint of knowledge processing, hypermedia and logic programming can and should incorporate each other. We will also discuss where logic programming and hypermedia meet in several respects.

# 1 Introduction

## 1.1 Knowledge Media

There are two kinds of work in the life of man. One is of a physical nature such as manufacturing and transportation. The other is an intellectual one such as planning and decision making. Physical work has required a huge amount of labor. In the old days, for example, transportation of goods was performed by laborers using a variety of tools, but now, using automobiles and railways, the physical power of man has been amplified.

What kind of evolution can be seen in man's intellectual work? Intellectual work is a problem solving process using empirical knowledge and sometimes a new idea.

Traditional tools for helping intellectual work are such media as books, documents, films and so on. They play a role of storage and communication media of knowledge.

Nowadays, as well as these traditional media, computers are playing a role of media which accumulates and propagates knowledge. Unlike passive memory, computers have an active feature in the sense that they can answer questions using stored programs. Namely, computers are active media [Kay]. We can see many concrete examples. Among them, word processors and spreadsheets running on personal computers are most noteworthy. They not only accumulate documents and tables, but also respond actively to requests from users. Let us call such media "Information Media" corresponding to the underlying information processing.

However, from the viewpoint of media which amplify one's power of memory and problem solving in intellectual working, information media is still underdeveloped. This is because information media understand accumulated items only as a collection of characters and numbers, not as a collection of knowledge. Information media can not derive any new conclusions or contradictions therefrom. A medium which really handles knowledge has to be able to derive new conclusions and contradictions, which is what "handling knowledge" actually means.

The ways in which computers handle knowledge have been intensively studied in Artificial Intelligence for many years. An expert system is one outcome. An expert system handles knowledge in the sense that it can solve problems using some sort of programs encoding some knowledge. However, it puts emphasis on its inference power. Its applications are restricted to specific domains because it can obtain good results using powerful inference rules with a relatively small amount of knowledge. Therefore, it hardly means that expert systems are media handling knowledge.

In place of the above information media and expert systems, active media which can amplify the knowledge processing power of man as automobiles do in physical work are highly desired. In his outstanding paper, Stefik calls such an active medium *A Knowledge Medium* [Stefik].

> A knowledge medium is characterized in terms of knowledge processes such as the generation, distribution, and application of knowledge and, secondarily, in terms of specialized services such as consultation and knowledge integration... AI research includes topics relevant to knowledge media... However, AI technology, as it now exists, does not function in an important way as a knowledge medium in our society. Its influence has been far less important to the creation and propagation of knowledge... The term "artificial intelligence" expresses the most commonly understood goal of the field: to build intelligent, autonomous, thinking machines... In contrast, the goal of building a knowledge medium draws attention to the main source and store of knowledge in the world today: people. (from [Stefik])

Stefik's statements strike us as profound; in fact the project developing Knowledge Media Station is an attempt to realize Knowledge Media inspired by his paper. A similar project is also proposed by Emden [Emden(c)] independently. Our project shares many features with his, especially in the respect that both adopt logic programming as the key technology.

In realizing Knowledge Media, we thought that the following four points were important.

1. Open knowledge representation
   In order to represent knowledge, man uses various methods such as texts, pictures and tables. However, there is no machine-interpretive language which is as easy to use and powerful as these methods. Knowledge Media should encompass these non-machine-interpretive knowledge representations in addition to machine-interpretive ones.

2. Knowledge processing
   Knowledge is alive in the sense that it can derive new consequences and contradictions through its interaction. Therefore, Knowledge Media should not only accumulate knowledge represented in various ways, but also fully utilize stored knowledge to generate new knowledge.

3. Knowledge systematization
   Usually knowledge appears chaotic. To review it from various viewpoints and relate one to the other, and hence organize it, are essential operations in knowledge processing. Therefore Knowledge Media should have knowledge systematizing tools beyond conventional file systems.

4. Interactive media
   Knowledge Media are such that they amplify one's power of memory and problem-solving. Therefore behavior of Knowledge Media should be transparent to users. Also Knowledge Media should be open to interaction whenever desired.

## 1.2   Overview of Knowledge Media Station

In designing the Knowledge Media Station fulfilling the four requirements above, we have selected logic programming and hypermedia as the base technologies for the following reasons.

- Although it is not necessary (in fact impossible) for computers to fully understand all the representation schemes, the representations that can be understood by computers should be declarative. Based on this, a constraint logic programming language is adopted as a knowledge representation language because of its clear semantics and readability. A logic programming language has another advantage in that it naturally introduces database facilities.

- Knowledge-base is reconstructed as hypermedia, a multi-media version of hypertext, together with knowledge systematizing tools, since it enables arbitrary network organization of unstructured knowledge with the help of powerful reviewing tool.

At present, Knowledge Media Station handles the seven forms of knowledge below:

- Programs written in a constraint logic programming language

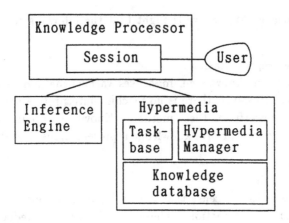

Figure 1: Architecture of Knowledge Media Station

- tables

- texts

- graphs

- drawings

- bit-mapped images

- menus

Knowledge Media Station consists of three subsystems, Hypermedia, Knowledge Processor and Inference Engine (Figure 1).

1. Hypermedia

   Hypermedia is the augmented knowledge-base. It stores and organizes knowledge of various forms in addition to constraint logic programs in arbitrary network forms. Hypermedia provides a tool, called *Knowledge Browser*, for reviewing the knowledge network.

2. Knowledge Processor

   Knowledge Processor provides a working environment called *a session* where a user can solve a problem interactively utilizing both Inference Engine and Hypermedia. Knowledge Processor also provides facilities for managing multiple working environments.

3. Inference Engine

   Inference Engine executes constraint logic programs.

The paper is organized as follows. In Section 2, we will discuss how knowledge is represented from scratch. A constraint logic programming language and hypermedia framework will be introduced for human friendly knowledge representation framework there. Section 3 is devoted to explain how knowledge processing can be realized in Knowledge Media Station. We will describe a meta-level environment which manages many knowledge processing environments in Section 4.

# 2 How Knowledge is represented

Knowledge Media Station aims at an active knowledge medium which not only stores and utilizes knowledge represented by well-formulated languages, but also enables users to integrate and organize this knowledge together with various types of knowledge. Knowledge Media Station is not an automatic knowledge processor, but an active medium which can communicate with people. People handle knowledge trivially. However, the way people represent knowledge is quite different from the way a computer does. Even in advanced AI software knowledge representation is very restrictive. It is clear that there is a big gap between human oriented knowledge representation and computer oriented knowledge representation. In order to reduce this gap, an active knowledge medium should handle knowledge of multi-media forms. There is folklore belief that knowledge processing is symbolic processing. This is half true. This is true when we think about thinking computers. But this is false when we think about computers communicating with humans.

Handling multi-media data is not enough for knowledge processing. The key issue is the integration of knowledge processing and multi-media data handling. Our first approximate solution to this issue is to extend the knowledge-base to hypermedia.

## 2.1 Hypermedia

In conventional computer aided document processing, each document is stored in a file and they are managed by their operating systems' file system. Recent advances in computer hardware and software enables more sophisticated document processing, namely hypertext [Conklin]. Hypertext consists of document database and window-based interface. A novel feature of hypertext is the concept of *a link* which directly connects documents. Owing to links, we could refer from one document to the other by just following links, not by calling a document by its file name. Modern WYSWYG interfaces realize this reference operation just by mouse operation and documents are displayed in separate windows. A link is a functionally simple concept, however its implication to document processing is enormous. In a large document database, usually they are mutually related. It is sufficient to be able to recall the manuals of some software. A link is a language which can directly represent such a relationship. It is beneficial to those who make mutually related documents and also to those who read them. We could say that a link brought us a totally new organization mechanism of documents. Before we didn't have such a mechanism.

Hypermedia is a multi-media version of hypertext. In hypermedia, we can organize and review mutually related documents, drawings and so on. In Knowledge Media Station, the knowledge-base is extended to have the functionality of hypermedia. This is why we call our knowledge-base "Hypermedia" (Hereafter the term 'Hypermedia' means the Hypermedia part of Knowledge Media Station. When we need to refer to the ordinary hypermedia, the term 'pure hypermedia' will be used).

Since a knowledge-base is the place to store knowledge, it is natural to keep not only programs (knowledge described in a machine-interpretive language) but also knowledge of various forms such as texts, tables, graphs, drawings, images and menus. Now the knowledge-base can be viewed as a network where an arc and a node correspond to a link and knowledge, respectively. Knowledge is one of the following six types; text, table, graph, drawing, image and menu. A program is treated as a text.

Such extension of knowledge-base enables the user to keep almost all kinds of knowledge related to a problem solving task. Furthermore the user can establish mutual relationship among knowledge in an arbitrary form using links. This is powerful, especially when a problem is complicated and needs various kinds of knowledge such as manuals, design sketches and statistics graphs.

## 2.2  A constraint logic programming language

Among various types of knowledge that Knowledge Media Station can handle, the one that can be automatically interpreted by a computer is the most important. Since other types of knowledge such as texts and graphs, are declarative in nature, that language should be also declarative. Knowledge Media Station adopts a constraint logic programming language, called $\tau$ , as the language for describing such knowledge. Constraint logic programming introduced the concept of "constraint" into logic programming by generalizing the logic framework so that it increases the declarative expressive power and the efficiency of logic programming. A good example of how it improves Prolog is the handling of numerical expressions. In Prolog, numerical expressions are processed in an ad-hoc manner. Thus when solving numerical problems a user is forced to program procedurally. Constraint logic programming languages regard numerical expressions as true constraints. Thus they make a user free from procedural programming. Generally, in constraint logic programming, one can solve a problem by describing constraints which a solution has to satisfy, not by describing procedures to find a solution.

Recently several constraint logic programming languages have been proposed [Colmerauer], [Jaffar], [Dincbas(b)]. $\tau$ shares many features with these predecessors. As constraint logic programming languages are supersets of Prolog, $\tau$ is also a superset of Prolog. Thus it inherits nice features of Prolog such as database facilities. In addition to function handling constraints, $\tau$ incorporates a module structure similar to that of ESP [Chikayama] and a frame representation similar to CIL [Mukai].

### 2.2.1  Constraints

One of the basic characteristics of constraint logic programming languages is the introduction of constraints which are managed independently from the ordinary order of execution. A constraint is evaluated when it obtains enough data to determine whether the condition is fulfilled or not. Otherwise the Evaluation of a constraint is postponed until sufficient data become available.

$\tau$ handles the following five constraints:

1. Not-equal (=/=)

2. Inequality (<, >, =<, >=)

3. Negation (not)

4. Linear and nonlinear equation

5. Finite domain

In the course of execution, many constraints may be suspended. Against these suspending constraints, the system does forward reasoning in order to derive stronger consequences. Such consequences include substitutions, failure. Constraints together with forward reasoning are called *active constraints* [Dincbas(a)]. In $\tau$ , active constraints are classified into ones relating to finite domain constraints, ones relating to interval constraints and ones relating to equations.

In addition to these pre-defined constraints, a user can make an arbitrary predicate behave like a constraint by putting invocation condition. An invocation condition specifies the condition that must be satisfied before the evaluation of a goal. The form of an invocation condition is similar to the mode declaration of Edinburgh Prolog. Given a predicate, an invocation condition specifies one of the following three for each argument; (1) it must be ground, (2) at least it has a principal functor, (3) anything. When a goal is to be evaluated and at least one of the arguments does not satisfy the invocation condition, then the evaluation of the goal is suspended.

## 2.2.2  Frame Representation

Frame representation enables the effective chunking of knowledge. $\tau$ provides the frame representation based on property lists. The approach is similar to CIL [Mukai]. The reason why we chose this approach is that representation based on property lists is simple and can incorporate unification naturally, though it may need much syntax sugar for high readability.

A property list is a set of pairs of property names and corresponding property values. Syntactically it is read and written in the following form.

```
George = {@, name!george, age!28, sex!male}
```

where @ indicates that this is a property list (and not a vector). The intended meaning of the above expression is that George is the frame description of a person whose name, age and sex are george, 28 and male, respectively. A value of the specific property can be accessed by <property list>!<property name>. For examples, George!name and George!age refer to george and 28, respectively.

A property list is additive, that is, one can add a new pair of a property name and a property value to the existing property list if the new pair is consistent with existing pairs. The new property value can be an unbound variable. Suppose that george married lisa. To represent the marriage, it is sufficient to add

```
George!wife = Lisa
```

where

```
Lisa = {@, name!lisa, age!26, sex!female}
```

Furthermore, if their home is not fixed, it is sufficient to add

```
George!address= NewAddress
```

New address would be put in the property list of George by just instantiating NewAddress
to the concrete address when it gets fixed.

Suppose that there are two objects, each described by property lists, X and Y. To
make these objects equivalent, it is enough to unify X and Y. Unification of two property
lists is basically a union of pairs of property names and property values, where if two
pairs share the same property name then corresponding values are unified. Unification
of two property lists succeeds if all the unification of property values sharing the same
property name succeeds. Otherwise, unification fails. Suppose that we have another
description about george:

```
Employee={@, name!george, task!programmer}
```

We can integrate these two descriptions by saying:

```
George = Employee
```

As a result, George and Employee become the following property list:

```
{@, name!george, age!28, sex!male,
    task!programmer,
    wife!{@, name!lisa, age!26, sex!female},
    address!NewAddress}
```

### 2.2.3   Other features

A program of $\tau$ is a set of *worlds*. A world is similar to a class of ESP. Like ESP,
$\tau$ also supports inheritance among worlds. Unlike ESP, $\tau$ allows a user to specify
integrity constraints for each world. These integrity constraints can be used to check
the consistency of a world definition.

$\tau$ does not provide any I/O primitives such as read and write. Generally in logic programming languages, there are three kinds of input/output operations. Putting goals
and adding clauses are two fundamental input operations. Returning answer substitutions is also an output operation. Regarding goals as input is the philosophy underlying
the incremental query approach [Emden(a)], [Ohki]. Sergot found that adding clauses
could be regarded as input and he proposed the query-the-user [Sergot]. Answer substitution is a fundamental output operation every Prolog interpreter has.

In Knowledge Media Station, we took an approach which realized declarative I/O
based on these three operations rather than introducing side-effect oriented read and
write operations. A mechanism similar to query-the-user was also implemented in $\tau$

This enables the user to add clauses on demand. Interactive querying and various interpretation mechanisms of answer substitution were also implemented. But they are realized outside the language, that is, in the level of the interpreter. This approach makes $\tau$ programs entirely I/O independent so that one program can incorporate different input and output interfaces. We believe that this has been achieved owing to the flexible control structure of constraint-based computation.

# 3 Knowledge Processing in Knowledge Media Station

In Knowledge Media Station, problem solving in a specific domain is done in a working environment called *a session*. A session can utilize both Inference Engine and Hypermedia and has the following features.

1. Reasoning with knowledge
   In a session, a user can solve a problem interactively using $\tau$ programs. Interactive query model and various interpretation mechanisms of answer substitution are provided.

2. Creation and editing of knowledge
   A session provides standard sheets for handling text, tables, graphs, drawings, images and menus. These sheets can easily be obtained by icon operations. They are displayed by overlapping windows, and changing their sizes, moving their positions and controlling mapping status can be done freely.

3. Systematization of knowledge
   Using the authoring tool of Hypermedia, a user can link one sheet to the other by mouse. By this link-operation, a user can systematize knowledge. Once links among knowledge have been established, a user can refer to related knowledge by following links using mouse. Knowledge Browser helps a user to get the whole structure of linked knowledge by drawing a network graph in which a node and an arc correspond to knowledge and a link, respectively.

## 3.1 Constraint logic programming: A framework for Interactive problem solving

First a session is explained mainly as a problem solving environment. From this viewpoint, a session has the following features.

1. It adopts an interactive query model based on incremental query [Emden(a)] and interactive query revision [Ohki].

2. It provides standard input and output interface between the Inference Engine and various types of knowledge such as texts, tables, graphs, drawings, images and menus.

### 3.1.1   Interactive query model

In ordinary Prolog interpreters, a goal statement is a conjunction of literals and specifies the conditions the solution must satisfy. Other goal statements before and after that are completely independent. On the contrary, in interactive query models such as incremental query and interactive query revision, a goal statement can be divided into several statements and they can be given incrementally. The interactive query model has the following advantages.

- The user does not necessarily enumerate all the conditions the solution must satisfy. This corresponds to the fact that the user is not always aware of all the conditions.

- The user can think about missing conditions by observing an intermediate answer substitution. This encourages incremental constraining of a problem.

- The user can use the same variable keeping the same content over goal statements.

The first points out the plausibility of incremental nature. The second points out the importance of visualizing intermediate states in incremental problem solving. We believe that these two points are essential in constraint-based computation.

Although interactive query models were first invented for Prolog, in some cases they work badly in Prolog. This is because of Prolog's dirty, non-declarative features such as I/O and ad-hoc arithmetic operations. It is now clear that constraint logic programming languages that overcome non-declarative features can nicely incorporate interactive query models. And the most important thing is that combined with constraint logic programming languages, the interactive query models can fully utilize its incremental nature.

A session is a working environment with multiple windows. One of them is called a *query window* and interfaces to Inference Engine. Query window adopts the interactive query models explained above with the following extensions:

1. It has the function of screen editor. Hence it can allow arbitrary editing operations against goals entered so far.

2. In order to handle backtracking in different goal statements and backtracking in the same goal statement in the same manner, we installed a table for keeping records from which goal we have to restart the execution.

### 3.1.2   Visualizing intermediate states

As already mentioned, in constraint-based computation, visualizing intermediate states is important for understanding the current status and thinking about the next step. A session provides various types of windows each of which monitors different aspects of the problem solving state.

1. Suspended constraints window
   It displays constraints currently being suspended because of a lack of data. Such

constraints include linear equations and user-defined goals with invocation conditions.

2. Variable window
   It displays variable names used so far.

3. Query reference window
   When a variable is pointed by mouse pointer, it displays the current value of the variable and all the queries (goals) referring to that variable.

4. Variable domain window
   When a variable is pointed by mouse pointer, it displays the current domain or the current interval of the variable if such constraint exists. A user can enter a concrete value for that variable from this window.

A method for monitoring parts of the current answer substitution other than query reference windows and variable domain windows is explained in the next subsection.

Among these windows, the suspended constraint window is the most important. In constraint-based computation, intermediate state is expressed by answer substitution and suspended constraints. Let $G$, $\theta$ and $C$ be a goal, answer substitution and suspending constraint, respectively. In such a situation, we could say that $G\theta$ is true if $C$ is true. This could be an answer if you can not know the truth value of $C$ or if you do not care about the truth value of $C$. This style of answer statement is called *qualified answer* by P. Vasey [Vasey]. We believe that the concept of qualified answer matches quite well with incremental constraint-based computation.

### 3.1.3 I/O interface with various types of knowledge

By replacing the ordinary query model by the incremental query model and extending the display mechanism of answer substitution, Emden et al. realized spreadsheet interface for Prolog [Emden(b)]. This increases the independence of a program and an input and output interface, so that a user can concentrate on description of problem domain without considering I/O interface.

Inspired by their idea, $\tau$ is intended to have no special built-in predicate for input and output. Instead a session provides standard types of knowledge such as texts, tables, graphs, drawings, images and menus together with input and output interface to Inference Engine. (Note that we use the term *types of knowledge* as *representation forms of knowledge*.) This extends the spreadsheet idea to various forms of interfaces, so that a user can try different I/O interfaces and choose a desirable one even after a program has been made.

Connection between Inference Engine and each piece of knowledge can be established by one-to-one correspondence between a special variable called *an entry variable* and *an entry* in the interpreter level. A session manages creating and maintaining of such connections. The difference between an entry variable and an ordinary variable is in their naming convention. A variable whose name follows the convention below is handled as an entry variable by the session.

```
<entry variable name> ::= <sheet id><entry id>
<sheet id> ::= S<number>
<entry id> ::= <alphabet><number>
```

`<sheet id>` is an identifier of the knowledge in a session and `<entry id>` is a local address of the entry in the knowledge. Thus a name of an entry variable uniquely specifies the corresponding entry.

An entry is a display object which can be interpreted differently depending on the type of knowledge. In case of a text, it is a region in a text string. In case of a table, it is a field whose address is specified by row and column. In case of a graph, it may be an amount of some item. In case of drawings, it may be the radius of a circle. In case of an image, it may be x-offset. In case of a menu, it may be a selection status of some item.

Connection between an entry variable and an entry works bidirectionally, that is, it can be used for input and output. Output: After solving the current goals, Inference Engine automatically propagates values of entry variables to the corresponding entries. And each piece of knowledge interprets them and reflects upon its display image. For example, if knowledge is of the text type, it inserts the value into the text string. Input: An action determining a value of an entry causes the insertion of the new goal. It is a unification of the entry variable and the value.

The mechanism described so far seems similar to that of access value. However, they are quite different since access values are parts of a program while we carefully separated a program part (entry variables) and an interface part (entries) and their connections are made outside a program. It is worth noting that a program with entry variables works as well without an interface part since in such a situation entry variables are treated as ordinary variables.

A constraint logic programming language together with interactive query model and input/output mechanism described so far has the following impact on applications.

1. It is easy to construct applications that invoke inference by input to texts, tables, graphs and so on. This is in fact an underlying mechanism of spreadsheet and form language applications.

2. It is easy to display the solution in a variety of forms. Furthermore, exchange of interface by transferring what is displayed in the table to the bar graph is easy to perform. This will help in understanding the intermediate solution and enrich the next step in interactive problem solving.

### 3.1.4 An example

Let us design a bridge circuit shown in Figure 2. Basic description about this circuit is given as follows according to physical laws:

$$E = R1 \times I1 + R2 \times I2$$
$$I1 = I2 + I5$$
$$I4 = I3 + I5$$

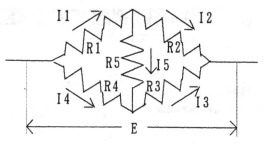

Figure 2: A Bridge Circuit

$$0 = R1 \times I1 + R5 \times I5 - R3 \times I3$$
$$0 = R2 \times I2 - R4 \times I4 - R5 \times I5$$

In Figure 3,Figure 4,Figure 5, three snapshots of the session solving this problem are shown. In Figure 3,Figure 4,Figure 5 , the window on the right side is the query window and the one on the lower left corner is the suspended constraint window which appears only in the first figure. Other windows, a table, a circuit and a bar graph, are used to display values of resistors and currents. In Figure 3, five equations above are found in the middle of the query window. Additional constraints are described below them. They specify the possible values of resistors and lower and upper bounds of currents. Note that entry variables are used to establish the bidirectional connection between variables such as $R_i$ and interface windows. In fact, lower and upper bounds were input through the table. Such inputs are translated into unification atoms and appended to the query window. The suspended constraint window shows part of the suspended constraints. Note that their forms are different from the original ones, since they have been transformed by the constraint solver.

Figure 4 shows the session just after the query window has received the last three statements which determine the value of $E$ to 100. indomain(R) is a built-in predicate which instantiates the argument to an element of the domain associated to the argument. These constraints are sufficient to determine the values of resistors and currents, which can be seen in respective positions. Now suppose that we need the circuit in which $I2 \leq 0.2$. Although this constraint is not satisfied at the current stage, it is sufficient to add the new constraint to the table as an upper bound of $I2$. Figure 5 shows the session right after this addtion. It is shown that a set of new values have been obtained owing to the backtracking mechanism.

## 3.2 Hypermedia: Systematizing and reviewing knowledge

### 3.2.1 Links

In a session, every knowledge sheet has a link icon in its label field. Figure 6 shows the layout of a sheet. A link icon indicates the place where links may exist and the menu of link operations is obtained by clicking this icon. For example, when one wants to connect two knowledge sheets, it is enough to select two sheets and indicate one as the starting node and the other as the terminal node.

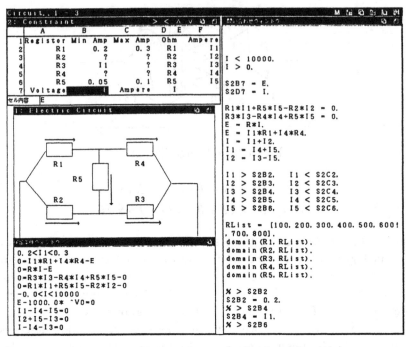

Figure 3: Session solving the Bridge Circuit(a)

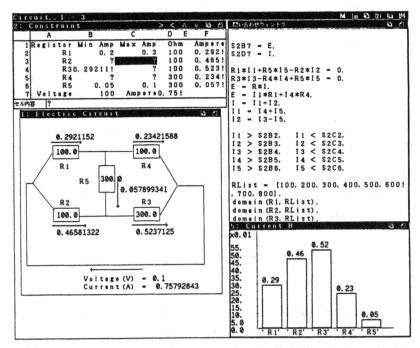

Figure 4: Session solving the Bridge Circuit(b)

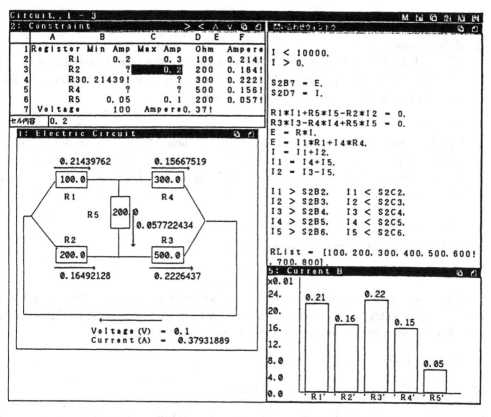

Figure 5: Session solving the Bridge Circuit(c)

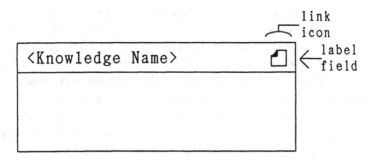

Figure 6: A Sheet

A link has the following features.

1. Bidirectional
   Although a link is established by specifying the two sheets as a starting node and a terminal, it works bidirectionally. Therefore, if there is a link between $K_1$ and $K_2$, we can reach from $K_1$ to $K_2$ and *vice versa*.

2. Multiple
   One knowledge sheet can have more than one link. When one tries to refer to connected knowledge by clicking a link icon, and there are several links, a menu listing all the destinations is presented. Each item in the list contains the following information:

   (a) Type: text, table, graph, drawing, image or menu

   (b) Display status: mapped or unmapped

   (c) Name: the name appearing on the label field

Furthermore, in a text sheet, a user can attach links to an entry. Such a link can point to another entry in the same text as well as an arbitrary knowledge sheet. Links established between entries support the following additional operations.

1. Exchanging the contents of entries

2. Copying the contents from one entry to another

Such operations can be used for selecting a desirable statement from predefined various statements and inserting it to an original text.

### 3.2.2  Dynamic Link

An entry with links in a text sheet behaves completely like part of the text. It moves together with the string it contains during editing. However, entries are managed separately from the text. A text with entries consists of the original text and entry definitions. Such management is advantageous when a text is a $\tau$ program and entries are used to attach comments to parts of the program text. Since the original text (a program) is not affected by entries, it can be safely compiled.

In some cases, it is desirable to embed entries with links directly in a program. Suppose that we want to dynamically change links attached to some part of the text. The easiest way to do that is to define the part to be an entry and to set there an object with links dynamically by a program. To achieve this it is necessary to embed links in a program.

We have introduced another type of entry called *a dynamic link* which is directly embedded in the text. A dynamic link can be created by indicating so when defining a link. An entry with a dynamic link behaves like an ordinary entries. It is intended to be used in a program text. A user should care about places to which a dynamic link is attached since it affects the original text. Currently an entry containing a string is safe to have a dynamic link and it is translated into a special term internally and safely compiled. When an entry variable corresponding to an entry in a text is instantiated to a string with a dynamic link, the string is displayed at the entry and the dynamic link is added to links that the entry already has. Once the dynamic link is added to the entry it behaves like an ordinary link. Therefore if it connects the entry with other knowledge a user can refer to it just by mouse operations.

We claimed that hypermedia and mechanized inference contribute to human problem solving. However, this brings up several questions. Are they just two independent tools? Where and how do logic programming and hypermedia meet? One promising solution to these questions is to handle links in a logic program. This enables dynamically reconfigurable hypermedia.

There may be several ways to handle links in a logic program. The way we took was just described above. Namely a dynamic link. It is equivalent to a string with links. Since a string is an ordinary data type that $\tau$ can handle, a dynamic link can be naturally introduced and it can be incorporated with other constructs of $\tau$.

Another possible way to handle links in a logic program is to see a link as a logical relation. Since a link is a binary relation between knowledge the idea is quite natural. Furthermore the idea can be easily extended to incorporate labeled links. Labeled links are an attempt to give meaningful key words to links so that a semantic structure can be immediately obtained from the network. Comparing to this approach, our approach can be called a non-labeling approach.

Labeling or non-labeling, which is better? Labeling approach seems attractive since it combines a link and logical relation naturally. However, we rejected this approach for the following reasons.

1. Success of the labeling approach depends on the set of words labeling links. An unsuitable set of words makes the system hard to use and hence the system becomes useless. However, as far as we know, there is no consensus about such a set of words. Nobody knows how many labels we need in what situation. We concluded that it was very dangerous to take this approach at such a premature stage.

2. The non-labeling approach is more flexible. It is so basic that it can simulate the labeling scheme.

### 3.2.3 Session browser

Usually a session includes many pieces of knowledge such as documents, histories of this task and idea sketches. They are mutually related and hence may be connected with each other. In such a situation, it is inevitable to grasp the whole structure of knowledge network in order to understand the various aspects of the problem to be handled. The session browser is a tool for reviewing that network. Figure 7 illustrates what it displays.

The network structure of knowledge can take an arbitrary form. The session browser displays an arbitrary network by converting it to the pseudo-tree structure illustrated in Figure 8. Given a network and an arbitrary node in it, the pseudo tree can be obtained by (1) labeling each node with the length of the shortest path from the give node, (2)

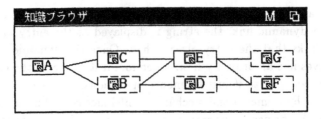

Figure 7: Session Browser

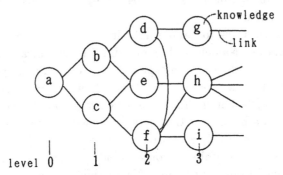

Figure 8: Pseudo Tree

displaying nodes in ascending order with respect to their labels. Pseudo tree has the following advantages. First, we can get several views of network by changing the root node. Second, by controlling the display depth (label number of observable nodes) we can review the network at various ranges.

Each node in a network graph gives information about its display status (mapped or unmapped), its name and its type. The following operations are achieved by direct manipulation of a node and a link by mouse.

- retrieval of knowledge

- removal of knowledge

- establishment of a new link between two pieces of knowledge

- removal of a link

- registration of the entire or part of a knowledge network which will be explained later

## 3.3  Powerful coexistence

A session is not only an environment for $\tau$ programming and execution, but also place to utilize Hypermedia. The ability to utilize both $\tau$ environment and Hypermedia enables a user to solve a problem with the help of mechanized inference while referring various kinds of knowledge such as documents describing background the task, graphs showing historical data and drawings illustrating ideas.

Figure 9 shows the two snapshots of the session for the management of the software development projects. A project is modelled as follows: (1) The entire software consists of several submodules. (2) designers and programmers are ranked according to their skills. (3) Productivity of a designer/programmer depends on his or her career, favorite languages and so on. The role of this session is (1) to confirm that the project has made progress as it is planned, (2) to make a report describing the current status and (3) to make an updated plan and estimate the cost of the reschedule if some delays have been found. In this task, various kinds of knowledge have to be utilized. They include schedules of the designers and the programmers, progress histories and reports, graphs analyzing costs and so on. They are mutually dependent, so that it is very dangerous to manage them separately.

However, owing to Hypermedia, the session can manage each piece of knowledge safely from its creation to its removal while keeping mutual relationship unchanged. The dependency graph can be displayed by the session browser if desired as shown in Figure 9 (a). Since Inference Engine enables to maintain logical relationships among an arbitrary set of entries, consistency among knowledge is also kept unchanged. Furthermore dynamic links controlled by $\tau$ programs enable to present appropriate references to related knowledge among a large amount of knowledge. Figure 9 (b) shows such a situation where one dynamic link (dynamic links are indicated by fat arrows) connects the progress summary to the list of sub-module progresses and the other the list to the explanation of the cause of the delay.

# 4    How Knowledge Processing Applications are Managed

In Knowledge Media Station, problem solving in a specific domain is done in a working environment called a session. Creation, saving, restoring and customization of more than one working environment is supported by *Knowledge Processor* so that the user can manage several problem solving processes in progress safely. The best way to explain Knowledge Processor is to explain what kinds of resources it manages.

## 4.1    Resources

Knowledge Processor manages four kinds of resources. These are sessions, tasks, knowledge and clusters.

**Session**  A session is a working environment utilizing Inference Engine and Hypermedia. A session can reside only in memory. By saving a session, we obtain a task.

**Task**  A task is a frozen session, which can be safely stored on a disk. A task keeps copies of all the knowledge used in a session. This is advantageous since once a session is

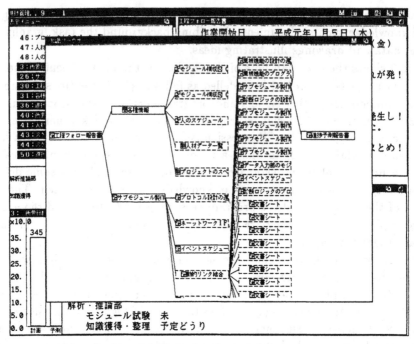

(a) Browsing knowledge

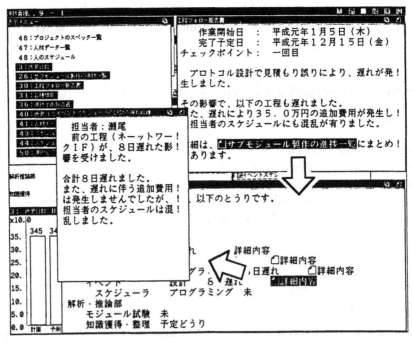

(b) Dynamic links

Figure 9: A Session for Managing Software Development Projects

frozen as a task its contents will never be affected by other sessions. A task also keeps the queries entered so far in a session with miscellaneous information such as window sizes and positions. Using such information, a session can be restored with the completely same appearance from a task. ¿From a task, arbitrary number of sessions can be generated. All these sessions have the same initial contents. Knowledge Media Station provides one special task called *a white task* which has nothing in it. A white task is used as the basis for making an entirely new task.

**Knowledge** Usually knowledge such as texts, tables, graphs, drawings, images and menus are encapsulated in a task. When a user wants to share some knowledge in one task with other, he can make them global so that they can be referred from any session. Such globalized knowledge is handled as *registered knowledge* by Knowledge Processor.

**Cluster** A cluster is a box which can keep the two kinds of resources above, tasks and knowledge. A cluster is used for organizing tasks and knowledge hierarchically.

## 4.2 Management of working environments

There are several advantages in saving and restoring more than one working environment:

- By modifying an original task and saving it, we can easily obtain customized tasks.

- Since when a task is opened it arranges everything automatically, it is comfortable even for users who were not involved in its making.

- Faithful restoration helps recall what was going and thus increases operation continuity.

- By opening several sessions from one task, we can easily extend works with different approaches in parallel.

- A user can work without fear of destroying other tasks.

Hypermedia can also keep tasks. Furthermore an entry can be connected with a task. Such a link is called *a task invocation link*. Following a task invocation link causes the opening of a session from the corresponding task. In fact, task invocation links add the command menu function to a text. The resultant text is more powerful and flexible than a menu in such respects that it allows a free text format, and command (task) invocation buttons can be inserted at arbitrary places.

These exentions of Hypermedia enables a user to keep almost all kinds of tasks related to a problem solving task and establish mutual relationship among tasks in an arbitrary form using links. This is powerful, especially when a problem is complicated and needs various kinds of tasks. This is also beneficial to those who want to understand a task.

In order to visualize various resources it may have, Knowledge Processor provides desktop facility, where resources are displayed as icons. In Figure 10, two styles of desktop are shown. Manipulations of resources such as opening/closing a session and reviewing knowledge in a session are all realized as icon and menu operations.

## 4.3  Knowledge Registration and Version Management

Figure 11 shows the structure of Hypermedia. Link manipulations are managed by Hypermedia manager. Links made in a session are stored in a task together with knowledge connected by them. In order to keep a task unchanged, it is not allowed to manipulate links from outside the task. When one needs to refer knowledge and links in a task different from the one keeping them, one should first register the knowledge. Knowledge registration is the operation that makes knowledge and links among them sharable. Registered knowledge and links are stored in knowledge database and link database, respectively, by Hypermedia manager. As shown in Figure 12, registered knowledge can be retrieved by specifying its name by any session, and knowledge connected with the registered knowledge by links can be referred to by tracing links.

When one modifies or updates knowledge and wants to keep old and new knowledge while sharing almost all properties such as name and links, the version problem arises. In Hypermedia, the version problem arises in registered knowledge, but not in knowledge encapsulated in a task. This is because a task shares nothing with other tasks. In fact, when a task is saved after modification of some knowledge in it, a completely new task is created.

When registered knowledge is modified and registered again with the same name, it is registered as a new version and links associated with the old version knowledge are extended to cover the new version. Figure 13 illustrates a simple case. Suppose that there are two pieces of registered knowledge, $A_1$ and $B_1$, and a link $l_1$. Let us assume that $B_1$ is modified to have a new link to $C_1$. Figure 13 illustrates what happens after the registration of $B_1$. The new version of $B$ is registered as $B_2$. $B_2$ can see $A_1$ and $C_1$ while $B_1$ can not see $C_1$. Note that $A_1$ can see both $B_1$ and $B_2$.

Although a destination menu is displayed when one piece of knowledge is connected with several pieces of knowledge, we can set default destination if destinations are all different versions of the same knowledge. Possible defaults are (1) fixed and (2) latest. In case of 'fixed', the knowledge with the same version as that of the source knowledge is retrieved. In Figure 13, if $A_1$ is the source, then $B_1$ is retrieved. In the case of 'latest', the latest version is retrieved.

## 4.4  Knowledge Browsers

In addition to the session browser, Knowledge Media Station provides two more browsers task browser and registered knowledge browser, each of which has a different view scope.

Task browser is a convenient browser which can review knowledge included in a task without opening a session, although task browser does not allow some operations which session browser allows. Given a task, it displays network graph (Figure 14) reflecting linking structure of knowledge included in the task.

Registered knowledge browser is a tool for reviewing registered knowledge. It has the

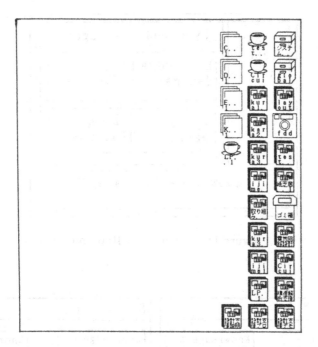

(a) Iconic Style

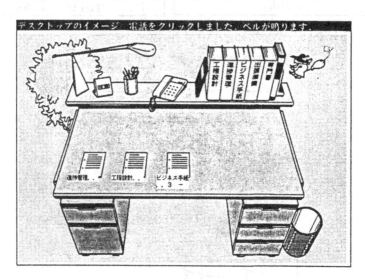

(b) Realistic Style

Figure 10: A Session for Managing Software Development Projects

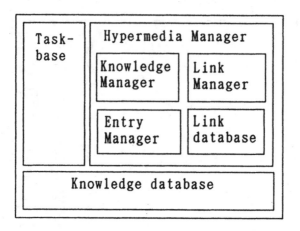

Figure 11: Structure of Hypermedia

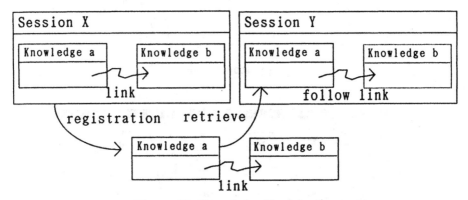

Figure 12: Knowledge Registration

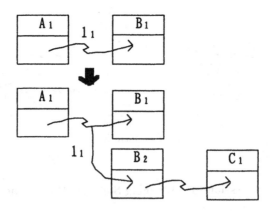

Figure 13: Version Management

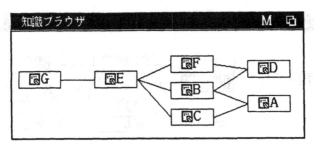

Figure 14: Task Browser

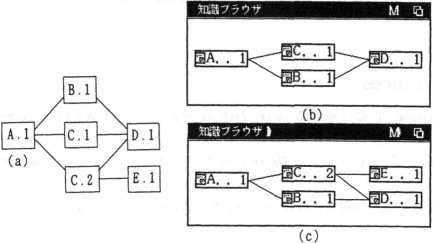

Figure 15: Registered Knowledge Browser

ability to provide several views according to versions of registered knowledge. Suppose that there is the knowledge network shown in Figure 15 (a). If we set default link to be fixed, then we have Figure 15 (b). And if latest, the browser displays Figure 15 (c). Registered knowledge browser is used mainly to grasp the network structure of registered knowledge and to search and retrieve specific knowledge. It can also be used to remove unnecessary knowledge.

When in a session registered knowledge is referred to, registered knowledge is automaitically copied into a session. Such knowledge is displayed differently by session browser. In Figure 16, $C$, $D$ and $E$ are examples of such knowledge. Manipulation of nodes corresponding to registered knowledge is also possible in the same way as ordinary nodes. However its effect is only valid in a session.

# 5 Current Status

Knowledge Media Station was developed on MELCOM PSI-II, a Prolog machine originally developed at Institute for New Generation Computer Technology. It is now running on it, and several applications have already been developed. These include user consultation system for complicated software, design assistant of architecture and diagnosis system for electric devices.

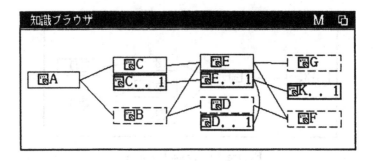

Figure 16: Viewing registered knowledge by Session-browser

# References

[Chikayama]   T. Chikayama, *Unique Features of ESP*, Proc. FGCS'84, 1984, pp. 292-298.

[Colmerauer]   A. Colmerauer, *Opening the Prolog III Universe*, Byte, Aug. 1987, pp. 171-176.

[Conklin]   J. Conklin, *Hypertext: An Introduction and Survey*, Computer, Sep. , 1987.

[Dincbas(a)]   M. Dincbas, *Constraints, Logic Programming and Deductive Databases*, Proc. France-Japan Artificial Intelligence and Computer Science Symposium, 1986.

[Dincbas(b)]   M. Dincbas et al. , *The Constraint Logic Programming Language CHIP*, Proc. FGCS'88, 1988, pp. 693-702.

[Emden(a)]   M. H. van Emden, *Logic as an Interaction Language*, Proc. of 5th Conf. Canadian Soc. for Computational Studies in Intelligence, 1984.

[Emden(b)]   M. H. van Emden, M. Ohki, A. Takeuchi, *Spreadsheet with Incremental Queries as a User Interface for Logic Programming*, New Generation Computing, Vol.4, No.3, 1985, pp. 287-304.

[Emden(c)]   M. H. van Emden, *Project 4.5*, Technical Report LP-6, Dept. of Computer Science, University of Victoria, 1988.

[Kay]       A. Kay, A. Goldberg, *Personal Dynamic Media*, Computer, Mar. , 1977, pp. 31-41.

[Jaffar]    J. Jaffar, J-L. Lassez, *Constraint Logic Programming*, Proc. POPL-87, 1987.

[Mukai]     K. Mukai, *Unification over Complex Indeterminates in Prolog*, Proc. the Logic Programming Conf. , 1985, pp. 271-278.

[Ohki]      M. Ohki, A. Takeuchi, K. Furukawa, *A Framework for Interactive Problem Solving based on Interactive Query Revision*, Proc. Logic Programming Conf. , 1986.

[Sergot]    M. Sergot, *A Query-The-User for Logic Programming*, Proc. the European Conf. on Integrated Computing Systems, Degano and Sandewall (eds.), North Holland, 1983.

[Stefik]    M. Stefik, *The Next Knowledge Medium*, The AI Magazine, Vol.7, No.1, 1986, pp. 34-46.

[Vasey]     P. Vasey, *Qualified Answer and Their Application to Transformation*, Proc. 3rd Int. Conf. on Logic Programming, 1986, pp. 425-432.

# cu-Prolog and its Application to a JPSG Parser

TSUDA, Hiroshi
HASIDA, Kôiti
Institute for New Generation Computer Technology (ICOT)
1-4-28 Mita, Minato-ku, Tokyo 108, Japan

SIRAI, Hidetosi
Chukyo University
101-2 Yagoto honcho, Showa-ku, Nagoya 466, Japan

### Abstract

This paper presents a symbolic constraint logic programming language *cu-Prolog*, and shows a simple Japanese parser based on JPSG (Japanese Phrase Structure Grammar) as a suitable application.

cu-Prolog employs *constraint unification* instead of the ordinary unification, and handles symbolic constraints in terms of user-defined predicates. The program clause of cu-Prolog is an expansion of Horn clause and is called *Constraint Added Horn Clause (CAHC)*. The constraint satisfaction mechanism of cu-Prolog is based on the unfold/fold transformation of logic programming.

Unlike most conventional CLP systems, cu-Prolog deals with constraints on the Herbrand universe to describe constraints on symbolic and combinatorial objects. In the application of natural language processing or of many AI problems, this kind of constraint is more important than those on numerical or boolean objects. In comparison with Prolog, cu-Prolog also has richer descriptive power, and is more declarative. In particular, cu-Prolog enables a natural implementation of unification-based grammar formalisms such as GPSG, HPSG, and JPSG.

## 1 Introduction

Prolog is frequently used in implementing natural language parsers or generators based on unification-based grammars[12] such as GPSG[5] and HPSG[11]. This is because Prolog is also based on unification, and therefore has a declarative feature. One important characteristic of unification-based grammar is also a declarative grammar formalization.

However, Prolog is not sufficient for handling declarative constraints because it executes every part of a program sequentially (left to right for AND process, and top to bottom for OR process) and because every variable of Prolog can be instantiated to any object. Constraints in unification-based grammar are therefore treated not declaratively but procedurally.

We developed a new constraint logic programming language *cu-Prolog* [15] that is free from the above defects of Prolog. In cu-Prolog, constraints in terms of user-defined predicates can be directly added to a program clause (Constraint Added Horn Clause) by using *Constraint Unification* [8] [1] instead of the ordinary unification. This paper outlines cu-Prolog and explains how it is suitable for implementing unification-based grammar formalisms showing a simple Japanese parser based on JPSG (Japanese Phrase Structure Grammar) [6].

## 2 cu-Prolog

### 2.1 Constraint Added Horn Clause (CAHC)

The following are the program clauses of cu-Prolog which we call *Constraint Added Horn Clauses* (CAHCs):

---

[1] The name cu-Prolog comes from an abbreviation of Constraint Unification. In these earlier papers, "constraint unification" was called "conditioned unification."

**[Def] 1 (CAHC)** <u>*Constraint Added Horn Clause*</u> *consists of the following three types of clause:*

$$
\overbrace{H}^{\text{head}} \quad ; \quad \overbrace{C_1, C_2, \ldots, C_m}^{\text{constraint}}. \qquad \text{(fact)}
$$

$$
H \quad :- \quad \overbrace{B_1, B_2, \ldots, B_n}^{\text{body}}; \overbrace{C_1, C_2, \ldots, C_m}^{\text{constraint}}. \qquad \text{(rule)}
$$

$$
:- \quad B_1, B_2, \ldots, B_n; C_1, C_2, \ldots, C_m. \qquad \text{(question)}
$$

*$H$ is called the* head *and $B_1, B_2, \ldots, B_n$ is called the* body.
*$C_1, C_2, \ldots, C_m$ constitutes a set of constraints (or null) on the variables occurring in the clause. The constraint must be, in the current implementation, a canonical form called* **modular**, *which is described later.*

Seen from declarative semantics, these three clauses are equivalent to the following three Prolog clauses. The Prolog clause is a special case of CAHC.

$$
H \quad :- \quad C_1, C_2, \ldots, C_m.
$$

$$
H \quad :- \quad B_1, B_2, \ldots, B_n, C_1, C_2, \ldots, C_m.
$$

$$
:- \quad B_1, B_2, \ldots, B_n, C_1, C_2, \ldots, C_m.
$$

## 2.2  Canonical form of the constraint

A constraint of CAHC must be satisfiable. In the current implementation, it is of the conventional canonical form, called *modular*.

**[Def] 2 (modular)** *A set of atomic formulas $C_1, C_2, \ldots, C_m$ is* <u>*modular*</u> *when*

1. *every argument of $C_i$ is variable ($1 \leq i \leq m$),*

2. *no variable occurs in two distinct places, and*

3. *the predicates occurring in $C_i$ are modularly defined ($1 \leq i \leq m$).*

The predicate occurring in the constraint of CAHC is an ordinary Prolog predicate of the following form.

**[Def] 3 (modularly defined)** *Predicate p is* <u>*modularly defined*</u>, *when the body of its every definition clause is modular or empty.*

For example, `member` and `append` are modularly defined. Then,

```
member(X,Y),member(U,V) is modular,
member(X,Y),member(Y,Z) is not modular, and
append(X,Y,[a,b,c,d]) is not modular.
```

## 2.3  Basic mechanism of cu-Prolog

cu-Prolog employs *constraint unification* [8] which is the normal unification plus constraint transformation (normalization).

In natural deduction format, the inference rule of cu-Prolog is as follows:

$$
\frac{\overbrace{A, \mathbf{K}; \mathbf{C}.}^{\text{goal}} \quad \overbrace{A' :- \mathbf{L}; \mathbf{D}.}^{\text{program}} \quad \overbrace{\theta = mgu(A, A')}^{\text{substitution}} \quad \overbrace{\mathbf{C}' = mf(\mathbf{C}\theta, \mathbf{D}\theta)}^{\text{constraint transformation}}}{\underbrace{\mathbf{L}\theta, \mathbf{K}\theta; \mathbf{C}'.}_{\text{new goal}}}
$$

$A$ and $A'$ are atomic formulas. $\mathbf{K}$, $\mathbf{L}$, $\mathbf{C}$, $\mathbf{D}$, and $\mathbf{C}'$ are sequences of atomic formulas. $mgu(A, A')$ is the most general unifier between $A$ and $A'$.

$mf(C)$ is a modular constraint that is equivalent to C. If C is inconsistent, the application of the above inference rule fails because $mf(C)$ does not exist. When C is divided into equivalent classes in terms of the variables as

$$C = C_1 + \cdots + C_n$$

then,

$$mf(C) = mf(C_1), \ldots, mf(C_n).$$

For example,

$$mf(\texttt{member}(X, [a, b, c]), \texttt{member}(X, [b, c, d]), \texttt{append}(U, V))$$

returns a new constraint $\texttt{c0(X)},\texttt{append(U,V)}$, where the definition of c0 is

```
c0(b).
c0(c).
```

and

$$mf(\texttt{member}(X, [a, b, c]), \texttt{member}(X, [k, 1, m]))$$

is not defined.

The constraint transformation mechanism is based on the unfold/fold transformation [13]. In the following discussion, we only consider the transformation of each equivalent class.

## 2.4   Constraint Transformation

This subsection explains the mechanism of the constraint transformation of cu-Prolog.

Let $T$ be a set of definition clauses of modularly defined predicates, $\Sigma$ be a set of constraints $\{C_1, \ldots, C_n\}$, $x_1, \ldots, x_m$ be the variables occurring in $\Sigma$, and p be a new m-ary predicate.

$\mathcal{P}_i$ and $\mathcal{D}_i$ are sets of clauses, and initially,

$$\mathcal{D}_0 = \{\texttt{p}(x_1, \ldots, x_m) : -C_1, \ldots, C_n.\}$$

$$\mathcal{P}_0 = T \cup \mathcal{D}_0$$

$mf(\Sigma)$ returns $\texttt{p}(x_1, \ldots, x_m)$, if and only if there exists a sequence of sets of program clauses

$$\mathcal{P}_0, \mathcal{P}_1, \ldots, \mathcal{P}_l$$

and every predicate in $\mathcal{P}_l$ is modularly defined.

In the above sequence, $\mathcal{P}_{i+1}$ is derived from $\mathcal{P}_i$ $(0 \le i < l)$ by one of the following three operations.

1. *unfolding*

   Select one clause $\zeta$ from $\mathcal{P}_i$ and one atomic formula $A$ from the body of $\zeta$. Let $\zeta_1, \ldots, \zeta_k$ be all the clauses in $\mathcal{P}_i$ whose heads unify with $A$, and $\zeta'_j$ be the result of resolving $\zeta$ with $\zeta_j$ upon $A$ $(j = 1, \ldots, k)$.
   [2]

   Then, $\mathcal{D}_{i+1} = \mathcal{D}_i$ and

   $$\mathcal{P}_{i+1} = \mathcal{P}_i - \zeta + \zeta'_1 + \cdots + \zeta'_k.$$

2. *folding*

   Let $\zeta (= A : -\mathbf{K}, \mathbf{L}.)$ be a clause in $\mathcal{P}_i$, and $\xi (= B : -\mathbf{K}'.)$ be a clause in $\mathcal{D}_i$, and $\theta$ be the substitution that meets the following conditions:

   (a) $\mathbf{K} = \mathbf{K}'\theta$, [3]

---

[2] The result of resolving $\xi (= H : -A, \mathbf{R}.)$ with $\zeta (A' : -\mathbf{B}.)$ upon $A$ is

$$H\theta : -\mathbf{B}\theta, \mathbf{R}\theta.$$

Here, $\theta$ is the most general unifier between $A$ and $A'$.

[3] For example, the most general unifier between two sets of atomic formulas $\{\texttt{f(a,b,X)}, \texttt{g(Y,c)}\}$ and $\{\texttt{g(d,U)}, \texttt{f(V,b,W)}\}$ is $\{\texttt{U/c}, \texttt{V/a}, \texttt{X/W}, \texttt{Y/d}\}$.

(b) **K** and **L** have no common variables, and

(c) $\zeta \notin \mathcal{D}_i$.

Then, $\mathcal{D}_{i+1} = \mathcal{D}_i$ and

$$\mathcal{P}_{i+1} = \mathcal{P}_i - \zeta + \{A : -B\theta, \mathbf{L}\}.$$

3. *definition*

Let $\zeta (= A : -\mathbf{K}, \mathbf{L}.)$ be a clause in $\mathcal{P}_i$, where **K** is one of the least non-modular atomic formulas [4] in the body of $\zeta$ and contains variables $x_1, \ldots, x_k$. Let p be a new k-ary predicate of the following definition:

$$\xi = p(x_1, \ldots, x_k) : -\mathbf{K}.$$

Then,

$$\mathcal{D}_{i+1} = \mathcal{D}_i + \xi$$
$$\mathcal{P}_{i+1} = \mathcal{P}_i - \zeta + \xi + \{A : -p(x_1, \ldots, x_k), \mathbf{L}.\}$$

The above three transformations preserve the semantics of programs as the least model semantics [13].

**Example.**

The following example shows a transformation of

$$\mathrm{member}(A, Z), \mathrm{append}(X, Y, Z).$$

Here, $\mathcal{T}$ is { T1,T2,T3,T4 }, where

```
T1 = member(X,[X|Y]).
T2 = member(X,[Y|Z]):-member(X,Z).
T3 = append([],X,X).
T4 = append([A|X],Y,[A|Z]):-append(X,Y,Z).
```

and

$$\Sigma = \{\mathrm{member}(A, Z), \mathrm{append}(X, Y, Z)\}$$

Step 1: A new predicate p1 is defined as

```
D1 = p1(A,X,Y,Z):-member(A,Z),append(X,Y,Z).
```

and

$$\mathcal{D}_0 = \{D1\} \quad \mathcal{P}_0 = \{T1, T2, T3, T4, D1\}$$

Step 2: Unfolding the first formula of D1's body (member(A,Z)), we get

```
T5 = p1(A,X,Y,[A|Z]):-append(X,Y,[A|Z]).
T6 = p1(A,X,Y,[B|Z]):-member(A,Z),append(X,Y,[B|Z]).
```

Then,

$$\mathcal{D}_1 = \mathcal{D}_0 \quad \mathcal{P}_1 = \{T1, T2, T3, T4, T5, T6\}$$

Step 3: By definition (p2 and p3 are new predicates) ,

```
T5' = p1(A,X,Y,[A|Z]):-p2(X,Y,A,Z).
T6' = p1(A,X,Y,[B|Z]):-p3(A,Z,X,Y,B).
D2  = p2(X,Y,A,Z):-append(X,Y,[A|Z]).
D3  = p3(A,Z,X,Y,B):-member(A,Z),append(X,Y,[B|Z]).
```

and

$$\mathcal{D}_2 = \{D1, D2, D3\} \quad \mathcal{P}_2 = \{T1, T2, T3, T4, T5', T6', D2, D3\}$$

Step 4: By unfolding D2,

```
T7 = p2([],[A|Z],A,Z).
T8 = p2([B|X],Y,A,Z):-append(X,Y,Z).
```

---

[4] For example, the least non-modular atomic formula of {p0(X,[a,b],Y),p2(U,V),p3(Y,Z)} is {p0(X,[a,b],Y),p3(Y,Z)}.

These clauses comprise a modular definition of p2. Now we have

$$\mathcal{D}_3 = \mathcal{D}_2 \quad \mathcal{P}_3 = \{\text{T1}, \text{T2}, \text{T3}, \text{T4}, \text{T5}', \text{T6}', \text{T7}, \text{T8}, \text{D3}\}$$

<u>Step 5:</u> Unfold the second formula of D3's body (append(X,Y,[B|Z]) ), and we have

```
T9  = p3(A,Z,□,[B|Z],B):-member(A,Z).
T10 = p3(A,Z,[B|X],Y,B):-member(A,Z),append(X,Y,Z).
```

Then,

$$\mathcal{D}_4 = \mathcal{D}_3 \quad \mathcal{P}_4 = \{\text{T1}, \text{T2}, \text{T3}, \text{T4}, \text{T5}', \text{T6}', \text{T7}, \text{T8}, \text{T9}, \text{T10}\}.$$

<u>Step 6:</u> Folding T10 by D1 generates

```
T10' = p3(A,Z,[B|X],Y,B):-p1(A,X,Y,Z).
```

Accordingly,

$$\mathcal{D}_5 = \mathcal{D}_4 \quad \mathcal{P}_5 = \{\text{T1}, \text{T2}, \text{T3}, \text{T4}, \text{T5}', \text{T6}', \text{T7}, \text{T8}, \text{T9}, \text{T10}'\}.$$

Every predicate in $\mathcal{P}_5$ is modularly defined. As a result, member(A,Z),append(X,Y,Z) has been transformed into a modular constraint p1(A,X,Y,Z) preserving equivalence, and the following new clauses have been defined.

$$\{\text{T5}', \text{T6}', \text{T7}, \text{T8}, \text{T9}, \text{T10}'\}.$$

## 2.5 Heuristics

Efficient constraint transformation calls for some heuristics. In the current implementation, one target atomic formula of the unfold transformation is selected in the following order of precedence:

1. An atomic formula of the finite predicate.

2. An atomic formula that has constants or □ (nil) in its arguments.

3. An atomic formula that has ground lists in its argument.

4. An atomic formula that has plural dependent variables.

5. The latest atomic formula.

Here,

**[Def] 4 (finite predicate)** *A predicate p is <u>finite</u>, when the body of its every definition clause is*

    *1. nil, or*

    *2. composed of finite predicates*

The above selection rule is effective in the following examples.

**Example 1** *Transformation of* m(X,Y),p(X) *, where*

```
m(X,□).
m([A|B],X) :- m(B,X).
p(□).
p([a]).
```

*If we always select the leftmost atomic formula, that causes an infinite loop because* m( ) *is always unfolded. By the above rule, however, because predicate* m *is infinite and* p *is finite,* p(X) *is unfolded at first, and the transformation soon terminates.*

```
_member(X,[X|Y]).
_member(X,[Y|Z]):-member(X,Z).
_append([],X,X).
_append([A|X],Y,[A|Z]):-append(X,Y,Z).

_@ member(X,[ga,no,wo,ni,kara,made,sae]),member(X,[to,he,ni,kara,sura,ga]).

solution = c0(X)
c3(ni).
c3(kara).
c0(ga).
c0(X0):-c3(X0).
CPU time = 0.017 sec

_@ member(A,Z),append(X,Y,Z).

solution = c14(A, Z, X, Y)
c15(X2, X2, X0, Y1, Y3):-append(X0, Y1, Y3).
c15(X2, Y3, X0, Y1, Z4):-c14(X2, Z4, X0, Y1).
c14(A0, X1,  [], X1):-member(A0, X1).
c14(A0, [A1|Z4], [A1|X2], Y3):-c15(A0, A1, X2, Y3, Z4).
CPU time = 0.000 sec
```

The first four lines are definitions of member and append. The lines that begin with "@" are the user's input atomic formulas (constraints). cu-Prolog returns the constraint (c0(X) and c14(A,Z,X,Y)) and its definition, which is equivalent to the input constraint. (CPU time is counted in 60ths of a second on SYMMETRY).

Figure 1: Demonstration of the constraint transformation

**Example 2** *Transformation of*

$$\text{fuse}(A, B, C), \text{fuse}(C, D, E), \text{fuse}(E, F, G)$$

*where*

```
fuse([],[],[]).
fuse([A|X],Y,[A|Z]):-fuse(X,Y,Z).
fuse(X,[A|Y],[A|Z]):-fuse(X,Y,Z).
fuse([A|X],[A|Y],Z):-fuse(X,Y,Z).
```

*The leftmost or rightmost selection causes an infinite loop. As* fuse(C,D,E) *alone has two dependent variables (C and E), it is selected by selection rule 4 and the transformation succeeds.*

## 2.6  Implementation

The source code of cu-Prolog is, at present (Ver 2.3), composed of 5,000 lines of language C on UNIX and MS-DOS.

Figure 1 demonstrates constraint transformation of cu-Prolog.

## 2.7  Comparison with related work

This subsection compares cu-Prolog with conventional approaches in logic programming.

### 2.7.1  Prolog

In Prolog, constraints are inserted in fixed places of the goal and processed sequentially. Prolog is not suitable for describing declarative constraints, and the execution may be inefficient when constraints are inserted in suitable places. On the contrary, in cu-Prolog, constraints are treated as such.

### 2.7.2  Bind-hook

As constraints are rewritten at every unification, cu-Prolog also has more powerful descriptive ability than the bind-hook technique. For example, **freeze** in Prolog II[4] can impose constraints on one variable, so that when the variable is instantiated with ground term, the constraints are executed as a part of the Prolog goal. Freeze has, however, two disadvantages. First, freeze cannot impose a constraint on plural variables at one time. For example, the following CAHC is not expressed by freeze.

$$f(X), g(Y, Z); append(X, Y, Z).$$

Second, since the contradiction between constraints is not detected until the variable is instantiated, there is a possibility of useless computation in the case of constraint deadlocking. For example, even after executing freeze(X,member(X,[a,b])) and freeze(Y,member(Y,[c,d])), X and Y are unifiable without evaluating the constraints. In cu-Prolog, f(X);member(X,[a,b]) [5] does not unify with f(Y);member(Y,[c,d]).

### 2.7.3 Constraint Logic Programming

Most of the constraint logic programming languages (CLP(R) [9], PrologIII, and so on) deal with constraints in terms of algebraic equations, constraints on numerical domains, such as those of real numbers and other things. They use an algebraic equation solver (for example, Gröbner bases) for the constraint solver.

However, in the problems arising in Artificial Intelligence, constraints on symbolic or combinatorial objects are far more important than those about numerical objects. To describe such kinds of constraint, cu-Prolog handles constraints on the Herbrand universe in terms of a sequence of atomic formulas with user-defined Prolog predicates, employing a constraint solver based on the unfold/fold transformation of logic programming. Strictly speaking, cu-Prolog does not conform to the framework of CLP(X), because the Horn clause does not have a canonical form and is not decidable. However, cu-Prolog fits well with the framework of the program transformation or partial evaluation.

## 3 A JPSG parser

As an application of cu-Prolog, a natural language parser based on the unification-based grammar has been considered first of all. Since constraints can be added directly to the program clauses that represent lexical entries or phrase structure rules, the grammar is implemented more naturally and declaratively than in normal Prolog. Here we describe a simple Japanese parser based on JPSG in cu-Prolog. CAHC plays an important role in two respects.

### 3.1 Encoding ambiguity as constraint

First, CAHC is used in the lexicon of homonyms or polysemic words. For example, the Japanese noun "hasi" has three meanings: bridge, chopsticks, or an edge. This polysemic word can be subsumed in the following single lexical entry.

$$lexicon([hasi|X], X, [\ldots sem(SEM)]); hasi\_sem(SEM).$$

where hasi_sem is defined as follows.

```
hasi_sem(bridge).
hasi_sem(chopsticks).
hasi_sem(edge).
```

The value of the semantic feature is a variable (SEM), and the constraint on SEM is hasi_sem(SEM). Note that predicate hasi_sem is modularly defined. This kind of ambiguity in the lexicon will be dissolved when other constraints are imposed on the variable in the subsequent parsing process. Without CAHC, such a lexical entry is divided into separate program clauses and the parsing process may be inefficient. Japanese has such ambiguity also in conjugation, postpositions, and so on. They can be treated in the same manner.

---

[5] member(X,[a,b]) is not modular, but is equivalent to p1(X) ,where

$$p1(a). \quad p1(b).$$

## 3.2 Encoding phrase structure rule as constraint

Second, a phrase structure rule is described naturally with CAHC. In JPSG [6], the FFP(FOOT Feature Principle) is:

The value of a FOOT feature of the mother unifies with the union of those of her daughters.

This principle is embedded in a phrase structure rule as follows:

$$\text{psr}([\text{slash}(\text{MS})], [\text{slash}(\text{LDS})], [\text{slash}(\text{RDS})]); \text{union}(\text{LDS}, \text{RDS}, \text{MS}).$$

However, this cannot be described in this manner in Prolog: either psr($\cdots$) or union($\cdots$) is always executed before the other.

## 3.3 Example of JPSG parser

Figure 2 gives a simple demonstration of the JPSG parser, and Figure 3 shows an example of treating ambiguity as constraint. The current parser treats a few features and has a small lexicon. However, the expansion is straightforward. It parses sentences of about ten to twenty words a second on SYMMETRY.

Since JPSG is a declarative grammar formalism and cu-Prolog describes JPSG as such, the parser can employ parsing algorithms independently. In the current implementation, we simply adopt the left corner parsing algorithm [1].

```
_:-p([ken,ga,naomi,wo,ai,suru]).

v[syusi]:[love,ken,naomi]---[suff_p]
|
|--v[vs2]:[love,ken,naomi]---[subcat_p]
|  |
|  |--p[ga]:ken---[adjacent_p]
|  |  |
|  |  |--n[n]:ken---[ken]
|  |  |
|  |  |__p[ga, AJA{n[n]}]:ken---[ga]
|  |
|  |__v[vs2, SC{p[ga]}]:[love,ken,naomi]---[subcat_p]
|     |
|     |--p[wo]:naomi---[adjacent_p]
|     |  |
|     |  |--n[n]:naomi---[naomi]
|     |  |
|     |  |__p[wo, AJA{n[n]}]:naomi---[wo]
|     |
|     |__v[vs2, SC{p[wo], p[ga]}]:[love,ken,naomi]---[ai]
|
|__v[syusi, AJA{v[vs2]}]:[love,ken,naomi]---[suru]
cat      cat(v, syusi, [], [], [], [love,ken,naomi])
cond     nil
True.
CPU time = 0.067 sec
```

The first line is a user's input. "Ken ga Naomi wo ai suru" means "Ken loves Naomi."

Then the parser draws a parse tree and returns the category and constraint of the top node. In this example, the constraint is nil because the sentence is not ambiguous.

Figure 2: An example of our JPSG parser

# 4 Final Remarks

Further study of cu-Prolog has many prospects. For example, to expand the descriptive ability of constraints, a negative operator or universal quantifier may be added. The constraint transformation mechanism should

```
_:-p([ken,ga,ai,suru]).

v[Form_675, AJN{Adj_677}, SC{SubCat_679}]:SEM_681---[suff_p]
 |
 |--v[vs2, SC{p[wo]}]:[love,ken,Obj0_415]---[subcat_p]
 |  |
 |  |--p[ga]:ken---[adjacent_p]
 |  |  |
 |  |  |--n[n]:ken---[ken]
 |  |  |
 |  |  |__p[ga, AJA{n[n]}]:ken---[ga]
 |  |
 |  |__v[vs2, SC{p[ga], p[wo]}]:[love,ken,Obj0_415]---[ai]
 |
 |__v[Form_675, AJA{v[vs2,SC{p[wo]}]}, AJN{Adj_677}, SC{SubCat_679}]:SEM_681---[suru]
cat      cat(v, Form_675, [], Adj_677, SubCat_679, SEM_681)
cond     c7(Form_675, SubCat_679, Obj0_415, Adj_677, SEM_681)
True.
CPU time = 0.050 sec

_:-c7(F,SC,_,A,SEM).
 F = syusi  SC = [cat(p, wo, [], [], [], Obj00_30]  A = []  SEM = [love,ken,Obj00_30]
 F = rentai  SC = []  A = [cat(n, n, [], [], [], inst(Obj00_38, Type3_36))]
 SEM = inst(Obj00_38, [and,Type3_36,[love,ken,Obj00_38]])
no.
CPU time = 0.017 sec
```

This is a parse tree of "Ken ga ai suru" that has two meanings: "Ken loves (someone)" or "(someone) whom Ken loves".
The ambiguity is shown in the two solutions of the constraint c7(F,SC,_,A,SEM).

Figure 3: An example of an ambiguous sentence

be more powerful in proportion to the expansion of the canonical form of constraints. We are revising the constraint transformation into a more complete one by using OLDT [14] resolution.

Current cu-Prolog deals only with the conjunction of constraints, but some linguistic phenomenon are explained as a preference between disjunctive constraints, such as the interaction between syntactic and semantic constraints in [10]. Considering the constraint hierarchy [3], such constraints will be treated in the framework of cu-Prolog.

Constraint-based partial aspects of Situation Semantics [2] are naturally implemented in an extended version of cu-Prolog [7]. By regarding a parser program as a set of constraints and the parsing process as the constraint transformation, syntactic as well as semantic ambiguity can be treated at one time.

For practical applications of AI in general and natural language processing in particular, one needs a mechanism for carrying out computation partially, instead of totally as described above, where constraint transformation halts only when the constraint in question is entirely transformed into the canonical form. So the most difficult problem one must tackle concerns itself with heuristics about how to control computation.

### Acknowledgments

This study owes much to the discussion with our colleagues in the JPSG Working Group (Chairman: Prof. GUNJI, Takao) at ICOT, Prof. YAMADA, Hisao, and Mr. ONO, Yoshihiko. The implementation of cu-Prolog was financially supported by ICOT.

## References

[1] A. V. Aho and J. D. Ullman. *The Theory of Parsing, Translation, and Compiling, Volume 1: Parsing.* Prentice-Hall, 1972.

[2] Jon Barwise and John Perry. *Situation and Attitudes.* MIT Press, Cambridge, Mass, 1983.

[3] Alan Borning, Michael Maher, Amy Martindale, and Molly Wilson. Constraint Hierarchies and Logic Programming. In *Proc. of 6th International Conference of Logic Programming*, pages 149–164, 1989.

[4] A. Colmerauer. Prolog II Reference Manual and Theoretical Model. Technical report, ERACRANS 363, Groupe d'Intelligence Artificielle, Universite d'Aix-Marseille II, October 1982.

[5] Gerald Gazdar, Ewan Klein, Geoffrey K. Pullum, and Ivan A. Sag. *Generalized Phrase Structure Grammar*. Basil Blackwell, England:Oxford, 1985.

[6] Takao GUNJI. *Japanese Phrase Structure Grammar*. Reidel, Dordrecht, 1986.

[7] Kôiti HASIDA. A Constraint-Based View of Language. Presented at *Workshop on Situation Theory and its Application*, 1989.

[8] Kôiti HASIDA and Hidetosi SIRAI. Jyokentsuki Tan'itsu-ka (Conditioned Unification). *Computer Software*, 3(4):28–38, 1986. (in Japanese).

[9] Joxan Jaffar and Jean Louis Lassez. Constraint Logic Programming. In *Proceedings of the 14th ACM POPL Conference*, pages 111–119, Munich, 1987.

[10] Mitchell P. Marcus. *A Theory of Syntactic Recognition for Natural Language*. MIT Press, Cambridge:Mass, 1980.

[11] Carl Pollard and Ivan A. Sag. *Information-Based Syntax and Semantics, Vol.1 Fundamentals*. CSLI Lecture Notes Series No.13. Stanford:CSLI, 1987.

[12] Stuart M. Shieber. *An Introduction to Unification-Based Approach to Grammar*. CSLI Lecture Notes Series No.4. Stanford:CSLI, 1986.

[13] Hisao TAMAKI and Taisuke SATO. UNFOLD/FOLD Transformation of Logic Programs. In *Proc. of Second International Conference on Logic Programming*, pages 127–137, 1983.

[14] Hisao TAMAKI and Taisuke SATO. OLD Resolution with Tabulation. In *Proc. of Third International Conference on Logic Programming*, pages 84–98, 1986.

[15] Hiroshi TSUDA, Kôiti HASIDA, and Hidetosi SIRAI. JPSG Parser on Constraint Logic Programming. In *Proc. of 4th ACL European Chapter*, pages 95–102, 1989.

# Table-Driven Bottom Up Parser in Prolog

Naoyoshi Tamura

Yokohama National University

156 Tokiwadai, Hodogayaku, Yokohama 240, Japan

Hiroaki Numazaki      Hozumi Tanaka

Tokyo Institute of Technology

2-12-1 Oookayama, Meguro 152, Japan

### Abstract

Various improvements have been made to the Bottom Up Parser in Prolog (BUP for short), such as speed up of processing time, describability for Extraposition Grammars and idioms and so on.

In this paper, we present another speed up method without spoiling these assets. The original BUP has no particular mechanism to choose one production rule deterministically; however, in our method the parser can restrain the nondeterminism by means of an action table and a lookahead. The principle of our methods is based on the correspondence between BUP and the LC(1) parser. The LC(1) parser can deterministically parse sentences which belong to a class of context free language called LC(1). We apply the parsing method for LC(1) to general context free grammars. The nondeterminism caused by the extension can be managed through the backtracking in the same way as the original BUP. We also present an implementation and experimental results from a practical-sized grammar with 560 production rules.

## 1   Introduction

Many speed up techniques [1] have been developed for BUP (Bottom Up Parser in Prolog) since Matsumoto and others presented BUP [2]. Moreover many improvements for BUP have been made, such as the describability by XG (Extraposition Grammars)[3], efficiency by TRIE structured dictionary and applicability to idiomatic phrases[4], and they are gathered into the LangLAB as a natural language processing environment[5]. Without spoiling these assets, we present in this paper a new speed up technique based on the LC(1) parser.

It is well known that there are some classes in the context free language, $LL(k)$, $LR(k)$ and $LC(k)$, for which deterministic parsing methods are proposed, respectively. Applying those parsing methods to context free grammars, parsing actions generally become nondeterministic. However, not all phases in the methods are nondeterministic, that is, there are some phases in which the parser can determine the next action. Our method is based on the LC(1) parser, which is appled to BUP to decrease the ambiguity (nondeterminism).

LR($k$)-based parsers are most efficient because they leave applicable productions as a closure which is a parsing state. In such parsers, [6], which have the graph-structured stack, are said to be the fastest methods. The LR parser is completely controlled with a lookahead (string), an action table and a stack, and the table is built only from productions (syntax rules) so users must write productions for each idiomatic expression. And the extraposition grammars [7], which are useful to write rules for relational pronoun phrases, are hard to describe. Although our method may not accomplish such efficiency as the LR parser, we aim at an acceleration with the fewest modifications without spoiling the inheritance accumulated during the development of the LangLAB.

High speed is always required for analyzers, so you might say that some high level language is more adequate for efficiency for some applications. But considering an analyzer on the developing environment, how one can build a high speed analyzer within the logic grammar or the logic programming is important. And users of the analyzing system don't want to rewrite their works through the improvement of the system. Therefore our modification comes to have significance.

In section 2 we explain the principle of our method comparing it with the LC(1) parser. In section 3 we present an implementation for a practical grammar. And finally in section 4 we show the experimental results of syntax analysis for an English grammar with about 560 production rules and we discuss our methods.

# 2  Principle

In this chapter we explain the principle to drive BUP with a table.

## 2.1  The principle of BUP

First we define the *left corner* and present the principle of BUP. In the followings of this paper we use $G = (V, \Sigma, P, S)$ to represent a grammar where $V$ represents a set of grammar symbols, $\Sigma$ a set of terminal symbols, $P$ a set of production rules and $S \in N$ the start symbol ($N = V - \Sigma$ represents a set of nonterminal symbols).

**Definition** (Left Corner)
  For a context free grammar $G = (V, \Sigma, P, S)$, we call $X_1 \in V$ a *left corner* of a production $X_0 \longrightarrow X_1 \cdots X_n \in P$ or simply a *left corner* (of some production).

In principle, the syntax analysis of BUP is a proof process (SLD-deduction) to show a theorem (2.7) from axioms (2.1),(2.3) and (2.5) for a context free grammar $G = (V, \Sigma, P, S)$. Here we define two predicates:
First let

$$LC(s, g, w)$$

represent that a subtree with its root $g \in V$ is built on a left corner $s \in V$ followed by a terminal string $w \in \Sigma^*$ as its leaves. And second let

$$ST(s, w)$$

represent a subtree with the root $s$ built on a terminal string $w$ as its leaves. Sometimes we call a subtree with the root named $g$ *goal* $g$, or *subtree* $g$.

The axioms are constructed as follows:

(1) For each production $s_0 \rightarrow s_1 s_2 \cdots s_n$, we make an axiom

$$LC(s_1, g, w_2 \cdots w_n w) \leftarrow \qquad (1)$$
$$ST(s_2, w_2) \wedge \ldots \wedge ST(s_n, w_n) \wedge LC(s_0, g, w)$$

which states that when there is a left corner $s_0$ with the root $g$ followed by a terminal string $w$ and there are subtrees $s_2, \ldots, s_n$ with terminal strings $w_2, \ldots, w_n$ as leaves, respectively, then there is a left corner $s_1$ with the root $g$ followed by a terminal string $w_2 \cdots w_n w$. This clause is depicted in Fig. 1 and is implemented as a rule of Prolog (2.2).

$$s1(G, DI, DO) : -$$
$$goal(s2, DI, D2),$$
$$goal(s3, D2, D3), \qquad (2)$$
$$\cdots,$$
$$goal(sn, \cdots, Dn),$$
$$s0(G, Dn, DO).$$

We call clause (2.2) a *BUP clause*. In procedural interpretation, when predicate $s1$ is called (which means subtree $s1$ is built in a bottom-up manner), the body of this clause becomes applicable. Then goal clauses (see below) to build subtree $s_2, s_3, \ldots, s_n$ are called in this order (in a top-down manner). When these are completed, left corner $s_0$ is also recognized, and the next BUP clause is called.

(2) This clause states that the recognized left corner $g$ of some production is itself the root of a goal subtree $g$.

$$LC(g, g, \varepsilon) \leftarrow \qquad (3)$$

where $g \in V$, and $\varepsilon \in \Sigma^*$ stands for a null string. For all nonterminal $s \in V$, we make the following unit clause in implementation.

$$s(s, X, X). \qquad (4)$$

We call this unit clause a *termination clause*. In the procedural interpretation, this clause represents that on the way building a subtree $s$ when a left corner $s$ is recognized $s$ can be regarded as the same $s$ that is the root of the subtree.

(3) (2.5) states that when a subtree $g$ is built on a left corner $s$ followed by a terminal string $w$ and there is a production $s \rightarrow a$ ($a \in \Sigma$), then there is a subtree with root $g$ on terminal string $aw$.

$$ST(g, aw) \leftarrow LC(s, g, w) \wedge s \rightarrow a \in P \qquad (5)$$

where $aw \in \Sigma^*$.

A Prolog implementation is shown as follows:

$$goal(G, DI, DO) : -$$
$$dictionary(C, DI, DIO), \qquad (6)$$
$$P = ..[C, G, DIO, DO],$$
$$call(P).$$

We call clause (2.6) the *goal clause*. The predicate

$$dictionary(C, DI, DIO)$$

states that the first element of the difference list $DI$ belongs to the category $C$ and the rest of the list is $DIO$. (2.6) means that, in the procedural interpretation, to build (in a bottom up manner) a subtree $G$ the analyzer reads a terminal and recognizes it as a left corner of the subtree $G$.

(4) The theorem to be proved is (2.7), which states that a tree with root $S$ (that is the start symbol of the grammar) is built on input string $x$ as leaves.

$$\leftarrow ST(S, x), \qquad (7)$$

The Prolog implementation corresponds to the initial query to the system.

$$:? - goal(s, X, []), \qquad (8)$$

where $s$ is the start symbol and $X$ is assigned to a string to be parsed.

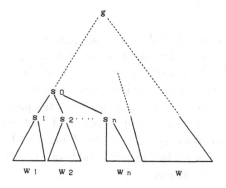

**Fig.1** The structure stated by statement (1)

## 2.2 Nondeterminism of BUP

Assertions of $wf\_goal$ and $fail\_goal$ introduced in the previous version of BUP are used to record the results of the analysis, which are represented as successes or failures of goal clauses, in order to eliminate the identical computations. However, they are not fundamentally used to reduce the nondeterminism. Here we study the nondeterminism of BUP. BUP has the nondeterminism as follows:

(1) When a left corner has been recognized, *the decision is how to select a production rule to which the left corner belongs.* That is, for a production rule represented as the form of (2.1), if there are any other productions with the same left corner as $s_1$, the matter is which production to select.

(2) When the name of a left corner is identical to the root name of the subtree which is the current goal, *the decision is to recognize it as the time when the goal is satisfied or when another left corner whose name happens to be identical to the root name is recognized.* That is, when a left corner $s_1$ is recognized, in other words when $LC(s_1, g, w)$ holds, if $s_1$ is equal to $g$, the matter is which rule to select, the form of (2.1) or (2.3). Essentially there is no nondeterminism for grammars with no left recursion.

(3) *Homonyms.* A parser usually consults a dictionary for the category and some information on words, so for homonyms there is nondeterminism in selecting one of them.

(4) *Augmentations.* There is sometimes nondeterminism in the semantic procedures (augmentations) written in production rules.

(5) *Disjunctions in a production rule.* Containing a left corner within the disjunction is prohibited in BUP. However, disjunctions in other structures are the same kind of nondeterminism as (1).

In these nondeterminisms (3) and (4) are essential without respect to parsing methods. And (4) is an advantage of the underlying nondeterministic programming language, such as Prolog, for the description of augmentation, which is not always allowed in many other languages. (5) is merely a descriptional convenience and we take it out of this research. So the essential nondeterminisms come from the parsing principle of BUP are (1) and (2), and we call these nondeterminisms the *adaptability* and the *left recursivity*, respectively. The principle of our speed up method mentioned in the subsequent section is to reduce the nondeterminism by the action table of LC(1) parser, taking note of the similarity between LC(1) parser and BUP.

## 2.3 Aho's LC($k$) [8]

In this section we introduce LC($k$) grammars (Left Corner Grammars with $k$-lookahead) and its deterministic parsing method from [8]. First of all, we define the left corner derivation.

**Definition** (left corner derivation)  Let $G$ be a CFG. We say that

$$S \underset{lc}{\overset{*}{\Rightarrow}} wA\delta \qquad (9)$$

if

$$S \underset{lm}{\overset{*}{\Rightarrow}} wA\delta \qquad (w \in \Sigma^*, \delta \in V^*) \qquad (10)$$

and the nonterminal $A$ is not the left corner of the production which introduced it into a left-sentential form of the sequence represented by (2.10).

In the followings $FIRST_k(\beta\gamma\delta)$ represents a set of substrings of the length not exceeding $k$ symbols from the first, derived from $\beta\gamma\delta$.

**Definition** $(LC(k))$

A CFG $G = (V, \Sigma, P, S)$ is an $LC(k)$ if the following conditions are satisfied: Suppose that

$$S \underset{lc}{\overset{*}{\Rightarrow}} wA\delta. \qquad (11)$$

Then for each lookahead string $u$ there is at most one production $\beta \to \alpha$ such that $A \overset{*}{\Rightarrow} B\gamma$ and

(1).  (a) If $\alpha = C\beta$, $C \in N$ then $u \in FIRST_k(\beta\gamma\delta)$ and

(b) In addition, if $C = A$, then $u$ is not in $FIRST_k(\delta)$;

(2). If $\alpha$ does not begin with a nonterminal, then
$u \in FIRST_k(\alpha\gamma\delta)$.

Condition 1(a) guarantees that the use of the production $B \to C\beta$ can be uniquely determined once we have seen $w$, the terminal string derived from $C$ (the left corner) and $FIRST_k(\beta\gamma\delta)$ (the lookahead string). (Fig. 2a)

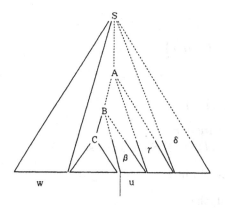

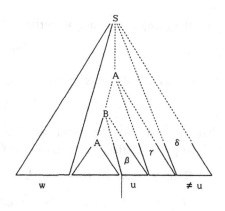

**Fig.2(a)** Case (1)(a)  **Fig.2(b)** Case (1)(b)

Condition 1(b) ensures that if the nonterminal $A$ is left-recursive (which is possible in
an LC grammar), then we can tell after an
instance of $A$ has been found whether that
instance is the left corner of the production
$B \to A\gamma$ or the $A$ in the left-sentential form
$wA\alpha$. (Fig. 2b)

Condition 2 states that $FIRST_k(\alpha\delta\gamma)$
uniquely determines that the production
$B \to \alpha$ is to be used next in a left-corner
parse after having seen $wB$, when $\alpha$ does not
begin with a nonterminal symbol. (Fig. 2c)

For each $LC(k)$ grammar we can construct
a deterministic parser, here we shall outline
the $LC(1)$ parser. Let $G = (V, \Sigma, P, S)$ be an
$LC(1)$ grammar. The parser uses an input

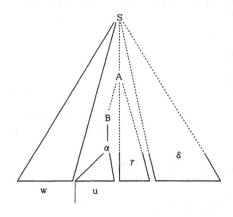

**Fig.2(c)** Case (2)

tape, a pushdown stack and an output tape. The set of pushdown symbols is $\Gamma = N \cup \Sigma \cup (N \times N) \cup \{\$\}$, where $\$$ denotes the bottom of the stack. A symbol appearing on top of the stack is interpreted as the current goal to be recognized, so the initial stack is $S\$$. The element of $N \times N$, $[A, B]$, is called an *lc pair*, and the first element $A$ represents the current goal to be recognized and the second $B$ does a left corner which has just been recognized.

The parser is driven with a *left-corner parsing table* $T$, which maps $\Gamma \times (\Sigma \cup \{\varepsilon\})$ to $(\Gamma^* \times (P \cup \{\varepsilon\})) \cup \{pop, accept, error\}$. The configuration of the parser is a triple $(w, X\alpha, \pi)$, where $w \in \Sigma^*$ represents the remaining input, and $X\alpha$ represents the *pushdown stack* with $X \in \Gamma$ on top, and $\pi$ is the output at this point.

The deterministic action of the parser is as follows:

(1). If $T(X, a) = (\beta, i), X \in N \cup (N \times N)$, then we write

$$(aw, X\alpha, \pi) \vdash (aw, \beta\alpha, \pi i).$$

(2). If $T(a, a) = pop$ then we write

$$(aw, a\alpha, \pi) \vdash (w, \alpha, \pi).$$

We say $\pi$ is a (left-corner) parse of $x$ if

$$(x, S\$, \varepsilon) \vdash^* (\varepsilon, \$, \pi),$$

where $\vdash^*$ stands for the transitive reflective closure of $\vdash$.

The parsing table $T$ is constructed from $G = (V, \Sigma, P, S)$ as follows:

(1) Suppose that $p_i : B \to \alpha$ is the $i$th production in $P$.

    (a) If $\alpha = C\beta$, where $C$ is a nonterminal, then
      $T([A, C], a) = (\beta[A, B], i)$ for all $A \in N$ and $a \in FIRST_1(\beta\gamma\delta)$
      such that $S \overset{*}{\underset{lc}{\Rightarrow}} wA\delta$ and $A \overset{*}{\Rightarrow} B\gamma$.
      Here, the parser recognizes a left corner in bottom-up.

(b) If $\alpha$ does not begin with a nonterminal, then

$T(A, a) = (\alpha[A, B], i)$ for all $A \in N$ and $a \in FIRST_1(\alpha\gamma\delta)$ such that $S \overset{*}{\underset{lc}{\Longrightarrow}} wA\delta$ and $A \overset{*}{\Longrightarrow} B\gamma$.

(2) $T([A, A], a) = (\varepsilon, \varepsilon)$ for all $A \in N$ and $a \in FIRST_1(\delta)$
such that $S \overset{*}{\underset{lc}{\Longrightarrow}} wA\delta$.

(3) $T(a, a) = pop$ for all $a \in \Sigma$.

(4) $T(\$, \varepsilon) = accept$.

(5) $T(X, a) = error$ otherwise.

## 2.4 Principle of Speed Up

The principle of our parsing method is based on the LC(1) parsing method introduced in the previous section to reduce the nondeterminism shown in the section 2.2 in the same way. The LC(1) parser is originally designed to parse sentences in LC(1) language deterministically. When the LC(1) parsing method is applied to a general context free grammar, a parser for that language is easily constructed, however, its parsing behavior becomes nondeterministic. But this nondeterminism is more restistic than that of BUP because of guidance by the lookahead mechanism. Moreover even if the parser seeks all solutions by backtracking in this nondeterminism, the cost of the parsing is at most the same as that of of BUP. This is the principle of our method and we present the detail of the method in this section.

### 2.4.1 Comparison between BUP and LC(1) Parser

There are many correspondences in the parsing process between BUP and LC(1) parser. In this section we present the comparison between BUP and LC(1) parser from the viewpoint of LC(1) parsing table construction.

(1) BUP Clause: A BUP clause of the form (2.2) represents the action which is the subject of the table construction process 1(a). An entry generated in the process 1(a) is used to direct the parsing action when a left corner $C$ is recognized in the construction of goal $A$. The action means making a new left corner $B$ after recognition of $\beta$, the rest of right hand side of the production $p_i$ which has the current left corner $C$.

(2) Goal Clause: The goal clause of the form (2.6) resembles the table construction 1(b). In the goal clause, the parser reads a symbol from input and regard it as a new left corner to call a BUP clause. On the other hand in the table construction 1(b), the LC(1) parser reads a symbol which is a left corner of the production $p_i$, and after the analysis of the rest of the right hand side of the production, the parser recognizes a new left corner $B$ which is the left hand side of $p_i$. The parsing action for a production with only one right hand side, moreover which is a terminal symbol, corresponds to that of goal clause in BUP.

(3) Termination Clauses: A termination clause of the form (2.4) is used when the recognized left corner has the same name as the current goal, and that timing corresponds to the action of the table construction 2. In BUP a series of processes have achieved the goal and terminated the processes, and in LC(1) the parser pops up the parsing stack at this timing.

### 2.4.2 "Which production to select ?"

In this section, based on the correspondence noted above we study a method to reduce the nondeterminism introduced in section 2.2, i.e. adaptability. Remember that adaptability is the nondeterminism in deciding one production when a left corner is recognized in some goal. From the discussion of (1) in the previous section there are correspondences between the action of BUP and an LC(1) parser and we can use the action table of the LC(1) parser without any modification. That is, we add a table reference mechanism into the BUP clause of the form (2.2).

For all production $p_i = s_0 \rightarrow s_1 s_2 \cdots s_n \in P$,

$$
\begin{aligned}
&s1(LC, DI, DO) : - \\
&\quad lh(C, DI), \\
&\quad t(LC, C, NLC, p_i), \\
&\quad goal(s2, DI, D2), \\
&\quad goal(s3, D2, D3), \\
&\quad \cdots, \\
&\quad goal(sn, \cdots, Dn), \\
&\quad s0(NLC, Dn, DO).
\end{aligned} \tag{12}
$$

In this rule $lh(C, DI)$ states that the category of the first element of difference list $DI$ is $C$, and $t(LC, C, NLC, p_i)$, which is used to look up the action table, is equivalent to the LC(1) parsing table entry

$$T([G, s_1], C) = (s_2 \ldots s_n[G, s_0], p_i),$$

where $LC$, $NLC$ are assigned the codes of lc pairs $[G, s_1]$, $[G, s_0]$, respectively. This clause states that when the lc pair of the current left corner and the goal is $LC$, and the lookahead is $C$ then the recognized production rule is $p_i$ and the lc pair of new left corner and the goal is $NCL$. Whether there is an entry for the lc pair $LC$ in the table corresponds to the reachability of BUP represented by a *link clause* (which will be seen later), moreover, such a constraint becomes more precise than the original link clause of BUP by combination with a lookahead. When the symbol $s_i$ ($2 \le i \le n$) is a terminal, we use $Dj = [si|Di]$ instead of $goal(si, Dj, Di)$, which corresponds to the LC(1) table construction (3).

### 2.4.3 "Whether a subtree has completed ?"

Now we study the second nondeterminism (left recursivity) mentioned in the section 2.2 (2), that is, the decision to select one of two, a goal subtree has completed or a left corner with the same name as root's is recognized. The decision corresponds to that of LC(1) parser as we showed in section 2.4.1 (3). Then we add a table lookup mechanism to termination clauses of the form (2.4). That is, for all nonterminal $s$,

$$s(LC, X, X) : -$$
$$lh(C, X),$$
$$follow(LC, C).$$
(13)

In this rule $follow(LC, C)$ is equivalent to the LC(1) parsing entry

$$T([s, s], C) = (\varepsilon, \varepsilon)$$

where $LC$ is assigned the code of the lc pair $[s, s]$. This rule states that recognized left corner $s$ has the same name as the root name of the goal subtree. Then the constraint is to check whether the lookahead symbol $C$ is allowed to follow $s$ or not, as you can see from the table construction (2).

### 2.4.4 Correspondence of goal clause

As we showed at section 2.4.1 (2), the action for the goal clause corresponds to that of the LC(1) parser when the parser proceeds a production with one terminal symbol of right hand side. To utilize this parsing method for ours, however, we need a little modification for the table construction as follows:

(b') $T'(A, a) = ([A, a], \_)$ for all $A \in N, a \in \Sigma$ such that

$$S \xRightarrow[lc]{\cdot} wA\delta \text{ and } A \xRightarrow{\cdot} a\gamma.$$

New goal clause corresponding to the above table entry is as follows:

$$goal(G, DI, DO) : -$$
$$dictionary(C, DI, DIO),$$
$$lc(G, C, LC),$$
$$P = ..[C, LC, DIO, DO],$$
$$call(P).$$
(14)

In this expression $lc(G, C, LC)$ is equivalent to the entry of new LC(1) parsing table

$$T'(G, C) = ([G, C], \_),$$

where the code of the lc pair $[G, C]$ is assigned to a variable $LC$. This is a constraint to check whether the lookahead symbol is a legal one. When the lookahead is legal, new lc pair $LC$ is made from the lookahead and the current goal $G$. Note that whether there is an lc pair of the left corner and the goal corresponds to the existence of the link clause in BUP.

# 3 Implementation

In this section we present implementational matters of a syntax analysis system, BUP-TD, based on some principles so far. We have been developing the system in order that it can be adaptable to a practical grammar with about 560 productions. There are some parts that must be efficient enough to deal with such grammar, even if they are not important in principle. We also present the matter of this kind. The analysis system is written in C-Prolog (interpreter) and implemented on Sun3/140.

## 3.1 Action Table

For our application, there are about 35,000 entries in the action table (except error entry). Because of this large size, at first one lookup for an entry took more than one second. In our implementation for BUP-TD, the action table are allocated on a static area by a C language program noticing that C-Prolog has a convenient interface with C programs, in which hashing is utilized with a key of a pair of a lookahead and a nonterminal or (the code of) an lc pair.

You may say that if some programs written in other than Prolog were allowed, then it would be better for speed up to write some essential part, extremely speaking whole the system, in a procedural language such as C. But in this research we take the position that only the effect of the table driven mechanism is interesting, so we can reduce other overheads as possible.

## 3.2 Lookahead Mechanism

The first element of an input string is categorized in BUP clauses, the goal clause and termination clauses. When a word has a homonym, its category and meaning must be consistent if it were referenced anywhere. On the other hand all possible categorizations must be examined. The simplest way to settle this problem is to prepare all possible combinations of category sequences, however, wastefully same computations often occur for some part of input string. In our implementation, when the dictionary is looked up the control is passed one predicate after another with the consistent information (i.e., category name) from the dictionary. Then we augment each predicate with two arguments as follows:

$$goal(G, ..., Fst, Fol),$$

and for a left corner $n$,

$$n(G, ..., Fst, Fol).$$

$Fst$ is assigned to the category name of the first element to be parsed. And $Fol$ represents the category name of the first element that follows the constructed subtree $G$.

Fig. 3 (b) is the augmented version of the original (Fig. 3(a)). Lookaheads flow from predicate to predicate through $Fst$ and $Fol$ as input string through the difference list. Predicate $lh(Fst, I)$ is modified so that it searches the dictionary only when $Fst$ is not bound. Fig. 3(c) shows an example of the termination clause where $35 denotes the code of lc pair [noun_phrase, noun_phrase].

noun_phrase(np(Det,adj(Adjs),n(Noun))) ⟶
        determiner(Det),
        adjectives(Adjs),
        noun(Noun).

**Fig. 3(a)** Some Rule in DCG

determiner(G,Det,Info,I,O,Fst,Fol) :-
        lh(Fst,I),
        t(G,Fst,NG,14),
        goal(adjectives,Adjs,I,I1,Fst,F1),
        goal(noun,Noun,I1,I2,F1,F2),
        noun_phrase(NG,np(Det,adj(Adjs),n(Noun)),
            Info,I2,O,F2,Fol).

**Fig. 3(b)** Augmented Version of Fig. 3(a)

noun_phrase($35,I,I,S,S,Fol,Fol) :-
        lh(Fol,S),
        follow($35,Fol).

**Fig. 3(c)** A Termination Clause

## 3.3  Coupling with Inheritance of BUP

Our method is essentially independent of the speed up and descriptive efficiency developed for the original BUP, and can be used together with such methods. At the beginning, we will explain how we made use of them. Fig. 4 represents an actual goal clause in both our BUP-TD and the original.

(1). *Augmentation* or *Semantic Attachment*: We can write augmentations anywhere in the production except the first like BUP, and the timing when the predicate is evaluated completely corresponds to that of BUP.

(2). *Link Clauses*: In BUP, link clauses assert that the left corner being constructed is a proper left corner of some subtree which is the current goal, and these assertions are precomputated from production rules (syntax rules) before actual syntax analysis. That is, $link(A, G)$ asserts that constructed left corner $A$ can be a left corner of some subtree $G$ and is identical with an lc pair $[G, A]$ in BUP-TD. In our method, an lc pair is used to search an item of the action table as an entry, which means that the existence of the item guarantees the lc pair is valid. Therefore the constraint by link clauses in BUP is completely included in our method.

(3). *wf_goal, fail_goal*: The success/failure of a goal is recorded as an assertion of a unit clause, $wf\_goal/fail\_goal$, which includes two arguments, the goal and the position in the input. By referring to this assertion the parser can omit the same computation which has the same goal and input position. In our method the same mechanism can be implemented, only the contents to be recorded are extended: The original $wf\_goal$ and $fail\_goal$ are as follows:

$$wf\_goal(G, I, A, O)$$

where $G$ represents a goal, $A$ semantic information, $I$ input string and $O$ the rest of the input, and

$$fail\_goal(G, I)$$

where $G$ represents a goal and $I$ input string. In BUP-TD, $wf\_goal$ and $fail\_goal$ are extended. That is,

$$wf\_goal(G, I, A, O, Fst, Fol)$$

and

$$fail\_goal(G, I, Fst)$$

where $Fst$ and $Fol$ have the same meaning explained in the section 3.2. The reason for this extension is to deal with the homonym of words, that is, to synchronize categories when recording the input string and when utilizing it.

(4). *Morphological analysis* and *TRIE structured dictionary*: Input strings are preprocessed by the same morphological analyzer that BUP uses, and the dictionary for it is also the same. Though we must modify the part for idioms a little, it is not critical.

(5). *XG*: We have not implemented the part for the extraposition grammars (XGs for short). Here we describe the outline of it. At first we show the essential part.

$$goal\_x(G, GARG, x(G, GARG, X1), X1, D, D).$$
$$goal\_x(G, A, X, Y, DI, DO) : -$$
$$\quad X = x(T, TARG, X1),$$
$$\quad T\backslash == G,$$
$$\quad P = ..[T, G, TARG, A, X, X1, Y, DI, DO],$$
$$\quad call(P).$$

These are written in the rear part of $goal\_x$ clauses (XG version of the goal clause), and called when ordinal $goal\_x$ clauses have failed. The action is as follows: At first (a) whether the goal is included in the X list, $x(G, GARG, X1)$, is examined. If it is included then the current goal is accomplished; otherwise (b) the first element of the X list is considered to be the next left corner like usual lookaheads and processed in this way. In this modification constraints with the action table are not used for (a).

The countermeasure for XGs are theoretically possible, however, there are some problems as to combinations with lookahead mechanism and $wf\_goal/fail\_goal$.

```
goal(G,A,I,O) :-
          (wf_goal(G,I,_,_)  ;
           fail_goal(G,X),!,
           fail ),!,
           wf_goal(G,I,A,O).
goal(G,A,I,O) :-
          dictionary(C,A1,I,IO),
          L=.. [C,G],
          call(L),
          P=..[C,G,A1,AA,IO,O],
          call(P),
          A=AA,
          assertz(wf_goal(G,I,A,O)).
goal(G,_,I,_) :-
          (wf_goal(G,I,_,_)  ;
           assertz(fail_goal(G,I)) ),!,
           fail.
```

**Fig. 4(a)** Original goal cluase

```
goal(G,A,I,O,Fst,Fol) :-
          ( wf_goal(G,I,_,_,Fst,_)  ;
           fail_goal(G,X,Fst),!,
           fail ),!,
           wf_goal(G,I,A,O,Fst,Fol).
goal(G,A,I,O,C,Fol) :-
          dictionary(C,A1,I,IO),
          lc(G,C,NG),
          P=..[C,NG,A1,AA,IO,O,_,Fol],
          call(P),
          A=AA,
          assertz(wf_goal(G,I,A,O,C,Fol)).
goal(G,_,I,_,Fst,_) :-
          ( wf_goal(G,I,_,_,_,_)  ;
           assertz(fail_goal(G,I,Fst)) ),!,
           fail.
```

**Fig. 4(b)** New goal clause

# 4   Experiments and Discussion

In this section we present experiments and we study the results.

## 4.1 Experimental Results

We show the experimental results in Table 1 from an application to 17 English sentences given in the appendix. The English grammar used for this experiment is a general purpose grammar, consists of 555 production rules in the DCG formalism with augmentations in order to eliminate illegal structures. The time shown in Table 1 is cpu time and does not include the time to picture the parse trees. The machine used in this experiment is a Sun 3/140 (clock 16MHz, memory 8MB) using the C-Prolog (interpreter).

We found the followings:

(1). Parsing speed is 1.47 sec. per a word in g BUP and 1.14 sec. in BUP-TD, which means 30% speed up is gained.

(2). BUP-TD is slower for sentence 5,7,10 than that of BUP. The ratio of this speed down is 4% (sentence 7) to 30% (sentence 30).

The principle of our method is to add additional constraints by the action table to the original BUP. Therefore there is no reason why the parsing speed becomes slower, except for overhead of the lookahead and the table lookup mechanism. This means these overheads defeat the speed up in sentence 5,7,10,15. In any case, the experiment is not much enough to discuss these phenomenon or to find common syntax structures in these sentences, so they will be studied as a future work.

According to [9], LangLAB (we call BUP in this paper) and SAX [10] are almost equal in parsing speed when driven on interpreter, however, on the compiler environment SAX is 5 to 10 times faster than LangLAB. The reason for this difference, [9] says, depends on the time cost of assertions of $wf_goal/fail_goals$ in interpretive mode. This point has also not been settled in our method; we think SAX is faster than ours.

## 4.2 Comparison and discussion

Here we compare and study (1)BUP and (2)our method (or the LC(1) parser). According to the discussion of the nondeterminism of BUP and our method in section 2.2, and the comparison of them in section 2.4.1, the speed up has its basis on a reduction of the nondeterminism of (a) "Which production to select ?" and (b) "Whether a subtree has completed ?" when a left corner is recognized. Next we study both of them.

- For (a) : Assume that there is no left recursion in production rules. We study the following time point of parsing:

  | current goal is | $g \in N$, |
  | recognized left corner is | $s_1 \in N$ and |
  | lookahead is | $c \in \Sigma$. |

  And let $s_0$ be the left hand side of a production whose first symbol of the right hand side is $s_1$ (i.e., the production is $s_0 \longrightarrow s_1 \cdots$). Furthermore let the probability that $g \overset{*}{\Longrightarrow} s_0\alpha$ holds be

  $$p_1 = P\{g \overset{*}{\Longrightarrow} s_0\alpha\}.$$

(1). The nondeterminism of BUP at this time point is to select one from

$$p_1 \times n_1(s_1) \qquad \text{rules(expected value)}, \qquad (15)$$

where $n_1(s_1)$ is the number of production rules which have $s_1$ as their left corner.

(2). Within production rules which have $s_1$ as their left corner, let $n_2(s_1, c)$ be the sum of the number of the productions whose second symbol of right hand can derive a string with lookahead $c$ at the first, and the number of productions whose right hand side consist of one symbol (i.e., only $s_1$) and the lookahead $c$ is derived from $\alpha$ such that $g \xRightarrow{\cdot} s_0\alpha$ [1].

Then the probability that $c$ is allowed as a lookahead is

$$n_2(s_1, c)/n_1(s_1). \qquad (16)$$

Therefore the nondeterminism in our method at the point we are discussing is to select one rule from

$$p_1 \times n_2(s_1, c) \qquad \text{rules(expected value)}. \qquad (17)$$

From (4.1) and (4.3), assuming that the speed up comes only from reduction of the nondeterminism, the ratio of the parsing speed of our method and BUP becomes

$$n_2(s_1, c)/n_1(s_1).$$

- For (b): In this case, when the parser is constructing a subtree $A$ (in bottom up manner), recognized left corner is also $A$. Let the lookahead at this time point be $u$, the parsing state corresponds to Fig. 2(b).

  (1). In the original method of BUP, the parser must consider two possibilities i. e. , one is to regard this state as the completion of the goal, and the other is to regard the recognized leftcorner as the middle to the goal even though recognized symbol $A$ does not occur at the first of right hand side the rule.

  (2). In our method, the parser cannot decide whether there is a left recursion or not, unfortunately. However, when a left corner is recognized, the constraint mentioned in (a) above can work. As a countermeasure for the left recursion, we are studying about a mechanism such as calling only the termination clause if the recognized left corner is not left recursive, which is predetermined before parsing.

---

[1] $n_2(s_1, c)$ is the sum of the number of productions such that $p_i : s_0 \longrightarrow s_1 s_2 \cdots$ where $s_2 \xRightarrow{\cdot} c \cdots$ or $p_j : s_0 \longrightarrow s_1$ where $g \xRightarrow{\cdot} s_0 c \cdots$

# 5 Conclusion

In this paper we presented a speed up version of BUP based on LC(1) parser.

First we gave the principle of BUP and listed reasons for the nondeterminism in parsing, two of which are important. Next we introduced the LC(1) grammar and the LC(1) parser. Comparing the parser with BUP, we found many correspondences between them.

Furthermore we showed the application of the principle of the LC(1) to BUP and explained an implementation of BUP-TD, that is, a table-driven version of BUP.

We also presented an experiment applying our method to a practical-sized English grammar. Our method gains about 30% speed up to some sentences. Finally we discussed the nondeterminism of BUP and our method, and found that some mechanism other than table drive is necessary.

The extension for Extraposition Grammars, a countermeasure for left recursion and an adjustment of the implemented system are left as future work. Noticing that there are some sentences for which our method took more parsing time than the original, programming technical improvements also seems to be necessary.

| sentence | no. of trees | no. of words | BUP | BUP-TD |
|---|---|---|---|---|
| 1 | 2 | 5 | 8.7 | 4.4 |
| 2 | 1 | 7 | 7.2 | 4.2 |
| 3 | 1 | 6 | 8.3 | 5.7 |
| 4 | 1 | 8 | 9.3 | 7.9 |
| 5 | 1 | 5 | 3.8 | 4.9 |
| 6 | 1 | 7 | 9.2 | 6.7 |
| 7 | 1 | 11 | 15.2 | 15.7 |
| 8 | 2 | 8 | 12.3 | 8.6 |
| 9 | 1 | 5 | 5.2 | 4.2 |
| 10 | 1 | 5 | 7.3 | 7.8 |
| 11 | 1 | 3 | 6.1 | 3.0 |
| 12 | 1 | 5 | 8.0 | 4.0 |
| 13 | 2 | 6 | 8.0 | 4.9 |
| 14 | 2 | 8 | 9.5 | 7.2 |
| 15 | 2 | 9 | 10.8 | 11.4 |
| 16 | 1 | 4 | 6.0 | 3.0 |
| 17 | 5 | 21 | 45.9 | 36.6 |

**Table 1** Comparison of the parsing speed of BUP and BUP-TD (in second)

# Acknowledgements

We are so grateful to Hiroshi Nakagawa, an associate professor of Yokohama National University for important comments on our study and the referees of this conference and J.Klavans for refereeing or commenting in the paper.

# References

[1] Tanaka,H., Kamiwaki,T., Okumura,M. and Numazaki,H. A Software System LangLAB for Natural Language Processing, *Proc. LPC'86*, pp.5-12, 1986.

[2] Matsumoto,Y., et al., BUP - A Bottom-Up Parser Embedded in Prolog, *New Generation Computing*, Vol.1, No.2, pp.145-158, 1983.

[3] Konno,S. and Tanaka,H., Processing Left-extraposition in Bottom Up Parsing System, *Computer Software*, Vol.3, No.2, pp.19-29, 1986.

[4] Kamiwaki,T. and Tanka,H., Idiom Handling by TRIE Structure Dictionary, *Proc. of LPC'85*, pp.329-340, 1985.

[5] Tokunaga,T., Iwayama,M., Kamiwaki,T. and Tanaka,H., LangLAB: A Natural Language Analysis System, *Trans. Inf. Proc. Soc. Japan*, Vol.29, No.7, pp.703-771, 1988.

[6] Tomita,M., An Efficient Augmented-Context-Free Parsing Algorithm, *Am.J.Comput. Linguist.*, Vol.13, No.1-2, pp.31-46, 1987.

[7] Pereirra,F.C.N., Extraposition Grammars, *Am.J.Comput. Linguist.*,

[8] Aho,A.V. and Ullman,J.D., *The Theory of Parsing, Translation, and Compiling, Volume 1 : Parsing*, Prentice-Hall, pp.362-367, 1972.

[9] Sugimura,R., et al., Comparison of Logic Programming based Natural Language Parsing Systems, *Preprints Work. Gr.for NL, IPSJ*, 57-2,1986.

[10] Matsumoto,Y. and Sugimura,R., SAX: A Parsing System based on Logic Programming Languages, *Computer Software*, Vol.3, No.4, pp.4-11, 1986.

# Appendix Sentences for Experiment

(1). Tell me when he came.
(2). Some of them were on the table.
(3). Did he give them to her?
(4). Could she have been given many of them?
(5). What should I do then?
(6). This is hard for me to do.
(7). He broke the vase her uncle had given up to him.
(8). You could break this vase with that hammer.
(9). You could break it up.
(10).Who gave her that book?
(11).who wrote it?
(12).By whom was it written?
(13).Where did he try to go?
(14).Why did you want John to attack it?
(15).How long will it take you to go there?

(16).I open the window.
(17).The annotations provide important information for other parts of the system that interpret the expression in the context of a dialogue.

# A Consistency Maintenance Mechanism for Subjective Judgments and Its Application

Toramatsu SHINTANI

IIAS-SIS FUJITSU LIMITED
17-25, Shinkamata 1-Chome, Ota-ku, Tokyo 144, JAPAN
E-mail: tora%iias.fujitsu.co.jp@uunet.uu.net

## ABSTRACT

In this paper, we propose a mechanism for maintaining consistency of subjective judgments. In the mechanism, subjective judgments of decision makers are extracted and used to select alternatives effectively. The subjective judgments are quantified by using AHP based pairwise comparisons. In order to maintain consistency of the comparisons, we exploit the TMS based nonmonotonic inference in the Prolog-based production system KORE/IE. By using the inference, the consistency of the comparisons is effectively maintained.

## 1. Introduction

Knowledge based systems support decision makers by using knowledge bases. It is necessary to construct and modify the knowledge bases beforehand in the decision support. It is tedious and consumes a lot of time for assembling and codifying knowledge in the knowledge bases. As an alternative means of articulating knowledge beforehand, we implement a system which extracts and dynamically uses information of decision makers in a decision process. The system is called CDSS(Choice Design Support System). CDSS is implemented on production system KORE/IE(Shintani 1988). KORE/IE is a fast production system on Prolog. The inference mechanism is realized by performing a recognize-act cycle in a similar manner as OPS5(Forgy 1981) in which the type of reasoning is forward chaining.

CDSS supports decision makers by structuring their knowledge and extracting their subjective judgments. Concretely, CDSS helps decision makers make a reasonable choice from alternatives. In the choice process, two processes are used. One is a process which clarifies attributes used for estimating the alternatives. The other is a process which determines the priorities of the alternatives by estimating the attributes. In the estimation, a pairwise comparison method based on AHP (Analytic Hierarchy Process)(Saaty 1980) is used. AHP is one of the weighting methods, and has an advantage of being able to treat subjective judgments of decision makers. However, in the method, it is difficult to maintain consistency of the judgments.

In this paper, especially, we focus on the mechanism for maintaining tconsistency and show the method for constructing the mechanism in CDSS.

## 2. The outline of CDSS

Fig.1 illustrates processes for decision support in CDSS. CDSS supports decision makers to create goals and their subgoals for problem solving. In the process CDSS uses subjective judgments of decision makers, and offers functions to clarify a structure of the problems. Knowledge of the decision makers is structured hierarchically through the process. In the hierarchy, elements which should be considered about the problems are arranged. The knowledge structured like this will be used as basic information for knowledge acquisition tools.

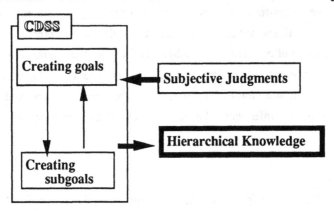

**Fig.1. The Processes for decision support in CDSS**

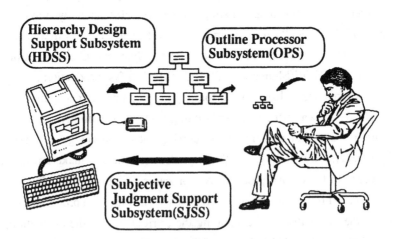

**Fig.2. The subsystems in CDSS**

CDSS is composed of (1)the Hierarchy Design Support Subsystem(HDSS), (2)the Subjective Judgments Support Subsystem(SJSS), and (3)the Outline Processor

Subsystem(OPS) as shown in Fig.2. The decision support processes in CDSS are achieved by combining and using these subsystems. HDSS helps to clarify elements which should be considered in the decision making process by arranging tthem hierarchically. The complexity in the problem is canceled through extracting relations among the elements and arranging the elements hierarchically. The hierarchy is treated visually as a graph by using a graph editor KORE/GET as shown in Fig.3. The editor provides functions for manipulating the graph. The functions of the editor include (1)editing nodes and arcs of the graph, and (2)drawing the graph in a visually well-organized form which enables us to easily grasp the structure of the graph. In the example illustrated in Fig.3, the graph is used for clarifying superiority or inferiority among alternatives at the third level by enumerating and estimating the elements (at the second level) which should be considered concerning a goal. The goal is shown at the first level of the graph.

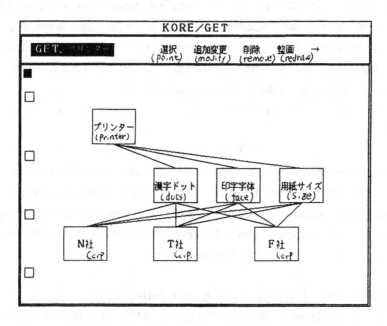

**Fig.3. An example of the graph (in Japanese)**

SJSS is used to quantify subjective judgments of decision makers by using AHP based pairwise comparisons. SJSS maintains consistency of the judgments. SJSS is discussed in more detail in Section 3.

OPS supports decision makers to arrange and structure their knowledge for problem solving. The organized knowledge is used and visually clarified as basic information for the decision support process in HDSS. CDSS provides a simulation function in the decision process by using HDSS and SJSS cooperatively. The function corresponds to a sensitivity analysis which is used to see how changing a judgment has an effect on a conclusion. Through the simulation, decision makers get information to evaluate and organize knowledge for the decision process.

## 3. The consistency maintenance mechanism
## 3.1. Quantifying subjective judgments

A decision maker can make better choices between elements of a problem by using the ratio scales which are obtained from his subjective judgments by using AHP based pairwise comparisons. The comparisons are used to determine the relative importance of the elements in a level with respect to the elements in the level immediately above it. A matrix is set up by carrying out all the comparisons. The matrix is called the pairwise comparison matrix. The pairwise comparison matrix is used to generate the ratio scale for clarifying the priority of the element in the level. The pairwise comparison matrix is a square matrix whose row (or column) consists of elements used for the comparisons. The content of the matrix is weighting number for the comparisons where if the value V for element $a_{ij}$ is determined then the reciprocal value $1/V$ is automatically entered in $a_{ji}$. The value V takes an integer which is less than 9. The larger the number, the more importantly the judgment is agreed upon.

In AHP, consistency can be checked by using the inconsistency ratio(I.R.) which can be represented as follows;

$$(\lambda_{max} - n)/(n - 1)$$

where $\lambda_{max}$, n are the maximum eigenvalue and the size of the pairwise comparison matrix respectively. If the I.R. is less than 0.1, the consistency is considered acceptable; otherwise is inconsistent. If inconsistency has occurred, we need to maintain the consistency by revising a few inadequate pairwise comparisons. However, it is difficult to find the comparisons. In the worst case it forces us to revise all the comparisons.

## 3.2. The Subjective Judgments Support Subsystem

The Subjective Judgments Support Subsystem(SJSS) provides a mechanism for automatically maintaining the consistency of the pairwise comparisons. The maintenance mechanism is realized by using rule based programming and a nonmonotonic inference function in KORE/IE(Shintani 1989). If inconsistency has occurred, inadequate pairwise comparisons are checked and revised first for maintaining the consistency.

### 3.2.1. The rule based process for pairwise comparisons

Fig.4 illustrates the process for pairwise comparisons in SJSS. In Fig.4, the symbol surrounded by a square represents a name of a rule. The rule "*start*" is used for initializing a state for pairwise comparisons.

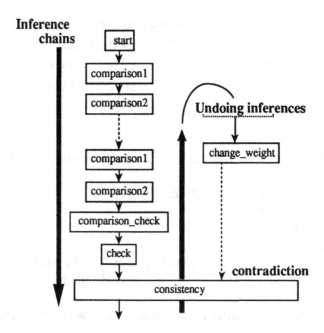

**Fig.4. The Process for pairwise comparisons in SJSS**

The rules "*comparison1*" and "*comparison2*" are used for obtaining a pairwise comparison matrix. The rule *comparison2* determines the reciprocal values and enters them into the matrix. The rule *comparison2* means that "*If the value of the cell in the C-th column, the R-th row of the matrix X is the weight W, and the value of the cell in the R-th column, the C-th row of the matrix X is undefined, then put the weight 1/W into the cell in the R-th column, the C-th row of the matrix X*". The rule *comparison2* can be described as follows;

```
comparison2:
  if matrix_element(name=X,column=C,row=R,weight=(W>0)) &
    -matrix_element(name=X,column=R,row=C)
  then
      add(matrix_element(name=X,column=R,row=C,
                              weight=compute(1/W))).
```

where a rule in KORE/IE consists of (1)the name of the rule (such as *comparison2*), (2)the symbol ":", (3)the symbol "**if**", (4)the LHS(Left Hand Side) which has some LHS patterns (such as "*matrix_element(name=X, ... )*"), (5)the symbol "**then**", (6)the RHS(Right Hand Side) which has some RHS actions (such as "*add*"), and (7) the symbol ".". The symbol "**&**" is a delimiter. The patterns correspond to compound terms of Prolog. The arguments are a sequence of one or more slot-value pairs. The pairs correspond to terms which have functions of arity 2 (e.g. =, \==, <, >). The second LHS pattern with the symbol "-" represents a negative pattern. In a matching process, the negative pattern is satisfied if no working memory(WM) elements match the pattern. The action *add* is used to create a new WM element and put the weight $W$ into the cell in the $R$-th column, the $C$-th row of the matrix $X$.

By the rule *comparison1*, weighting numbers are inserted and grouped into the matrix. The rule *comparison1* can be described as follows.

comparison1:
 if matrix(name=$X$,status=making,size=$S$,element=($E > 0$))
 then
  modify(1,[element=compute($E$-1)]) &
  column_row($S$,$E$,$C$,$R$) &
  qa_weight($X$,$C$,$R$,$W$,*Default*) &
  (*Default* == assumption,
   add_assumption(matrix_element(name=$X$,column=$C$,
              row=$R$,weight=$W$))
 ;
  add(matrix_element(name=$X$,column=$C$,row=$R$,weight=$W$))).

where the execution of RHS actions correspond to that of Prolog goals. The fourth RHS action is executed based on the OR control structure in Prolog. In the execution of the action *qa_weight*, pairwise comparisons are obtained, and a decision maker declares his belief for the pairwise comparisons. The fifth argument *Default* of the action *qa_weight* returns the status of the belief. The action *qa_weight* keeps the information of the comparisons in a database. The information is used to avoid the comparisons which had been already performed previously when the rule will be triggered by the nonmonotonic inference mechanism in KORE/IE. If a cell in the $C$-th column, the $R$-th row of the matrix $X$ is already filled by the weight number $W$ the action *qa_weight* returns the number $W$ with the belief *Default*. There are two type of the belief which are (1)assumption and (2)fact. Concretely, the decision maker can group the weighting numbers into two classes such as (1)temporary(or assumption) numbers and (2)reliable(or fact) numbers which can be generated by using the actions *add_assumption* and *add*, respectively. The actions are defined as predicates of Prolog. The action *add_assumption* is used to create a new assumption in the WM, and keep the temporary number $W$ and the information of the cell in the database. If inconsistency has occurred, the temporary numbers are checked and revised first for maintaining the consistency.

The rule "*comparison_check*" checks whether the matrix is filled or not. The rule "*check*" i used for getting the I.R. of the matrix.

## 3.2.2. The TMS based mechanism for maintaining the consistency

If the I.R. comes to be greater than 0.1, SJSS finds the causes for the inconsistency, and revises the causes by using the TMS(Doyle 1979) based inference mechanism in KORE/IE. The causes correspond to inadequate pairwise comparisons. The TMS based mechanism provides some advantages as follows: (1)In order to realize flexible pairwise comparisons, a decision maker can represent his belief for the pairwise comparisons. (2)The system can dynamically manage the order of the comparisons for realizing efficient comparisons. For example, SJSS can omit some redundant pairwise comparisons and check the consistency of each comparison dynamically by exploiting the Harker's method(Harker 1987).

The rule *"consistency"* is used for achieving the action *"contradiction"* if the I.R. is greater than 0.1. The action is used to find an inadequate assumption and resolve an inconsistency by revising the assumption. The action provides a TMS based function for maintaining consistency among pairwise comparisons. In SJSS, by using the action, the inconsistency is resolved by decreasing a temporary number of I.R. in which the number will come to be less than 0.1.

The outline of the algorithm for the action *contradiction* can be shown as in Fig.5.

*Step 1:* Get a list L of assumption on which an inconsistency depends. Go to Step 1-1.

*Step 1-1:* Sort the list L by using a specified strategy. Go to Step 2.

*Step 2:* If the list L is empty then stop the action and the action becomes a failure; otherwise go to Step 3.

*Step 3:* Get an assumption from the list L, which is the first element(that is, $L_{head}$) of the list L (that is, $L=[L_{head}|L_{tail}]$), and backtrack to the inference step which includes the assumption. Then, assert a negation of the assumption. Go to Step 4.

*Step 4:* If a new inconsistency is detected, then undo the result of Step 3, let $L=L_{tail}$, and go to Step 2; otherwise remove the data which depend on the assumption, and go to 5.

*Step 5:* Stop the action. The action succeeds.

### Fig.5. Sketching the algorithm for the action *contradiction*

The list L corresponds to the nogood-set of TMS. In TMS, assumptions in the nogood-set are checked in an arbitrary order. The feature of the algorithm shown in Fig.5 is to provide a function to check the assumption in a specified order. By specifying the order the algorithm can resolve the inconsistency effectively. The rule *consistency* can be described as follows:

consistency:
    if matrix(name=$X$,inconsistency_ratio > 0.1)
   then
      (contradiction(*Assumption*,decrease_IR)
      ;
       otherwise(*Assumption*,decrease_IR,new_weight).

where the action *contradiction* is used in the RHS. If the action *contradiction* fails, the first argument of the action *contradiction* returns a list of assumptions which corresponds to the nogood-set. The second argument of the action is used for indicating a strategy which sorts the list of the assumptions. The strategy is defined as a Prolog predicate which has an argument. The strategy is used at Step1-1 in Fig.5. In SJSS, by using the strategy *decrease_IR*, the assumptions in the list are arranged in decreasing order of the amount of number which is increased and decreased for revising the temporary numbers. If the second argument is not indicated, the list obtained at Step 1 is directly used in which the assumptions are arranged in order of generating them.

In the RHS, if the action *contradiction* fails, the action otherwise is activated. The action *otherwise* resolves inconsistency in the same manner as the action *contradiction*. However, there are two main differences between the actions. One is that the action *otherwise* is used for revising some assumptions at the same time. Second is that the action *otherwise* directly revises the temporary numbers in the list *Assumption* by using a specified procedure which is indicated at the third arguments. The reason for the direct revision is that in a forward chaining production system the simultaneous revision of the numbers corresponds to achieving the revision during each recognize-act cycle. Namely, the action *otherwise* includes a function for the rule *change_weight* mentioned in the next section. The simultaneous revision needs to be achieved only when the rule *consistency* is firing.

### 3.2.3. Revising the pairwise comparisons

A rule is needed to concretely revise an assumption because the action *contradiction* only negates the assumption by asserting the negation of the assumption as shown at Step 3 in Fig.5.

The rule "*change_weight*" is used for concretely revising the assumption(that is, an inadequate pairwise comparison), which can be described as follows;

change_weight:
    if \matrix_element(name=$X$,column=$C$,row=$R$,weight=$W$)
   then
      new_weight($W$,$W2$) &
      add(matrix_element(name=$X$,column=$C$,
                    row=$R$,weight=$W2$).

where the LHS pattern corresponds to the negation of the inadequate comparison which needs to be revised. The negation is generated by the action *contradiction* if the action finds the comparison as an assumption. By firing the rule *change_weight*, the inadequate comparison is revised. In order to revise the comparison, the RHS action "*new_weight*" is used. The action changes the old weighting value "*W*" to the new weighting value "*W2*" which contributes to decrease the I.R. of the matrix. The range of the change takes ±2 because we assume that the old value is not so inadequate for the consistency. If the I.R. comes to be less than 0.1, the action *contradiction* stops and the consistency is automatically maintained.

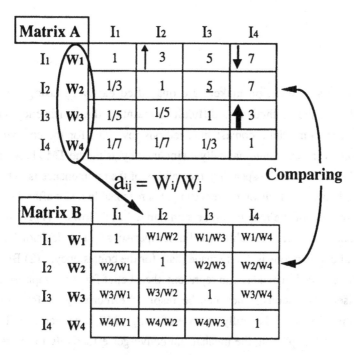

**Fig.6. Setting up Matrix B from Matrix A**

It is well known that it is difficult to determine the range of the change in which we need to decrease the maximum eigenvalue of a pairwise comparison matrix mentioned in Section 3.1. In order to concretely determine the range, we exploit the feature of the matrix based on AHP. Fig. 6 shows how the range is determined. It shows two pairwise comparison matrices which are Matrix A and Matrix B. An element $a_{ij}$ in Matrix A is obtained by performing a pairwise comparison between elements $I_i$ and $I_j$. In Matrix A, the direction of the arrows are used to represent the range of the direction in which the upper and down arrows indicate increasing and decreasing, respectively. The amount of increasing and decreasing is represented by using three kinds of arrows(that is, thin, normal, and thick) in which the thicker the arrow, the more the change is taken.

In order to determine the arrows, we set up Matrix B from Matrix A as shown Fig.6. Namely, Matrix B can be set up by using the weight of each element, which is computed from Matrix A. By exploiting the theory of AHP, the element $a_{ij}$ in Matrix B are defined as $W_i/W_j$ in which $W_i$ and $W_j$ are weights of the elements $I_i$ and $I_j$ in Matrix A, respectively. The I.R. of Matrix B comes to be 0 by using the method based on AHP. Matrix B corresponds to the ideal matrix in which pairwise comparisons of any problem are consistently performed. So, by gradually bringing Matrix A close to Matrix B, the I.R. of Matrix A will decrease effectively. Namely, the range of the change mentioned above can be determined by comparing Matrix A and B.

## 4. Conclusions

Subjective judgments of decision makers are quantified easily by using the pairwise comparison method. In the method, it is difficult to maintain the consistency among the comparisons. In order to maintain consistency, tedious revisions for the comparisons are required. In CDSS consistency is automatically maintained by using the TMS based inference mechanism in KORE/IE. Generally speaking, the validity of the maintenance is to be checked by decision makers. However, decision makers can get a reasonable result after the automatic maintenance. The reasons of the results can be summarized as follows: (1) By using AHP method, decision makers can perform almost valid comparisons. The decision makers can assume that the initial comparisons is not so inadequate for the consistency. (2) By using the TMS based mechanism, decision makers can represent their belief for the comparisons. If the inconsistency is arisen, the inconsistency can be resolved effectively by focusing on the assumption based comparisons. Generally, in case of using TMS, a convergence becomes a matter of concern. In our approach, the mechanism converges effectively to the reasonable result by using domain knowledge (that is, Matrix B mentioned in Section 3.2.3). (3) By restricting the range of the change (that is, ±2) for the comparisons, decision makers get reasonable result after the automatic revisions.

CDSS is similar to the frameworks of MORE(Kahn 1985) and MOLE(Eshelman 1986) which are knowledge acquisition tools. MORE and MOLE is used to obtain diagnosis knowledge from decision makers and structure them by using a domain depend interview method. The main feature of CDSS is that CDSS supports decision makers without the domain knowledge and the specified interview method. The future subject is that we enhance CDSS in order to realize a knowledge acquisition tool by adding functions for constructing and refining a model of a problem domain.

## Acknowledgment

The author would like to acknowledge the continuing guidance and encouragement of Dr. Mitsuhiko Toda, IIAS-SIS. The author is deeply grateful to Mr. Susumu Kunifuji IIAS-SIS, for reading the draft of this paper and giving him many valuable comments. This research has been carried out as a part of Fifth Generation Computer Project.

## References

[Boose 84] J.H.Boose: "Personal construct theory and the transfer of human expertise", Proc. of AAAI-84,pp.27-33,(1984)

[Doyle 79] J.Doyle : Truth Maintenance System, Artificial Intelligence Vol.12, pp.231-272(1979)

[Eshelman 86]L.Eshelman, et al. :"MOLE: A knowledge acquisition tool that uses its head", Proc. of AAAI-86, pp.950-955,(1985)

[Forgy 81]C.L.Forgy : OPS5 User's Manual, CMU-CS-81-135, July,(1981)

[Harker 87] P.T.Harker: "Incomplete pairwise comparisons in the analytic hierarchy process", Math. Modelling,9,pp.838-848,(1987)

[Kahn 85] G.Kahn, et al. :"MORE: An intelligent knowledge acquisition tool", Proc. of IJCAI-85,1, pp.581-584(1985)

[Saaty 80] T.L.Saaty: The Analytic Hierarchy Process, McGraw Hill(1980)

[Shintani 88] T.Shintani: "A Fast Prolog-Based Production System KORE/IE", Logic Programming: Proceedings of the Fifth International Conference and Symposium(edited by R.A.Kowalski and K.A.Bowen), MIT Press,pp.26-41,(1988)

[Shintani 89] T.Shintani: "An Approach to Nonmonotonic Inference Mechanism in Production System KORE/IE",LNCS 384, Logic Programming'88, Springer-Verlag,pp.38-52(1989).

# Logic Design Assistance Using
# Temporal Logic Based Language Tokio

NAKAMURA, Hiroshi     NAKAI, Masaya*     KONO, Shinji**

FUJITA, Masahiro***     TANAKA, Hidehiko

Department of Electrical Engineering, The University of Tokyo
*THE DAI-ICHI KANGYO BANK
**Sony Computer Science Laboratory
***FUJITSU LABORATORIES Ltd.

## Abstract

In this work, a logic design assistance system using *Tokio* is presented. Tokio is a logic programming language which is based on Interval Temporal Logic. Therefore, Tokio can specify both concurrency and sequentiality accurately and easily. In this system, the behaviors at both the algorithmic level and the register transfer level are given in the same language: Tokio. This is one of the most outstanding characteristics. In this paper, we mainly present a data path verifier at the register transfer level. This verifier is a core part of the assistance system.

## 1   Introduction

Presently, we are constructing a logic design assistance system using *Tokio* [1][2][3]. Tokio is a temporal logic programming language, adopted as a hardware description language in our assistance system.

We regard the logic design flow as follows.

First, the designers specify the algorithm of the behavior to be designed. Then, the behaviors at the register transfer level is derived from this abstract form by the designers. This deriva-tion is assured by simulating the descriptions. The designers also give the structure of the data path to be designed. Although there have been many reports on synthesizing the data path automatically from the behavioral description [4], the derived data paths are not yet as satisfactory as those which are designed manually. are difficult to improve. On the other hand, the designers have images of the data path to be designed even at an early stage in the actual design process, because they have designed many similar circuits. The designers are constructing the frames of the data path while they are deriving the behavior at the register transfer level. Our strategy is to utilize positively the designers' experience. Then, the consistency of the two descriptions is checked automatically. Even though a good data path can be synthesized automatically from the behavior in the near future, the process of improvement will still have to be done manually. Therefore, an automatic consistency-check process is important.

In this design flow, the following three points are important for the behavior description language.

- The behavior is specified in an executable form.

- The behavior at both the algorithmic level and the register transfer level are given in the same language.

⁰This work is partially supported by Grand-in-Aid for Encouragement of Young Scientists, The Ministry of Education, Science, and Cultures, No.01790381

• Sequentiality and concurrency can be specified accurately and simply.

Tokio meets these requirements, and therefore provides smooth logic design assistance.

**Structure of the Assistance System** The structure of the assistance system is shown in Figure 1.

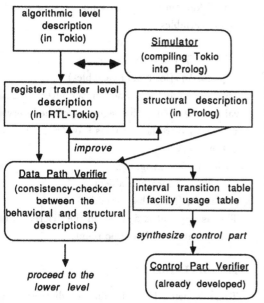

Figure 1: Structure of Logic Design Assistance System

The designers, at first, specify the algorithm of the behavior in Tokio. Then, the register transfer level description is derived. This derivation is assured by the already-developed simulator [3]. The register transfer level description is specified in RTL-Tokio which is a constrained form of Tokio. Both behaviors in Tokio and RTL-Tokio (Register Transfer Level Tokio) can be simulated on the same simulator.

The designers also give the structure of the data path in Prolog. Then, the "Data Path Verifier" verifies whether the behavior can run on the given structure. If there exists an error, the strucure and the behavior are modified to rectify that error, and then they are verified again. Otherwise, the design proceeds to the lower level such as logic synthesis. In the process of verification, both the *interval transition table* and the *facility usage table* are derived, from which the control part is synthesized. As for the control part, this system is connected to our already-developed verification system [7].

**Contents** Temporal logic programming language Tokio and RTL-Tokio is introduced in Section 2. Then the data path verifier is explained in Section 3. This verifier is the core part in the proposed assistance system. In section 4, this verifier is applied to an example and its result is presented. This paper is concluded in Section 5.

## 2 Temporal Logic Programming Language Tokio

### 2.1 Tokio

*Tokio* [1][2][3] is a logic programming language which is based on first-order Interval Temporal Logic [5]. Intuitively, Tokio is an extension of Prolog with an addition of the notion of time sequence. Therefore, Tokio can describe an algorithm as flexibly as in Prolog.

**Tokio operator** The expression

head :- p,q.

denotes that the goals p and q are executed in the same interval where the predicate head is defined. Concurrent execution is represented in this expression.

head :- p && q.

The *chop* operator && illustrates the sequential execution of the two goals p and q. This operator divides the interval of head into the two sub-intervals as shown in Figure 2. The goal p is executed in the former interval and q is executed in the latter interval.

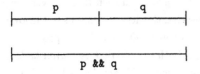

Figure 2: Chop Operator

Another principle operator is *next* operator @.

head :- @p.

This expression represents that the goal p is executed in the next interval to the current interval where head is defined. The next interval starts at the next clock to the current clock and ends at the same clock as the end of the current interval. The next interval is illustrated in Figure 3.

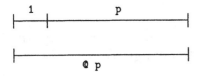

Figure 3: Next Operator

The following operators are defined by these operators mentioned above.

- # p :
  The *always* operator # indicates that the goal p is executed in all the subintervals of the current interval.

- keep(p) :
  The *keep* operator is similar to the always operator except that the goal p is not executed in the final subinterval of the current interval.

**Tokio Variables** A Tokio variable is a sequence of Prolog variables along the time sequence. Variables in Tokio can have different values at each time(clock), whereas variables in Prolog do not change their values.

There are two kinds of variables in Tokio.

- *global variable* :
  This variable retains its value unless a new assignment to that variable occurs. The name of this variable begins with a character "*".

- *local variable* :
  This variable changes its value along with the time sequence. The name of this variable begins with a capital letter.

In Tokio, there are two kinds of assignments to the variables.

- temporal assignment :
  $P < - Q$  (for local variables)
  $*p <= *q$  (for global variables)
  This assignment is defined on the interval. The values of Q or $*q$ at the beginning of the interval are assigned to the variables P or $*p$ at the end of the interval.

- immediate assignment :
  $P = Q$  (for local variables)
  $*p := *q$  (for global variables)
  This assignment is defined on the discrete time and executed at that time point.

## 2.2  RTL-Tokio

Tokio is defined on the idea of discrete time sequence. The semantics of Tokio depends on what "the discrete time" represents in the hardware. If "the discrete time" represents the next clock in the hardware, the description corresponds to a synchronous circuit. When "the discrete time" represents the absolute time, then the description may correspond to an asynchronous action within one clock. Due to this flexibility, Tokio can describe the behavior a different levels.

RTL-Tokio is a hardware description language at the register transfer level and a constrained form of Tokio where the discrete time indicate the machine cycle. The constraints are concerned with variable and backtracking.

**Variable** The global variables represent the data of the registers or memories because they hold their values. The local variables also represent these data indirectly. The immediate assignment of the global variables such as "*q := *p" is prohibited in RTL-Tokio because no data are transferred to registers or memories without time passing. Moreover, both the global and the local variables cannot have list structured values.

**Backtracking** Tokio has two kinds of backtrackings. One is the backtracking which occurs usually in Prolog and the other is the backtracking of the time sequence. Since the behavior of the hardware is decidable, RTL-Tokio should not backtrack. In order to prevent RTL-Tokio from the former backtracking, the syntax of RTL-Tokio is constrained as follows,

```
head(arg) :- localCond, !, recursiveCall.
head(arg) :- localCond, !, actions &&
        actions && ... && recursiveCall.
```

localCond should be evaluated at the beginning of the interval The number of conditions may be greater than or equal to 0. "actions" should not include any recursive predicate calls, whereas "recursiveCall" may include them. Consequently, only tail recursion (that is, loop structures) are to be permitted in RTL-Tokio.

The latter backtracking (that is, the backtracking of the time sequence) occurs because the length of each interval is chosen undecidably. (Details are mentioned in [1]). In RTL-Tokio, every temporal assignment is executed in length 1. The length of each interval is decided under this constraint. This constraint represents that the data transfers between registers are executed in one machine cycle.

## 2.3 Description Example

We use a simple program that computes the square root using Newton's method as an ex-

```
Y := 0.222222 + 0.888889 * X;
I := 0;
    DO UNTIL I = 4 LOOP
    Y := 0.5 * (Y + X/Y);
    I := I + 1;
    ENDDO;
```

(a) Algorithm of Newton's Method

```
main(X) :-
    Y <-  0.222222 + 0.888889 * X, X <- X
    && sub(X,Y,0).
sub(X,Y,C) :- C = 4,!, write(Y).
sub(X,Y,C) :- !,
    A <- X / Y,X <- X, C <- C,Y <- Y
    && B <- A + Y,X <- X, C <- C
    && Ans <- B / 2, CC <- C + 1, X <- X
    && sub(X,Ans,CC).
```

(b) Newton's method in Tokio

```
start([H|T]) :- main(H),@T = T, @start(T).
start([]) :- true.
main(X) :-
    Y <-  0.222222 + 0.888889 * X, X <- X
    &&   sub(X,Y,0).
sub(X,Y,C) :- C = 4,!, write(Y).
sub(X,Y,C) :- !,
    A <- X / Y, X <- X, C <- C, Y <- Y
    && B <- A + Y, X <- X, C <- C
    && Ans <- B / 2, X <- X, CC <- C + 1
    && sub(X,Ans,CC).
```

(c) Pipelined Newton's method in Tokio

Figure 4: Examples in Tokio

ample. Figure 4-(a) is an algorithm with four repetitions. The same behavior in Tokio is Figure 4-(b). Figure 4-(c) shows a pipelined behavior of (b). In the description of (c), main is called by start. Since start is called every clock recursively, main is also initiated every clock. Hence, this description indicates a pipelined behavior. The difference between (b) and (c) is the predicate start which indicates the initiation of each pipeline. This shows that Tokio has enough power to specify a behavior of hardware at the algorithmic level.

**Transforming Tokio into RTL-Tokio** Figure 5 shows the register transfer level description in RTL-Tokio which is derived from the algorithmic description. In this description, latency (the number of time units between successive initiations) is lower than that of Figure 4-(c) in order to avoid conflicts of registers (that is, global variables) in RTL-Tokio.

```
:- static([adr,input1,input3,reg1,
          reg2,reg3,reg4,output]).
:- static(memory).
start :- !,
    init && main.
init :- !,
    *memory(1) <= 1, *memory(2) <= 2,
    *memory(3) <= 3, *memory(4) <= 4,
    *memory(5) <= 5, *memory(6) <= 6,
    *memory(7) <= 7, *adr <= 1.
main :- *adr = 8, !, true.
main :- !,
    input && stage1 &&
    main, (stage2 && last_stage && true).
input :- !,
    *input1 <= *memory(*adr),
    *adr <= *adr + 1 &&
    *reg1 <= 0.222222 + 0.888889 * *input1.
stage1 :- !,
    *reg2 <= *input1 / *reg1 &&
    *reg2 <= *reg2 + *reg1 &&
    *reg1 <= *reg2 / 2 &&
    *reg2 <= *input1 / *reg1 &&
    *reg2 <= *reg2 + *reg1 &&
    *reg3 <= *reg2 / 2,
    *input3 <= *input1.
stage2 :- !,
    *reg4 <= *input3 / *reg3 &&
    *reg4 <= *reg4 + *reg3 &&
    *reg3 <= *reg3 / 2 &&
    *reg4 <= *input3 / *reg3 &&
    *reg4 <= *reg4 + *reg3 &&
    *output <= *reg4 / 2.
last_stage :- !, write(*output).
```

Figure 5: Pipelined Behavior of Newton's Method in RTL-Tokio

Transforming Tokio into RTL-Tokio is nothing but deriving a behavior at the register transfer level. This process includes operation scheduling, operation allocation, and register allocation. As shown in Figure 5, registers in the data path are declared as global variables. The process of register allocation in the structure is equal to the process of replacing local variables by global variables in RTL-Tokio. Whether the register allocation succeeds or not is detected by

simulating the derived RTL-Tokio descriptions. Operation allocation in the structure is verified by a "Data Path Verifier" explained in the next section.

# 3 Data Path Verifier

## 3.1 Overview

The structure of the data path verifier [6] is as shown in Figure 6. The inputs to this system are the behavior description in RTL-Tokio, the structure description in Prolog, and the operation rules in Prolog. The operation rules in Prolog can be regarded as a part of the structure.

This verifier checks whether the behavior can run on a given data path without data conflict. If a certain facility (hereafter, facility represents operators, busses, or paths of the data path structure) is occupied by more than one data-transfer at the same time, it results in an error. The assumptions in the verification are as follows.

1. All the data transfers occupy the necessary paths and operators during the whole time period specified in the behavior.

2. Operations in the behavior are linked to the operators in the structure description using the operation rules.

3. Names of the registers and memories in the behavior are the same as those in the structure description.

From another stand point, one type of operations should be linked to one type of operators. That is, '+' is realized by an adder and '> 1' is realized by a shifter. We introduce operation rules for their wide applicability. Since the behaviors at different levels are described in the same language Tokio, this system can be applied to the verification at higher level than the register transfer level, if the required operation rules are provided. As for this application, it is desi-

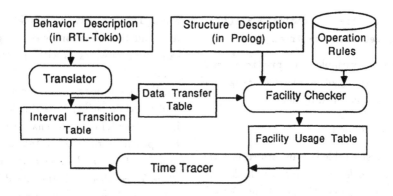

Figure 6: Structure of Data Path Verifier

able that registers and memories in the behavior are linked to those in the structure without the last assumption. This remains to be solved.

The process of this verification is divided into the following two stages.

• To find sets of facilities in the structure which are occupied by the data transfers in the behavior. This stage is executed by the *Translator* and *Facility Checker*.

• To check whether any facilities are occupied for more than one data-transfer simultaneously. This stage is executed by the *Time Tracer*.

In the following subsections, we first briefly explain the format of structure description, and then explain each part of this data path verifier.

## 3.2 Structure Description

The structure of the data path is specified in Prolog. Since a hierarchical structure can be expressed in this format, the other widely-used structural description languages can be translated into this style easily.

There are three types of declaration as follows.

• type( type-name, facility-name, module-name ).

"type(aa,bb,cc)." represents that a facility of name bb in the module cc belongs to the group of the type aa. The module name of the top level is reserved as *top*.

• path( path-name, input-port, output-port ).
This expression represents the network between the facilities. To declare the bit-width explicitly, the following syntax is prepared.

path([p412,[0,15]],[bus1,[out,[0,15]]],
        [add1,[in,[0,15]]]).

Fundamental bit-width can be declared as
  bit_width(0,15).
With this statement, all the path statements without bit-width declarations are interpreted as 16 bit-width paths.

• func( function, output-port, input-port, signal-line ).
This declaration represents the function of each type.

## 3.3 Translator

At first, the RTL-Tokio description is translated into the *interval transition table* and the *data transfer table* by the translator. The interval transition table represents the transitive relations between the intervals. From this table, state transition table is also derived. During the process of obtaining the *interval transition table*, the length of each interval is determined. The data-transfers occurring in each interval are listed in the data transfer table. The unification information is also listed in this table. For example, suppose the following description.

```
head :-A = *reg1, predicateCall(A).
predicateCall(X) :- *reg2 <= X.
```

Here, the local variable X in `predicateCall` is equal to the global variable `*reg1`, if `predicateCall` is called by `head`.

## 3.4 Facility Checker

The data transfer table is transformed into the *facility usage table* by the facility checker using the *operation rules*. The facility usage table consists of a set of facilities in the data path which are occupied by the data-transfers listed in the data transfer table. This transformation is done in accordance with the following steps.

- Find the operator or a set of operators which realize the operation of each data transfer.
- Search for data paths from the source register to the input of the operator and from the output of the operator to the destination register.

In the first step, care must be taken that one operation is realized in several ways. For example, the operation of 'multiplied by 2' is realized not only using a multiplier, but also using an adder or one-bit shifter. In order to find all the candidates, therefore, both the functions of the facilities and the rules of the equivalent operations should be given in advance. The rules are called the operation rules as shown in Figure 6. The former is declared in the structure descriptions as follows.

```
func(add,[[adder,out]],
    [[adder,in1],[adder,in2]],[adder,cnt]).
```

The latter is also given in the following Prolog form.

```
opSame([[multi,X,2],[shift_left,X],
    [add,X,X]]).
```

The operation rules are constructed in advance, but the user is allowed to add any necessary rules. The fact that the functions of the facilities and the operation rules are given in the same form provides us with smooth design assistance.

If the facility usage table cannot be obtained or if a certain facility is used twice in the same interval, the RTL-Tokio behavior cannot run on the specified structure. In the case that a certain facility is used in separate intervals, the *Time Tracer* checks whether the different intervals occur simultaneously or not.

## 3.5 Time Tracer

This part checks whether there exist any intervals which occur simultaneously and occupy the same facility. We have implemented two algorithms, that is, backward trace and forward trace. Details of the two algorithms are as follows.

**[1] backward trace**

**stage1** All the pairs of intervals which occupy the same facility are found.

**stage2** For a given set of intervals found in stage1, the concurrency check begins. Suppose the initial set of intervals be $A_0 = \{I_a\}$ and $B_0 = \{I_b\}$. In case that $I_a$ follows $I_c$ or $I_d$ and $I_b$ follows $I_e$ or $I_f$, $A_1 = \{I_c, I_d\}$ and $B_1 = \{I_e, I_f\}$ are obtained as the predecessor. Here, $I_i$ contains the information of predicate calls. Using the interval transition table, the backward trace continues in this way and constructs the $A_{i+1}$ and $B_{i+1}$ from $A_i$ and $B_i$ with recording the transitive conditions.

- If $\exists int, 0 \leq \exists i; int \subseteq A_i \cap int \subseteq B_i$ hold and the transitive conditions from $int$ to $I_a$ are not exclusive of those from $int$ to $I_b$, $I_a$ and $I_b$ are proved to occur simultaneously. This result in the design error.
- Suppose $A_n$ and $B_n$ be the newly obtained sets. If $0 \leq \exists i < n; A_n \subseteq A_i \cap B_n \subseteq B_i$ holds or either $A_n$ or $B_n$ is empty, $I_a$ and $I_b$ are proved not to occur simultaneously.

**stage3** For all the pairs listed in stage1, stage

is applied. The obtained results in the previous stage2 are used to cut off the same trace. This method decreases the execution time but increases the required memory.

**[2] forward trace**

**stage1** The initial interval $I_{init}$ is selected. $S_0 = \{I_{init}\}$.

**stage2** The set of intervals $S_{i+1}$ next to $S_i$ are obtained by tracing the interval transition table forward. The obtained intervals are recorded with the transition conditions. Suppose $S_n$ be the newly obtained set, if $0 \leq \exists i < n$; $S_n \subseteq S_i$ holds or all the transition is traced, the execution halts.

**stage3** All the elements in the set $S_i$ occur simultaneously unless they have exclusive transitive condition. Intervals which occur simultaneously and use the same facility are searched for.

In both the two algorithms, care must be taken that there exist some alternative sets of the facility usage. Whether there are any candidates avoiding the facility conflict is checked after the process of either backward or forward time trace.

For the given two transitive conditions, they are judged as exclusive only if they have the exclusive conditions at the same time spot. In order to consider exclusive conditions over time passing, linear programming method should be introduced.

# 4 Result Evaluation

## 4.1 Experimental Result

We have applied the data path verifier to the behavior of Figure 5. The given data path is shown in Figure 7 (except for dashed line).

In this example, one conflict is detected. The output of the verifier is shown in Figure 8. Figure 8 indicates that addA is used in (input/0,1,2) and (stage2/0,1,2) and these intervals occur simultaneously.

```
% Facility Checker
[((input/0,1,2),0)],1
 and
[((stage2/0,1,2),0)],1
 may conflict in
[[mltAaddA,[addA,[in1,[0,7]]]],
 [reg3addA,[addA,[in1,[0,7]]]]]

% Time Tracer
[((main/0,2,3),0)]
[((input/0,1,1),0)]
 [((input/0,1,1),1)]
 [((input/0,1,2),0)]

[((main/0,2,3),0)]
[((stage2/0,1,1),0)]
 [((stage2/0,1,1),1)]
 [((stage2/0,1,2),0)]

These may happen at the same time.
```

Figure 8: A Part of Output

Here, "(input/0,1,2)" represents "(predicate-Name/arity, clauseNumber, intervalNumber)". Thus, "(input/0,1,2)" denotes the second interval of the first predicate whose name/arity is input/0. This conflict is removed by adding one path to the data path (dashed line in Figure 7), and by modifying the behavior as shown in Figure 9.

We have altered the repetition times of the behavior. The verification halts only after all the conflicts are detected. The results are shown in Table 1. This verification system is implemented using SICStus-Prolog on SUN4/260. In this table, the intervals which includes data transfers are counted as the "Number of Intervals". "Number of Backward Trace" is the number of the pairs which are listed in the stage1 of the backward trace.

## 4.2 Evaluation

The required time for the translator and the facility check are linearly proportional to the scale of the behavior description. The number of backward traces is $_NC_2$ in the worst case,

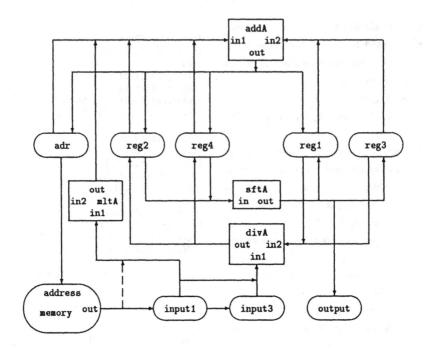

Figure 7: Data Path for Computing Square Root using Newton's Method

| Number of Repetitions | Number of Intervals | CPUtime (sec) | | | | Number of Backward Trace |
|---|---|---|---|---|---|---|
| | | Translator | Facility Check | Backward Trace | Forward Trace | |
| 2 | 8 | 0.54 | 3.02 | 2.27 | 0.45 | 6 |
| 4 | 14 | 0.72 | 4.58 | 19.62 | 0.64 | 28 |
| 8 | 26 | 0.98 | 7.92 | 273.9 | 0.99 | 120 |

Table 1: Results of Verifying Circuit for Computing Square Root

```
input :- !,
    *input1 <= *memory(*adr),
    *reg1 <= 0.222222 + 0.888889
            * *memory(*adr).
stage1 :- !,
    *reg2 <= *input1 / *reg1 &&
    *reg2 <= *reg2 + *reg1 &&
    *reg1 <= *reg2 / 2,*adr <= *adr+1 &&
    *reg2 <= *input1 / *reg1 &&
    *reg2 <= *reg2 + *reg1 &&
    *reg3 <= *reg2 / 2,
    *input3 <= *input1.
```

Figure 9: Modified Behavior (just modified part)

where $N$ is the number of intervals. In contrast, the transition table is traced once during the forward method. The required time for one forward/backward trace increases exponentially with the degree of the concurrency of the behavior and to the number of condition branches. As for this example, the degree of concurrency is 2 and the number of condition branches is 1. This is the reason why the method of forward trace is very efficient in this case. The method of backward trace is not suitable for verifying the whole description. This method, however, is still useful for verifying properties such as whether certain two intervals can occur simultaneously or not.

## 5 Conclusion

We have presented a logic design assistance system, and explained mainly a data path verifier at the register transfer level. In our system, temporal logic programming language Tokio has been adopted as the behavior description language. It is the characteristic of this system that the behaviors at the levels between the algorithmic level and the register transfer level are described in the same language Tokio.

The data path verifier has also been applied to an example and its capability has been discussed. To apply this verifier to larger examples remains to be solved.

## References

[1] T. Aoyagi, M. Fujita, and H. Tanaka. Temporal Logic Programming Language Tokio. In *Logic Programming Conference '85*, pages 128–137, Springer-Verlag, 1985.

[2] M. Fujita, S. Kono, H. Tanaka, and T. Motooka. Aid to Hierarchical and Structured Logic Design using Temporal Logic and Prolog. In *Proceedings.Pt.E*, pages 283–294, IEE, 1986.

[3] S. Kono, T. Aoyagi, M. Fujita, and H. Tanaka. Implementation of Temporal Logic Programming Language Tokio. In *Logic Programming Conference '85*, pages 138–147, Springer-Verlag, 1985.

[4] M.C. McFarland, A.C. Parker, and R. Camposano. Tutorial on High-Level Synthesis. In *25th Design Automation Conference*, pages 330–336, ACM/IEEE, 1988.

[5] B. Moszkowski. A Temporal Logic for Multi-Level reasoning about Hardware. In *CHDL '83*, IFIP, 1983.

[6] H. Nakamura, M. Fujita, S. Kono, M. Nakai, and H. Tanaka. A Data Path Verification System using Temporal Logic Based Language Tokio. In *IFIP WG10.2 Working Conference on the CAD Systems Using AI Techniques*, IFIP, June 1989.

[7] H. Nakamura, M. Fujita, S. Kono, and H. Tanaka. Temporal Logic Based Fast Verification systems Using Cover Expressions. In *VLSI '87*, pages 99–111, IFIP, 1987.

# Lecture Notes in Computer Science

This subseries of the Lecture Notes in Computer Science reports new develop
ments in Artificial Intelligence research and teaching – quickly, informally and at a
high level. The type of material considered for publication includes preliminary
drafts of original papers and monographs, technical reports of high quality and
broad interest, advanced level lectures, reports of meetings, provided they are o
exceptional interest and focused on a single topic. The timeliness of a manuscrip
is more important than its form which may be unfinished or tentative. If possible, a
subject index should be included. Publication of Lecture Notes is intended as a
service to the international computer science community, in that a commercia
publisher, Springer-Verlag, can offer a wide distribution of documents which
would otherwise have a restricted readership. Once published and copyrighted
they can be referred to in the scientific literature.

**Manuscripts**

Manuscripts should be no less than 100 and preferably no more than 500 pages in length.

They are reproduced by a photographic process and therefore must be prepared with extreme care according t
the instructions available from the publisher. Proceedings' editors and authors of monographs receive 75 fre
copies. Authors of contributions to proceedings are free to use the material in other publications upon notificatio
to the publisher. The typescript is reduced slightly in size during reproduction; best results will not be obtaine
unless the text on any one page is kept within the overall limit of 18 × 26,5 cm (7 × 10½ inches). On request, th
publisher will supply special paper with the typing area outlined.

Manuscripts should be sent to Prof. J. Siekmann, Institut für Informatik, Universität Kaiserslautern, Postfac
30 49, D-6750 Kaiserslautern, FRG, or directly to Springer-Verlag Heidelberg.

---

**Springer-Verlag, Heidelberger Platz 3, D-1000 Berlin 33**
**Springer-Verlag, Tiergartenstraße 17, D-6900 Heidelberg 1**
**Springer-Verlag, 175 Fifth Avenue, New York, NY 10010/USA**
**Springer-Verlag, 37-3, Hongo 3-chome, Bunkyo-ku, Tokyo 113, Japan**

---

ISBN 3-540-53919-0
ISBN 0-387-53919-0